PROBLEMS OF INDIAN EDUCATION

PROBLEMS OF INDIAN EDUCATION

Dr. M.U. Qureshi

ANMOL PUBLICATIONS PVT. LTD.
NEW DELHI - 110 002 (INDIA)

ANMOL PUBLICATIONS PVT. LTD.
4374/4B, Ansari Road, Daryaganj
New Delhi - 110 002
Ph.: 23261597, 23278000
Visit us at: www.anmolpublications.com

Problems of Indian Education

First Published, 2005

ISBN 81-261-2413-X

PRINTED IN INDIA

Published by J.L. Kumar for Anmol Publications Pvt. Ltd., New Delhi - 110 002 and Printed at Mehra Offset Press, Delhi.

Contents

Preface

It gives me great pleasure in presenting to the readers a new book, titled: Problems of Indian Education. It really departs from the general view that education is the solution of all human problems. In fact, solution itself has to face many a problem — some created by us and some others due to frequent changes in the world order. Globalization has a generous effect on our daily life and education is not beyond its reach.

Foundation of every nation is the education of its people. Education is the most important constituent of a good citizenship. It implies cultivation of mind to make life tolerable. But, system and style to educate the people in our country is rather outdated, it is non-systematic and unrealistic. It is totally academic and not problem oriented. It also does not provide genius qualities.

A big problem regarding our education is the present examination system. Keeping these problems in mind Government of India had announced a new education policy in 1986 with special emphasis on the education of women, delinking of jobs from degrees and to provide equal opportunities for all.

Here is a book on an old subject, with a new approach. All related and significant issues have been written about, in a clear and logical style so as to inspire the readers instantly for independent thinking on the subject after getting necessary 'food for thought.'

The subject matter of this book is arranged and presented in such a manner that it may fully cover every aspect of the related issues. The language used is very simple and understandable. It makes the book useful for the entire spectrum of readers.

The Editor is extremely thankful to various authors, whose works, he has liberally referred to.

Nothing is perfect in itself, it is likely that some mistakes might have occurred in this book too. The undersigned will feel grateful to the readers, if they forward their valuable suggestions.

Editor

1

Introduction

Today, we are independent. But, despite political independence, have we become really independent? And, if we have not, then why? The reason for this is that our educational system has not broken from tradition, its basis is the system employed in the time of our slavery. Besides, we have also had to face numerous problems in the educational sphere. In this period of crumbling belief and faith, not only our country but the entire world has lost all sense of direction. As a result, the older generation wants to tie down the rising generation, breaking completely from tradition, has become filled with anger, and is now bent upon revolution. We are finding it difficult to discover the path of synthesis and harmony at least apparently, there is no possibility of arriving at a compromise.

The Difficulties

1. *Problems of the Objectives of Education :* If our education from 1947 till the present is categorised as the aimless education of the aimless, it would be no exaggeration. The reason for this is quite explicit - we do not have before us a proper plan or sketch for building our nation. A nation does not undergo development by

the building of dams and construction of factories and mills, but through the process and medium of education. There is a famous Chinese proverb, which says, "If you plan for a year, plant grain; if you plan for ten years, plant trees, if you plan for a hundred years, plant men:" And in our case, the kind of nation that will be built or created is not evident even from the declaration on the national plan for education.

At present, the many problems that are afflicting education have one sole cause at their root which is aimlessness. According to Dr. Radhakrishnan, the objective of education is the discovery, and the development through proper training, of an individual's inborn qualities. Universities should fulfill these two prime duties towards their students.

The significant fact before our country today is that is needs of self-reliance in foodgrains, economic development and more employment, social and national unification, and political development can be fulfilled only through the training of students in character, in profession and practice, and development of literacy, artistic and cultural interests. And these, in reality, are the objectives of education.

2. *Problem of Primary and Compulsory Education* : The major problem confronting Indian education is the problem of compulsory primary education because the level of literacy has been very low. This shows that primary education has not expanded to the desired extent. Besides, many political, social, religious, economic and geographical factors are creating obstacles in the path of expanding primary education. This problem has been made even more complex by such contributory factors as the curriculum of primary education, problem of school, wastage and stagnation, and many administrative difficulties.

The important aspect of the problem in primary education is the failure to fulfil the promise of the Constitution, according to which it is the duty of the state to provide for the education of all children upto the age of 14; this is stated in Article 45 of the Constitution. States have remained indifferent towards the fulfilment of this promise. In the third Five Year Plan, efforts in this direction were made, but in the fourth, this ideal was assumed to be the cause of educated unemployment. In the fifth plan, it was clearly assumed that the objective of compulsory and universal education could not be fulfilled. It was assumed that only 75 per cent of the children could be provided education.

3. *Problem of Secondary Education* : Secondary education is the backbone of the country's development, and it is unfortunate that there is no uniformity at this level in our country. The curriculum is spread over 12 years in some states, over 11 years in others and over 10 in yet others. Besides, problems relating to curricula, administration, training of teachers, financial aid, etc., have combined to create obstacles. Among its numerous problems are those of the objectives of secondary education, its limits, form, curriculum, guidance, administration, substitution, finance, evaluation and examination, and the problem of a proper life for students.

Despite this, there has been considerable progress in secondary education. Between 1951 and 1974, the enrolment went up six times in the case of boys and 13 times for that of girls, though this is an average for the different rates of growth achieved in various states. With reference to the total population, admission of girls at the primary stages has decreased. Besides, secondary schools have also been afflicted with problems relating to resources, teachers and facilities. The central problem at this level is that of qualitative growth, though there is also the problem of education lacking a vocational bias.

4. *Higher Education* : Higher education, too, has been facing numerous problems in our country. In the main, it has failed to help students to earn their livelihood, and it has continued to expand despite the absence of employment. Its failure in this regard is the result of many factors. University education is lacking in direction because of political pressures, the sovereignty of universities themselves, the quality of student life, lack of finance and absence of clearly defined objectives. The country lacks any concrete plan for taking advantage of higher education, and because of this many contradictions have crept in. Higher education is

suffering from the problems inevitably linked with expansion. The enrolment in arts, commerce and science has risen from 3.2 million in 1968-69 to 3.5 million in 1974. Besides, since most institutions of higher education are located in cities, its benefit goes mainly to students living in urban areas: In addition, there is need for intellectual development, new curricula for the universities, etc.

5. *Problem of Technical Education* : India undoubtfully needs technical education for its rapid development, because, a variety of highly skilled technicians are required for exploring the country's considerable natural resources. But, education in this sphere has suffered mainly from a lack of proper planning. As a consequence, while many individuals received training in one branch of technology, there was a complete absence of trained personnel in other branches. This has led to unemployment. Even today, our technical education is handicapped by lack of proper planning, absence of textbooks, absence of teachers, lack of laboratories and other facilities. Its problems can be rooted out in only one way-linking it with employment. It is necessary to plan, for technical education in the light of manpower needs.

6. *Problem of Special Education* : The need for social education and adult education is indicative of the illiteracy prevailing in our country, because in proportion to the population, the percentage of literate individuals is very small. Besides, the very concept of social education has always lacked clarity. In this sphere, the main problem lies in not finding suitably devoted workers. Besides the administrative structure has also succeeded in covering this education with a veil of intellectuality, with the result that, instead of being something intimately concerned with the masses, it has become only a subject for intellectual discussion. This is despite the fact that, in the fifth plan, social education has been linked with continuous education. Because of this, social education is being expanded through such schemes as private candidature in examinations and correspondence education institutions. However, the problem of literacy is at the same level as in 1974. In the Sixth Plan, it has been given national importance.

—

7. *Problem of Teachers* : The problem of teachers also afflicts Indian education. It is the teacher who is the link between education and the student. Teachers have become even more dissatisfied, since the new scales of pay favoured by the Kothari Commission were not implemented. The responsibility for this dissatisfaction rests securely with our popular government which has continued to neglect the builders of the nation in its own selfish interests. Recognising the importance of teachers, the Kothari Commission has said that a concrete programme for the professional training of teacher is essential for bringing about qualitative progress. The money spent upon teacher training can bring forth the maximum dividends, since the money spent is less but its return in the form of a qualitative improvement in the education of lakhs of individuals is enormous.

The factors which influence the improvement of education and its contribution to national development are- the qualities, ability and character of the teachers. These are undoubtedly of the greatest importance. Nothing is more important than inducting good teachers into this profession. There should be professional training and the availability of satisfactory working conditions, which can influence them profoundly. The investment in the education of teachers can bring manifold advantages because the financial investment is less, but the advantages gained in the context of general education are comparatively much more.

8. *Student Unrest :* The new problem that has arisen because of lack of foresight in education is given the name of student dissatisfaction or student unrest. The violence and destruction indulged in by our students in the entire country over the last 15 years has proved beyond doubt that there is some serious fault in our educational structure. Though the phenomenon emerged somewhat late after independence, the entire world has seen with open eyes the anger of the younger generation and the repressive attitude of the older generation. The students who were used before independence to wave the national flag and make clamorous demands for the country's freedom came to raise the flag against the same leaders who had once inspired them. This came about

because of lack of direction. This has come to be called student indiscipline. When its causes were analysed, it was discovered that the students trained by crushed and dissatisfied teachers can never turn to constructive activity. Consequently, the discontentment of teachers also came to the fore in the form of the teacher's movement. This led to the opening of a new chapter, the arrest of teachers by their own students. Now, the teacher has been compelled to give up the selflessness of Dronacharya and to engage in a struggle for survival. This struggle still continues. From this, it is evident that the dissatisfaction of the students can be eradicated only when the structure of education is completely reshaped.

9. *Administration and Planning* : The educational system today is suffering from the problems inherent in a dual administration. The administration imposed by the Centre and the States is obstructing education at the local and individual levels. This system of providing grants is also defective. Besides, officials concerned with administration and inspection are ignorant of the real problems of schools, teachers and students. Hence, their decisions fail to benefit the educational system. If education is to be utilized for national development, there is great need for able and efficient administration and suitable educational planning. Hence, there is an urgent need for a suitable administrative and planning mechanism.

10. *Guidance and Counselling* : Education aims at the complete development of the individual. Today, education is based on psychology, and efforts are made to adjust students at a mass level with society, despite their individual differences. In India, the advantages of guidance and counselling services is available only to the privileged and so those lacking in opportunities remain in the condition of deprivation.

11. *Problem of Finance* : Indian education has been singularly unfortunate in that, whenever a crisis occurred, the budget of every other department remained unchanged while that of education suffered major reductions. Besides, only 2.3 per cent of the national income is usually spent on it. Other countries spend as much as 7 per cent of the national income on education. In the

fifth plan, 2.3 per cent of the national income was kept apart for education, although it was planned to be increased to 4.7 per cent by 1981. The present situation is such that even if more resources are allocated for education but remain linked to traditional techniques, which have been the cause of colossal wastages, even the basic needs of educational reform will not be fulfilled for this, the present stagnation must be brought to an end.

12. *Problem of Moral and Spiritual Values* : It is becoming increasingly clear that the main cause of the decline in national character is the absence of growth and development in moral and spiritual values. The Education Commission has paid particular attention to this problem.

13. *Problem of Inequality* : The glaring fact before us today is that educational opportunities are being exploited mainly by the privileged, and that is why many brilliant individuals in society fail to develop their capacities, and the nation is deprived of their potential. Almost 20 crore individuals are living far below the ideal level of existence in our country. For children belonging to this class, equality in the opportunities for education are inconceivable as long as special provisions are not made for them. This problem is being tackled to some extent through the policy of reservations, but it is also taking the nation towards a crisis. But, if such reservations are based on income, the result will be the eradication of a caste-based communalism, and also provide equal opportunities to children in the educational sphere.

14. *Problem of Educational Structure* : The educational structure is not uniform throughout the country; it is different in different states, and, as a result, we do not find mobility in the educational system. If the educational structure is made uniform, it will be possible to achieve a growth in social unity.

Difficulties of Qualitative Nature

The Kothari Commission reflected on the problems of education, considering every aspect and form of education, with the exception of medical sciences. The Commission has made an effort to come to terms with all kinds of problems inherent in the educational world. However, it was found that the Commission's statement of purpose was riddled by inconsistencies. What happened was that instead of solving existing problems, the Commission became the cause of numerous other problems. It gradually became clear that the crossroads at which education now found itself was the age old crossroads, with which we have been familiar since antiquity.

1. *Qualitative Growth in Education* : One important basis of qualitative improvement in education is the pay given to teachers. The pay scales considered adequate by the Commission failed to attract the teachers. This is not surprising, in view of the rising price index. In fact, the pay scales are shameful. Connected with this problem is the obstinacy of State governments, of which the government of Uttar Pradesh has provided an excellent example, Institutions are being compelled to face numerous intractable problems in implementing the new scales of pay. The redtapism of the Education Department must be held responsible for creating many problems.

The teachers movements give an inkling of the revolution which is brewing. Glancing at this state of affairs, the erstwhile Minister of Education, Dr. V.K.R.V Rao was compelled to observe that he had often become aware of the neglect of Indian teachers, which had been going on for decades. This neglect took two forms—denial of an adequate livelihood, denial of any suitable opportunities for his own professional development. Though some steps had been taken in this direction after independence, they were woefully inadequate. On the other hand, the teacher had adopted the method of revolution. In addition, there was a gradual assimilation of external vested interests in this movement, and consequently, the bright and respected image of the teacher in society was undergoing distortion. Dr. Rao did not deny the fact that a revolution was, in fact, necessary. In certain circumstances, revolutions become inevitable, but when they are organised by teachers, they should be in consonance with dignity of teachers so that the feelings of students, guardians and society towards the teachers should not be poisoned, and the teachers' respected image should not be destroyed.

On the other hand, the government had its own limitations. But, Dr. Rao admitted that it was the duty of administrators, politicians and elected representatives not to close their eyes towards the problems of teachers. If the government could not meet the demands of teachers because of limitations of resources, it could at least listen sympathetically to the teachers and explain to the teachers the reality of the situation. For certain unavoidable needs, available resources could be improved, while for others, steps could be taken to find a solution in the near future.

Dr. Rao's ideas are very far from reality, though he is perfectly aware of reality because of his close contact with education in the past. He is also aware of the problems of education. But the atmosphere of ministership surrounding him compels him to a kind of duplicity. This is nothing new in his case. Every teacher who became a minister soon moulded himself to the atmosphere surrounding ministers. The language of administration is marked by 'should', not by 'this is so'. In brief, what this means is that the problem cannot be solved as long as the distinction between professions and deeds continues. In fact, the commission has left no stone unturned in giving birth to class differences. The pay scales applicable to teachers, from the primary to the university level, give not even a slight indication of the principle of 'equal pay for equal ability.'

2. *Problem of Language* : The problem of language has also added to the problem of education. The Kothari Commission is also responsible for highlighting and intensifying this problem, because it raised a storm of controversy over this question. It was perhaps not aware of the truth that Hindi is the language of the nation, and that it was being prevented from taking its rightful place by political machinations and manipulations. Dr. Ramdhari Singh Dinkar has explicated the three-language formula in the following terms: We may suppose that a student of Bengal learns Bengali in (a) and English in (b). This allows him the freedom to fulfil the requirement of (c) by studying either French or Marathi. In the same way, if a student of Bihar studies Hindi in (a) and English in (b), he may learn Urdu or Russian to fulfil the requirement of (c).

This elaboration is based on the Commission's following formula.

(a) Mother tongue

(b) The state language of the Union or any parallel state language

(c) any new Indian or European language different from those under (a) and (b).

3. *Social and National Unity* : The Commission laid stress on the generation of national and social unity, but without clarifying how this objective was to be achieved. Besides, the Commission also failed to elaborate the meaning of Indian democracy. Dr. Sampurnanand has commented that no one dares argue that the objective of education in Soviet Russia, the U.S.A., England and France is not the comprehensive development of the country's citizens but the values which are declared to be the objective of western democratic countries are different from the values enumerated by the proponents of the Soviet Russian ideology. What is called dictatorship or tyranny by one country is called democracy by another. The term 'democracy' is one which should be clearly defined because when national and social unity reaches the hands of a dictator like Hitler, it becomes a most potent vehicle of evil.

4. *Work Experience vs. Basic Education* : The Commission has sought to introduce practical work experience at every level of education and to make education dynamic and productive. Despite the passage of considerable time since the publication of the Commission's report, no State has summoned up the courage to implement its curriculum. They see it as the productive system of Basic Education. On the contrary, the truth is that the scheme of practical work experience is the death knell of basic education. Our state governments try to imitate others or to delay action-whenever it is a question of accepting any responsibility concerning education. Dr. V.K.R.V Rao is of the view that education should be brought into close relationship with life and production. Nevertheless, before initiating this programme, the preexisting economic situation should be observed carefully. Only then can

there be any hope of success. He favours emphasis upon those schemes which do not involve economic problems, for instance, students should be given holidays during the days when they can work on their farms at home, or cooperate with their parents in other ways. By such means, education can be brought into ever closer contact with life, and it will be able to make progress as an effective instrument of society.

5. *Curriculum and 'Teacher Training* : Dr. Rao has pointed out that the view that teachers nowadays have no interest in their work was gaining currency in society. He feels this to be completely unfounded. He suggests that the same remark applies with equal truth to doctors, administrators, politicians and workers. It is a pervasive fact, a national disease. Then how can teachers remain free from its taint? For this, we need dedication, self-confidence, intimacy, and the creation of human values.

In order to increase the teacher's desire for better scholarship and greater ability, there should be some institutions whose membership should evolve great honour upon its possessor. The rules pertaining to such institutions should be based upon the objectives and activities in the educational sphere favoured by the people as a whole. Dr. Rao expresses the feeling that the honour bestowed by institutions of such a nation will be more inspiring and dignified than the awards distributed by the administrative machinery.

There is frequent mention of the decline in quality and standards in education. Qualitative, improvement presupposes the following three things- (1) Adequate material and physical resources should be available in schools, i.e., such things as libraries, buildings, laboratories, apparatus, materials, etc. (2) Capable teachers should be recruited and there should be provisions for training during employment or period of service, and (3) there should be an environment suitable to studying, and teaching in every institution. Of the three, the last factor is the most important, and it becomes possible only when teachers devote themselves dedicatedly to the task of teaching. Caution is also needed to ensure that the teachers' work is not unduly interfered with by persons not connected with education, the administration or the government. Achieving this is not as simple as it may appear. For this, it is necessary to generate the right awakening in society, it is not something which can be achieved by preparing a curriculum or providing the right text-books. Instead, it will be necessary to organise conferences and meetings at state levels for the organisers and administrators of schools in rural areas so that they are aware of their true responsibilities, and are able to manage schools in the best possible way.

Other Problems : From the viewpoint of education, our country is undoubtedly lagging far behind other countries. It has also faced a number of other complex problems. A solution to these problems was offered in the form of the Kothari Commission. Despite this, she path seems completely unchanged. Though government statistics give some satisfaction, the fact remains that education is in the doldrums. One must ask: why does such a state of affairs exist? The reason lies in the misunderstandings harboured by the government as well as the people as a whole, in the wrong techniques adopted, and in the fact that their basis is private self-interest.

The Kothari Commission made a telling point in its observation that education must be given the form of a complete process; teachers must be given the opportunities to maintain their existence; national development should be given the greatest attention to maintain the nation's very existence. It recommended that education in agriculture, industry and other professions should be made a part of the educational structure. It advised that the principle of an education coextensive with life should be adopted.

1. *Need for an Educational Plan* : The great educational plan for the next twenty years is unique. Its characteristic principle is that the development of the nation comprehends the development of the individual and the development of the individual contributes to the development of the nation. Because of this, the plan exhibits a touching faith in antiquity while at the same time, it gives expression to an attachment, faith and love for the future based on reason, not superstition.

2. *The Question of Existence* : On considering the question of existence, we are faced with certain old convictions which have assumed the form of questions. The Kothari Commission has sought an answer to the problem posed by the late Jawaharlal Nehru - Can we associate scientific and technological progress with the progress of the mind and the progress of the soul? We can never be untrue to science because it puts before us the fundamental truths and facts of life. In spite of this, can we not be assured and confident about the facts which India has additionally honoured and observed? We have to take firm steps toward industrial progress, while remembering that all material thing turn to dust and ashes in the absence of charity, patience and wisdom. (Introductory page of Education Commission, para 22, 1.86).

3. *What is to be Done* : We must remember that the aim of education is to build the nation. While many factors influence nation building, in the final analysis, this objective can be achieved only through (1) self-reliance in foodgrains (2) economic development (3) political development (4) social and national unity (S) development of human resources (6) national awakening (7) growth of democratic values. This objective is possible of attainment only through a revolutionary change in education.

4. *Suggestions by the Kothari Commission* : On the subject of the complete report of the Kothari Commission and the problems it gave rise to, it can be said that it is a very significant educational plan. Society has to resort to modernisation in order to educate itself. It must make an attempt to bring into existence an educated class comprehending citizens belonging to every class, deeply imbued with the qualities characteristic of India, so that it can raise the educational standard of the average citizen. The present age with its lack of faith and sense of direction has brought aimlessness not only to our country but the whole world, and as a result the old generation wants to shackle the younger generation in its own dogmas, customs and traditions. On the other hand, the new generation is filled with the furious desire for a revolutionary change. It is becoming difficult to find the path of accommodation and adaptation.

1. Generation unrest and gap was observed obviously after independence. Students unrest now become a common regular phenomena having its roots in politics. Political leaders gave wrong direction to the youths under the names of political youth organisations.
2. Teachers were exploited by society of haves. They have followed the path of confrontation against the Government for their jobs, social, economic and cultural security and for the survival of their own-selves.
3. The problem of national language still remains unsolved. Though Hindi is declared as a link language of nation, yet it could not get its right place due to the reasons known to all.
4. There is nothing obvious between the masses and the administration. Multi-tier system of education is found in the country which is ultimately responsible for creating drama on the stage of nation.

Therefore the following points should be kept in mind while planning for the education

1. Development of national consciousness should be the important aim of education. For this we should be aware of : (i) our cultural heritage (ii) its revaluation and (iii) firm faith in future.
2. For the qualitative improvement of education due emphasis be given to teacher education. For this (i) right type of persons should be attracted towards teaching profession (ii) they must possess high character, spiritual and moral values (iii) and must have professional wealth.

Development of the Nation

Ours is a country known by the name of India; ours is the nationality-Indian; ours is the Constitution which has a common goal of achieving justice- social, economic and political; freedom of expression of thought, of development and availing opportunities, achievement of integration national, social and emotional; attaining the common bonds of fraternity and unity.

Needless to say that all these ideals and goals cannot be achieved until and unless we do not overhaul the entire curriculum, method of teaching, rather the entire system of education with our national objectives in view. It is a bare truth that uniformity at all standards of education to bring out a coordination in the prevailing system which is eventually a state subject is the dire need of the hour.

Explosion of Population

There is population -explosion and that has left a vacuum in providing the equalization of opportunities in the realm of education. The ratio between the teacher and the taught is inadequate. Dearth of foodgrains, economic development, lack of employment opportunities, wide gap between the privileged, domination of the narrow loyalties under the guise of ideology, religion, language, state, caste, creed, etc., are some of the hurdles which require immediate consideration with a concrete follow up programme if national reconstruction is to be made with sincere efforts so that we may not only be able to solve the gigantic problems our country is facing at present but also raise the status of Bharat.

Change in Society

Education is a powerful tool for social change. Society goes on under a continuous process of change. Emerson was right when he asserted that it is not wealth or high pillars which make a man. Education can build a nation and can lead the entire nation on the path of progress. It is only through education that we can inculcate the feeling of self-sacrifice, patriotism, critical and analytical thinking, character building etc., which may ultimately transform an individual and society as a whole. For that we will have to evolve a national policy on education. History gives an evidence that it is only the educated elite which has brought a change in the world. Education trains the mind and leads an individual towards critical thinking and analogical outlook.

Education is not something which may be discussed in an isolated water-tight compartment; it requires aims, contents, teaching points, students, teacher, time table, vocational efficiency. Keeping in view the needs of society and the national objectives and exploitation of the manpower to raise the status of the country in the international sphere. The national development has its base in economic progress and productivity. If we want to bring out a social change we will have to see the modernization without sacrificing the gems of our rich cultural heritage

Contrary to Productivity

Only a handful of elite dominate all walks of life. This control is due to the ignorance of the people. The privileged always rule over unprivileged and the former have been exploiting them like any thing. This tendency has been widening the gap between haves and have-nots. The social unrest caused through this can only be removed if the following programmes are implemented.

— Science as a basic component of education and culture.

— Work experience as an integral part of general education, especially at the secondary school level to meet the needs of industry, agriculture and trade, and improvement of scientific and technological education and research at the university stage with special emphasis on agriculture and allied sciences.

As for the question of the adoption of science along with culture, India has been following the same from times immemorial. It is only ignorance which is giving impetus to the technology based on experience rather than science. Work experience is a system which provides opportunities for self-employment and prepares a man for the job in his future and present. That is why the Kothari Commission visualised for vocationalization of secondary education.

Integration of the Nation

There is a lot of diversity in our country. Language, provincialism, factionalism, regionalism, religion have been disturbing the nation's peace and order. National integration can only be achieved through cultural and moral integration. This needs stability in character. For this the following programme should be implemented.

— Introducing a common school system of public education.

— Making social and national service as an integral part of education at all stages.

— Developing all modern Indian languages and taking necessary steps to enrich Hindi as quickly as possible so that it is able to function effectively as the official language of the Union, and

— Promoting national consciousness.

Phase of Modernization

We can breath in a traditional society but we cannot live the life in it in the sense of the term. In the fast running world, there is always struggle for existence. We can exist only when we go ahead by maintaining the progress of science and technology. "Indian society of today is heir to a great culture. Unfortunately, however, it is not an adequately educated society and unless it becomes one, it will not be able to modernize itself and to respond appropriately to new challenges of national reconstruction or take its rightful place in the comity of nations," the National Commission says. For achievement of six major universities has been recommended.

Spiritual and Moral Values

Modernization does not mean that the social, moral and spiritual values be neglected and not given due importance. It is the age of conflict of culture, materialism and ethical values. It is the conflict between discerning and non-discerning, between values, patterns and concepts and man! He is missing his path.

Now education should be accepted as a powerful means of social revolution. There should be radical changes in education. We need quality but along with action. There should be close coordination of plan and execution. We have to go, rather rush with the world in this race. It is a challenge, but who will accept it, you, he or the legislative members, students, teachers, guardians, government, public, who,? Who will decide the fate?

The Menace

Napoleon once told his soldiers to have faith in God, but also to keep their powder dry, because even God could not make we-gun-powder usable. This remark seems to apply appropriately to the social forces bringing about rapid changes in today's volatile society. Education today is equivalent to Napoleon's powder and politics to God. Our powder-that is, education- has become so wet that it cannot be modified and improved in accord with circumstances. And, though politics is God, it cannot dry this wet powder. It is because of this wetness that the student and the teacher of today are completely helpless in providing society with the necessary sense of direction. The corrupt politics and society of today have completely altered the values of life. Human values now have different, unheard of definitions. National values have been swallowed by selfishness.

The life of every nation receives its truest sustenance from its system of education. A living educational system is the foundation of a life full of vivacity and energy, and it is the educational system which gives impetus to society and the life of the nation. It creates, shapes and moulds the national character. The bases of educational policy are the purposes and aims of the nation, for the fulfilment of which the country's administrative system must be possessed of honesty, dynamism and efficiency. These factors advance a nation's interests and take it towards its objectives through the medium of the educational system, and make it prosperous and contented. The individual and the nation are complementary units. In the event of any imbalance or disharmony between the two, both are destroyed. Adjustment with passing time, adaptation to a changing environment are bitter truths of life. A nation must not loose its sense of direction as time passes and circumstances change.

The history of education in India after independence establishes clearly that changing times have brought aimlessness, loss of a sense of direction. In this period of uncertainty, the life of our country is standing at the crossroads, immobile, lifeless, bewildered. It is seeking in vain for the right direction.

Our Constitution made education a subject to be dealt with by the States, not by the nation, a cruel mistake for which the new generation is paying. The acceptance of invisible responsibilities in the sphere of general and higher education was, for the Centre, no more than an escape, a flight from circumstances. Article 45 of the Constitution is a dead letter, a mere pronouncement. Even the question of achieving its implicit objective does not arise.

1. *The Politics of Education* : In theory, the basis of the politics of education is the Constitution, which we ourselves have framed and adopted, but it has completely neglected national character, and it was on the basis of this Constitution that our politicians played cruelly and willfully with the future of the nation. These politicians turned their entire energies to the physical or material development of the country. This led to cracks in dams, silence of generators producing electricity, immobilized wheels of the railways, roads leading to nowhere, and aeroplanes sitting idly on the ground. All this happened because the basis or content of education has been hollow. Our politicians lacked the foresight needed to prepare a blueprint for creating the foundation necessary for nation building.

The educational system and educational process in each state have differed so radically from those in other States that instead of encouraging national and emotional unity, it is disunity and alienation which have been promoted. Granting pensions to those who participated in the anti-Hindi movement in Tamil Nadu is an index of this national degeneration. Today, we have arrived at a stage in which citizens of one region face difficulties in working in or doing trade with other regions. Regional imbalances prove the view that making education a state subject was like subjecting the country to slow poisoning.

2. *Political Alienation* : The educational system and the social, political and economic circumstances, and the social and psychological diversity have all helped to evolve educational

politics as the politics of alienation. And, today, because of this alienation, there is strong discontent in every individual's mind. Every individual is dissatisfied and anxious. It would have been far better if a single educational current had flowed through and enveloped the entire country. Such an education would have aroused social and national awareness. But narrow political interests ignored this vital national need. The consequences of such narrow-mindness are before us. When a troubled mind whispers the word of revolution into one's ears, one is advised to maintain harmony between enthusiasm and commonsense, but this policy does not apply to these politicians.

Today, education has come to be regarded, in the political field, as a device for catching votes. This has entangled the educational class in political alienation, leading to confusion. One must wonder why no attention is being paid to this. Each one of our political parties raises its voice in favour of far-reaching changes in education. But these slogan-mongering parties are devoid of any national awareness, though they include members even of the party in power. In the recent election, students were given misleading and false assurances and the result was that these assurances themselves became a halter for the politicians.

3. *Neglect of Teacher* : In this field of educational politics, the present state of the teacher is not merely pitiable, it is worse. The one link that maintains the balance and liaison between bureaucrats, polycrats and students has been eliminated. Chancellors of universities do not think it necessary to take the advice of teachers when they are faced with student problems and student movements. It is the teachers who are asked to organise examinations, but directions are issued by the university administration, which drunk in the glory of its power over teachers, overlooks every important aspect.

The alienation pervading our universities and colleges has further intensified social differences, because of which harmony and balance have become impossible to maintain. Even such basic ideals as equal pay for equal work or equal pay for equal ability have been trampled underfoot. The Kothari Commission was right when it observed that, unfortunately, on the whole, our school system lacks any concrete traditions for the development of national unity and national consciousness. What is needed for developing national consciousness and cultural awareness and evaluation is an inspired devotion. This is completely lacking.

4. *Impact of Active Politics* : Now, the sole task of the teacher has degenerated into pointing out some important question and dictating the simplest possible answers to them, thus completing the courses of study. The teacher, today, is no better than an insignificant servant, who, on the one hand, must bow low before superiors, officials or suffer their anger, and on the other hand, suffer the indignities heaped upon him by his students. The general degeneration of social character is evident from numerous incidents every day. Our political parties have organised students unions into destructive forces. This is as true of one as of another student union, irrespective of whether they bear the name of Youth Congress, Vidyarthi Parishad, Yuvjan Sabha, Yuva Janta or any other name. All that students do is to wear the appropriate badge and organise political mass fights. A clear symbol of the crisis in education is the fact that central ministers and members of parliament take the deepest possible interests and give vent to their fiercest political loyalties in the elections to the students union of Delhi University.

Political statements also aggravate the crisis among students. In 1974, one newly elected minister of Uttar Pradesh went so far as to declare that students would be promoted without examinations. As a result, the entire order and timing of examinations has gone haywire. Examinations in most universities are postponed from March to May, and then again to August, when they are actually held. With the result, students suffer the loss of one full academic year.

The express demand of our time and our environment is that students should not be dragged into politics, that their creative energies should be employed to generate 'a national spirit. But, nothing concrete has been done in this direction. Our political leaders have yet to find the key to this problem.

It is a strange anomaly that, at the national political level, the education minister is not a minister of cabinet rank. One wonders why the chief executive authority in the educational sphere, though education is regarded as the foundation for nation building, is not provided with a suitable rank. This fact clearly suggests that our legislators are perpetrating a huge fraud upon the nation. State ministers of education are in an even worse position, since their voice echoes hollowly and ineffectively in the schools owned and managed by industralists and self-styled social workers. Managers of educational institutions reap rich harvests in a period in which the politics of education is riddled with corruption.

If we are to think of education in the context of a national awakening, it is necessary to change our present Constitution. As long as the articles of the present Constitution, relating to education,, stand unchanged, we cannot ever dream of a healthy educational system. Hence our objective should be-one nation, one Constitution and one educational system. In the last analysis, there should be no provision for private enterprise. Otherwise, we will continue to wander and roam, as we have been doing till the present.

The Causes

The crises in education actually arose as soon as we got independence. In our ignorance, we thanked our fortune for the social structure we had inherited from our period of slavery to a foreign power. We were so deeply obliged for that we accepted it as an invariable part of our life. Before independence, we were staunch opponents of Macaulay's educational system. After independence, ironically enough, the makers of our nation and a few vested interests began regarding Macaulay as a messiah. They recklessly adhered to Macaulay's ideas, with the result that his educational system sowed the seeds of casteism and class conflict in our society and in our educational world. Education of a particular group led to the emergence of a class of bureaucrats and politicians, while on the other hand, a governing class was created in the name of education of the people. It was this class conflict that has led to the crisis in education.

The crisis in education has overwhelmed the whole world, because the rise in population brought forth increasing numbers of students. The opportunities of education did not keep pace with the rise in population. Despite this, the expenditure on education increased at a rapid pace. At the same time, education began to grow in, the form of a local industry or enterprise, and hence the crisis in education is the product of many factors.

1. *Increase in Population* : The population has risen rapidly all over the world, while at the same time, the death-rate has registered a dramatic fall. It was only natural that the problem of providing the means of living for this increased number of people should confront the world. Educational opportunities did not increase in the same proportion, and consequently, an educational emergency arose all over the world. It is also true that a nation's educational system is closely linked with the struggle for life. There is inadequacy of money, teachers and classrooms, but there is no paucity of students. The gravity of the educational crisis confronting the world can hardly be delineated through maps.

2. *Differences due to Local Factors* : Though the educational crisis is universal, local differences have created much variety in its form and context at different places. However, the model of this crisis is the same in every country, a model which was variously called Change, Adaptation and Disparity. Since 1945, the world has witnessed a remarkable scientific and technological revolution. And, the consequent unregulated changes in educational policies led to educational crisis and conflict.

Reasons Behind

The major reasons responsible for the universal educational crisis are the following- (1) Increasing desire for education, (2) Lack or inadequacy of the means to education. (3) the internal permanent agency of education, (4) the structure of society. With the development and extension of the field of knowledge and science, the desire for education in the common people has increased, and as a result, the need for expanding education was felt. The change in the prevailing educational values in the traditional system gave rise to the view that national development was possible only through the maximum utilization of the nation's educated manpower.

Education and society must undergo adaptation in order to overcome this crisis, without which the structure of both must necessarily undergo degeneration. In order to face this challenge, the resources of domestic life, as distinct from the resources of national life, have to be adopted. Money is needed, but the allocations made for education in the national budget are not sufficient to provide all the means of education. Consequently, the optimum utilisation of the nation's manpower, should take place with a view to quality, efficiency and productivity. Transformation is possible only through ideas, courage and determination. It is here that the responsibility of the planners of education increases manifold. Each nation needs an educational system suited to its circumstances and resources.

Responsibility

Education is not the panacea for all the ills of society. Education-does not have adequate time to seek and provide a cure for all of society's varied ills. For the same reason, education cannot satisfy and fulfil all of society's ambitions. Education is, in fact, a faith, on the basis of which the individual undergoes development for his own benefit and the benefit of society. In providing the means for human development, the wastage that results is not due to education, but due to the circumstances of society. An important question must be asked here: Can a dogmatic faith provide assistance to any specific system in the process of rational analysis? The answer to this dogmatism gradually erodes reason in education and undermines foresight The system of education seems to combine the teaching of folk songs with that of science and technology, it is a cruel satire on education. At the same time, from the social viewpoint, such means also suffer misuse because these means fail to satisfy the real needs of society.

On the other, it is no less a fact that, even in the absence of means, an educational system for society can be evolved by putting faith in the philosophy of 'Know Thyself.'

1. *Attitude towards the Teaching Profession* : With changing circumstances has come a change in the attitude towards teachers and the profession of teaching. With the invention of new methods of teaching and modern teaching aids, the teacher can increase his efficiency. But, the explosion in knowledge, which is also responsible for the educational crisis, has not been able to give the requisite impetus to the teaching profession. Classes are still devoid of new knowledge. Consequently; there has come about an imbalance between the expectations from education and its achievements.

2. *Dogmatism* : One cause of the educational crisis is the dogmatism of teachers. There was a time when the dogmatic farmer hesitated in introducing the new methods of farming in his field, but today, the same situation is found with regard to teachers. The position of small schools is similar to that of small and scattered fields. They are lacking in the means for research. One cause of the fragmentation of education is the transference of traditional knowledge from one generation to another, because of the traditions practised in society. Today, education is bearing a heavy load of responsibility, but, in the existing circumstances, the fulfilment of this responsibility is a complex and difficult task. The task of educating the nation is no easier than the task of putting man on the moon. Hence, in the sphere of educational conflict, it is essential to get victory over the dogmatism inherent in this sphere.

Input-output Process

Input		*Output*
		Creation of stalled persons in the field of
1. Knowledge	1. Educational aims	1. Family
2. Values	2. Contents	2. Trade
3. Goals	3. Students-teachers activity	3. Leadership
4. Population and qualified manpower	4. Finances	4. Cultural
		These are developed by-

Contd...

Input		*Output*
5. Economic output and income	5. Physical items	1. Fundamental knowledge
		2. Physical and mental abilities
		3. Value, attitude and motivation
		4. Logical power
		5. Creativity
		6. Cultural praise
		7. Social responsibility
		8. Knowing the modern world

Table given rise to many questions through the use of such terms as management, technology, efficiency, quality; etc. In reality, all these combine to give rise to the educational process as well as the crisis in education.

National Problem

In his work *'World Educational Crisis'*, Philip H. Coomb has delineated the educational crisis in many countries, of which India is one. This crisis in India has been viewed and analysed from various points of views, such as-policy on admission, inefficient administration, students at the primary level, dropouts, economic growth, economic expenditure, college population, problems of teachers, etc.

The Kothari Commission has reflected on the educational crisis in terms of Input and Out put the three spheres examined by it are:

1. Transformation of the internal form of the educational method, so that it can be brought into intimate relationship with the life, needs and ambitions of the nation.
2. Qualitative improvement in education so as to make the

standards achieved by it adequate, and to ensure that such standards keep on improving with the aim of making them comparable to standards in the international sphere.

3. Expansion of educational facilities according to the needs of the population and stress upon equality of educational opportunities.

The three problems point towards the educational crisis. Hence education has been considered in the context of the problem of national development. Our nation's problems are-self-sufficiency in foodgrains, economic development, universal employment, social and national unification, and political development. Consequently, education must be made to conform to the lives, needs and ambitions of the people. The crisis in education can be rooted out only when education becomes flexible enough to change along with social dynamism and mobility.

Changing Pattern

Once, during a seminar, an informal discussion on educational objectives brought to light the fact that in India, the determination of educational priorities did not exist. After the analysis of the curricula of many states, it was found that they were incapable of fulfiling any educational purpose. It was felt that educational curricular are formulated merely to bestow priority on the choices indulged in by some Commissions.

Whenever I go to schools, I am overwhelmed by the feeling that we are indulging in a gigantic game in the name of education. After a glance at the results of examinations and marks obtained by my own children, I am compelled to view with alarm the yawning gap between profession and practice. On talking to lady and gentlemen principals of schools, I feel that the whole blame rests squarely on the shoulders of teachers. In talks with teachers themselves or the office bearers of teachers unions, the entire blame shifts to the government, but when I glance helplessly at the predicament of my own children, I feel that the entire fault lies with the parents themselves. The present day analysis of the educational process turns into mutual recrimination and shifting of the responsibility and blame to others. The unfortunate victim of this game of passing the buck is the helpless student.

Books on education have always provided impressive lists of the objectives of education, because they include such things as social, individual, professional, and cultural development, proper utilization of leisure and entertainment, integral development, spiritual development, and external or physical development. Students appearing for examinations learn such lists by rote, though they cannot imbibe them. They win freedom after learning of such objectives in the way best suited to them. I often see and meet many old teachers who never obtained any training anywhere, never studied the elaborate explanation of educational foundations in the context of the philosophy of education, never possessed any practical knowledge of educational psychology, and yet their students are performing their duties devotedly and faithfully in many walks of life. The success with which these untrained teachers have achieved the objectives of education is worthy of imitation.

The teacher of today receives training. In the context of its philosophical, sociological and psychological foundations, the curriculum of training is completed in one or two years. During training, he takes a variety of oaths-that he will be a devoted teacher, adopt the scientific and psychological methods of teaching, etc. But, when he enters the sphere of action his entire training goes overboard. His acquired skill becomes worthless, and like his predecessors, he anxiously waits for the 'pay-day' after making motions of having done his duty. An artificial dissatisfaction enters his life. Possibly, it may be difficult to find a better instance of the projection of reproach.

The questions staring us in the face are- why do such things happen? Have we strayed from our objectives? We are feigning ignorance, and hence, we cannot find an answer to these questions. And so, we come to feel that both our vision and our sense of direction have suffered distortion and mutilation.

Soon after independence, Dr. Radhakrishnan pointed out, on the basis of the suggestions of the Commission, that the objective of education is to discover the innate qualities of the individual and to develop them by training. Universities should fulfil these obligations towards their students. In fact, these obligations should be fulfilled not only by universities but by each and every educational institution. It is obvious that these objectives imply the development of a healthy mind. Personalities themselves lacking in harmony and balance; of which there is no dearth in any sphere of education, have failed to make students balanced and harmonious.

The crucial and challenging question before our country immediately after independence was the question of survival, or of existence. Man's existence is founded on material goods and the nation's existence on thought, awareness and consciousness. These latter elements bear a direct relation to education. Education has its beginnings at the primary level, but the suggestions of the Radhakrishnan Commission were adopted, and once again the Secondary Education Commission was granted the responsibility for determining and achieving the objectives of education. This Commission made its first attack on educational objectives. It profoundly observed that the political, social and economic circumstance had changed and new problems had emerged. It had become necessary to make a careful examination and redetermine the objectives of education at every level. This statement applies not only to the present situation, but also to the future evolution of education, the future of nature and social system, in which education has to modify itself, and to which education must adapt itself.

Consequently, the foundation for the development of democratic citizenship, professional efficiency, personality and leadership was given the following shape- (1) students should be given training in character so that they may be able to take part in the democratic process, (2) students should be given practical and professional training so that they may contribute to making the country economically prosperous, (3) students should be prepared for literary, artistic and cultural interests, which are essential for man's integral development and expression of self; in the absence of this, the country's culture will be underminded.

It is clear that the country's educationists had determined the objectives of education in conformity with the potential needs of the new democratic nation. But by the time the year 1964 came, it was felt that the implementation of the objectives of the 1953 Commission had been faulty. Students were taught mob behaviour in the name of democracy, anarchistic behaviour in the name of organisation, ignorance in the name of knowledge, irresponsibility in the guise of devotion and dedication, disbelief in the name of faith, and rights in the name of duties. The outcome was that the three points of the educational wheel-the teacher, the student and the curriculum-continued to sink steadily into a quagmire from which there was, for them, no emerging.

The declared purposes of the Commission of 1964 caused an explosion whose echoes can be heard even today. The truth of the matter is that society does, in reality, want to build the nation, but the management of society is in the hands of profiteers and black marketeers who are short-sighted and conscious only of their immediate interests. So, they regard the expenditure on education as no better than the money spent on a charity. The results of such negligence are before us. The student movements and the teacher movements are the result of this exploitation and torture. This has made it painfully evident once again that we have failed to achieve the objectives we ourselves created.

In restructuring educational objectives, we have kept before us the vision of national development. We have reflected on the possible modifications in the prevailing educational system. We have laid stress on determination and patience. Hence, the objectives of education have been determined in the new context, which comprehends such things as self-reliance in foodgrains, economic development and employment, social and national unification, development, etc.

Objectives of education have remained more or less the same in all ages. The main aim has always been-giving direction to society and the individual. But in this context, the dominating pattern has been that of the individual. Individuals have proved lethargic and negligent in honouring educational objectives, irrespective of whether these individuals are managers or legislators, teachers or parents, students or any others. Each one has given priority only to his own convenience. The teacher does not bother about fulfilling the objectives of education but about completing the course, as though that were the sole objective of his effort. The principal's sole objective is a satisfactory result. The management aims solely at grabbing money, by means fair or foul. Parents feel satisfied when they have sent their children to the prison of the school. What all this means is that there is so much variation and instability in the patterns and models of individuals that the aid which a liberal attitude has given them itself prevents them from regaining their balance.

Today, the contexts have altered. The negligence of the last twenty five years may have cheated no one else, but it has certainly cheated the younger generation. The founders of education, who have indulged in the worst possible exploitation of and injustice towards students, should now beware. For the present, student unrest is only a foreshadow of its real self, but it has indicated that the objectives of education, modes of teaching, behaviour, all must be changed; if they are not changed, students will replace those who was responsible for education.

These questions keep flashing through my mind. I see that the form of education lies entangled in the legislative assembles of states, the chairs of ministers, the files of secretaries and the helpless shortsightedness of our legislators. There is a need for dedication to the nation, for development of the nation, for its cultural development, for religion, morality and character. All its needs are lost sight of in the futile exercises in manpower planning and determination of the objectives of education, and devising suitable plans and schemes for achieving them. It is impossible to forecast when our nation will arise from its long slumber, when it will look at itself and the people with new eyes. What I wonder is whether our people have the necessary courage, dedication and ability?

The Resolution

The following steps will have to be taken to resolve the educational crisis in the country:

1. Educational values must be remoulded and reshaped from the social, moral and spiritual viewpoints.
2. Education must be linked with production. Science, practical experience and professionalisation will be elements in this education.
3. A uniform system of school education must be implemented for social and national unification. A programme for national and social service will have to be implemented. The language policy will have to be geared to achieve national unity. A national awareness will have to be generated.
4. Education must be linked with modernization.
5. Teachers must be given a position of respect and honour, a high social position.
6. Administration of education must be improved.
7. Stress must be laid on job oriented education.

2

Social Problems

Stage of Development

Education is a life-long and a never-ending process which continues throughout life. As time passes, changes keep on occurring, and every individual has necessarily to pass through these phases of change. The criterion of success for any individual is the extent to which he can adapt himself to changing circumstances. Keeping in mind this viewpoint, the Education Commission has opined that, in a democracy, the function of adult education is to give to every individual the opportunity for obtaining the kind of education he wants, the kind of education which can contribute effectively to his individual prosperity, professional progress as well as his social and political life. The Education Commission has greatly enlarged the scope of adult education by saying that the field of adult education is as vast as life itself.

India has, for a long time, suffered from a very low percentage of literacy. During the British period, Lord Macaulay's educational policy did much to alleviate this illiteracy, and though, during this period, the British government did, in theory, accept the importance of public education, in practice it did little to achieve this goal. Whatever little was actually achieved was the result of the following three forces- (i) Rise of a middle class in urban areas. (ii) The cooperative movement in the villages. (iii) Growth of political consciousness among the people.

Of these, it was the third factor which contributed the most, and it is. the same political consciousness which has made the future of adult education bright. Till the end of the World War I, satisfactory progress was made in this direction. Adult classes were run exclusively as night classes, and the teacher working in these classes was given an additional allowance.

The cooperative movement was started in 1905, and people felt that it was impossible to make it successful without becoming literate. Hence arrangements were made for creating libraries, and stress was laid upon the reading of newspapers. Gradually, universities set up adult education sections in their extension departments.

The growth of adult education can be divided into four periods:

First Phase : During this period, adult education suffered a blow because of the economic depression. The political movement raised the demand for adult franchise. The soldiers in the army were also infused with a strong national spirit when they returned home occasionally from their duties. By 1926, the number of cooperative committees had risen to 80,182. They conducted 100 night schools. In the Punjab, there were 3,784 adult schools in 1926-27, in which 98,414 students were enrolled. In Bombay, there were 27 schools in 1922 while in Uttar Pradesh, 6 municipalities managed night schools for providing adult education. Similar efforts were being made in the other provinces also.

Second Phase : This was a period of political turmoil, but many new schools came into existence during the time. Some missionaries, such as Dr. J.J. Lucas, Dr. J.J.H. Lawrence and Mr. Daniel prepared new books for adults in the Roman script. During this period, not much progress could take place in Punjab, because in 1936-37, it had only 189 schools with an enrolment of 4,988 students. Two experiments, however, were carried out in

Punjab. (i) Normal school teachers were inspired to organise libraries in villages for adult education ; and (ii) Cultural centres were set up in villages.

Similar experiments were also carried out in Bombay, Madhya Pradesh, etc., and many new institutions took birth, among them the Rural Reconstruction Association, Adult Education League, Literacy Association, Seva Sadan Social League, etc. The Travancore University began to send sets of books to rural libraries from its own collection for the purpose of adult education.

Third Phase : During this period, nationalist governments were set up in the provinces. Dr. Sayad Mahmood, the education minister of Bihar, himself went to villages, equipped with a blackboard and chalk, to educate the villagers. Dr. Rajgopalachari himself wrote textbooks and ran a strong movement for literacy over a period of three months. Teachers of primary schools made valiant and commendable efforts to spread literacy in villages, and as a result, 12,000 people were made literate within these three months. In this way, for the first time the responsibility for adult education was grasped by the Indian mind, and the government took this onerous task into its own hands. New curricula were formulated. The medium of teaching was changed. Books, posters, film shows and other things were recognised as instruments of adult education.

At this time, literacy movements were launched in Assam, Bengal, Bihar, Uttar Pradesh, Orissa, and Jammu and Kashmir, keeping in mind local conditions and needs. New textbooks were prepared for the neo-literates in regional languages, and a separate department for adult education was formally created. After 1942, the urge towards education and literacy grew even stronger in the country, the outcome of which was that by 1947 as many as 9,50,002 adults were made literate, and 6,33,896 books were distributed among them. The Talukka Library and the Bombay City Adult Education Committee were set up in Bombay, An Education Expansion Department was established in Uttar Pradesh, while comparable organisations quickly sprang up in other parts of the country also.

The period 1942-47 was a very difficult one for adult education because it was buffeted on the side by the nationalist movement, and on the other by the instability and indecision of the government. Despite this, the movement continued because the people were keen to receive education.

Education for Adults

After independence a central education advisory committee was constituted. The committee then set up a council to reflect upon the potential for adult education. This council took adult education out of the limitations of a knowledge merely of letters and raised it to the level of authentic knowledge, and, as a result, adult education was rechristened social education. A plan for social education was put before a committee of State ministers of education on February 19-20,1949, and the Government of India distributed Rs. 60 lakhs to the States for adult education.

Social education centres were established in Bihar, where, in order to speed up the pace of social education, such programmes as touring drama troops, troops of folk dances and hymn singers, etc., were organised. In Madras, libraries were developed, and a training camp for teachers was organised under the auspices of social education. Similar work was also done in Bombay. In Madhya Pradesh, literature was prepared in Hindi and Marathi. In Uttar Pradesh, Etawah a project was initiated. It was later assimilated with the development programme and social education officers came to be appointed. The Government of India, too, has played an active role through such organisations as the Institute of Audiovisual Education, the All India Radio, the Institute of Social Education, which became involved in preparing literature and discovering new techniques of adult education as well as the training of teachers.

The Kothari Commission, in particular, is extremely conscious of the need for and the importance of adult education. In one of its statements on this subject, it says that though, to its observation, the history of adult education in India is not an old one, literacy had risen to 29.3%, a fact which clearly implied that the movement should be suitably accelerated. In the sixth plan, the programme of adult education is being implemented on a national scale.

Aims and Objectives

Adult education must be looked at from a new perspective. In planning for education in backward areas, it must be remembered that the adult has already gained experience of life but in receiving education he consciously regresses to his childhood stage. At the same time, he has many memories of family responsibility and of his contribution to the economy of the family. He has to discover and form social, political, constitutional and mutual relationships. Though he may be illiterate, these elements form his background. He does not possess extensive knowledge of society, but he has the requisite ability to learn all this. He can easily learn reading, writing and counting. Hence, it is essential that the adult should be properly understood before an attempt is made to teach him.

Social education is corrective or remedial education. Those who never got a chance to go to school, or could attend school only for a short period, find that their social education has remained incomplete. The deficiency can be made up through social education.

Today, many terms have become prevalent in the sphere of social education:- Adult education, social education, informal education, continuous education, etc. Each one of these terms is indicative of adult education, but they differ conceptually from each other. The general and obvious meaning of adult education is the teaching of adults. Bryson has said that education, in every situation and in every condition for the individual is what constitutes adult education. Organ and Bundy define it as the adult individual's conscious attempt to learn. Rheins, Fenster and Hadley believe that adult education implies the education related to the individual's professional, individual and social life. The concept of a social education is a more comprehensive one in as much as it comprehends reading, writing, counting, etc., and even more, becoming a skilful and useful citizen. The term social education has been coined because the purpose is to arouse civil awareness in the individual. Humayun Kabir believes that it is a means to develop civic consciousness and social solidarity. In it, attention is paid to literacy, the creation of an educated mind, and the growth of a powerful citizenship for the nation.

S.N. Mukerjee : Social education is roughly inclusive of all the informal education that is given to adults. In India, it has two aspects- (i) adult literacy, i.e., the education of those adults who have not received any kind of education in schools, and (ii) continuous education for literate adults.

Barker : His view is that adult education constitutes that education which an individual receives on a part-time basis while continuing in his occupation.

Bryson : According to him, adult education comprehends all those activities which are related to the normal life of the individual, which have some importance for education, in the doing of which the individual has to utilise only one part of his total intellect.

K.G. Sayyidain : He sees adult education as inclusive of education of politics, of citizenship and also of morality.

Humayun Kabir : His opinion of adult education is that it aims at the development of an educated mind in an illiterate individual.

Implied in the concept of social education is the fulfilment of the needs of adults-economic efficiency, increased knowledge and the growth of cultural possessions. The objectives of social education can be pinpointed as follows:-

Remedial : Here, the purpose is to increase the individual's original or innate talent.

Vocational : In this case, the purpose is to impart commercial and industrial knowledge in urban areas and knowledge pertaining to agriculture and domestic activities in rural areas.

Health : Social education aims at acquainting adults with the basic principles of good health and the various means of maintaining hygienic conditions.

Social Skill : The objective of social education is to train the individual in maintaining harmonious relations with friends and companions, leading a satisfactory family life, and becoming conscious of one's rights and duties in society.

Recreational : In order to raise the mental level of adults, adult education seeks to develop the habit of healthy recreation. The varied means of entertainment available today have not had a desirable impact upon the minds of the people, but healthy recreation helps the individual develop his life along the right path.

Self Development : Social education aims at enabling the individual to bring about his own harmonious development by developing a thirst for knowledge, forming an individual philosophy of life and evolving a creative and aesthetic approach to life. Thus, it becomes apparent that the foregoing objectives of social education fulfil four important goals of our- national life:-

Growth of Civic Sense : Through social education, those who have been left behind in the race of progress are enabled to overtake others and to march in step with them, thus, being enabled to perform their tasks with the cooperation of others.

Utilization of National Resources : Having been influenced by adult education, adults are enabled to fulfil national objectives in their own respective spheres. Lenin said that socialism can never come through an illiterate populace because the illiterate is isolated from politics. Lenin's opinion may, or may not, apply truthfully to socialism, but it is certainly an axiom in the field of good citizenship.

Creation of Cooperative Associations : Through social education, the adult individual achieves economic as well as social progress, and thus becomes enthusiastic about the creation of cooperative associations.

Growth of a Social Viewpoint : Society as a whole cannot evolve a particular social viewpoint if its members are uneducated. For instance, the realisation that "we are Indians" can be developed and rooted deeply only when the people are educated.

On the whole, it can be said that our country needs adult

education for a social and political revolution. It can, on the one hand, develop emotional and national unity among the people, and on the other, develop self-confidence, fearlessness and skill in the individual. In fact, the success of democracy depends, to a very large extent, upon social education.

Different Institutions

Social education is the responsibility of society. In a democracy, every educated individual contributes to the shaping of society in his own individual way. And, the greater the extent to which society shoulders this responsibility, the better is it for society itself. Thus, (a) the government, (b) private institutions, and (c) universities and training institutions contribute to the spread of social education. At the governmental level, many ministries perform this task through a variety of programmes. Social education is imparted to the masses through (i) correspondence courses, (ii) vocational adult education, (iii) training of adult educators, (iv) agricultural and other professions, (v) public libraries, and (vi) museums, etc.

Area of affect : Social education is an educative process that continues through life, and hence its field is very vast. It is inclusive of spread of literacy, knowledge of rules pertaining to the safeguarding of health, vocational training for improving economic condition, feeling of citizenship, awareness of rights and duties, and healthy entertainment. In determining its scope, the following points are kept in view:-

1. Social education comprehends those subjects which are not taught in schools or those which are neglected.
2. It brings about a change in human attitudes.
3. It either reduces or eradicates the differences in social and individual progress, something which should be done through (a) knowledge, (b) deeds and (c) determination.

The Significance

Every individual today is a useful part of society. The purpose of social education is that the adult population should be educated in such a way that it may be able to improve its own life, develop the desire to create a better and a modern society instead of adhering to the traditional society, and also have faith in, the future of its nation. The responsibility for the field work in social education, including adult education, rests with the state governments and the administration of union territories.

In view of this, the importance of social education can be specified in the following terms:-

1. Social education provides the foundations for the success of democracy.
2. It is the lamp of hope for the uneducated.
3. It brings about the political, intellectual and social development of adults.
4. It inspires the aesthetic development of adults.
5. It strengthens the cultural aspect of community life.
6. It prefers new media of expression and forms of recreation.
7. When all other facilities are available in society, the existence of illiteracy is a blot.

Five Year Plans

First Plan : In the first five year plan, the education ministry provided financial aid to various projects to ensure the progress of the social education programme. Ideal community centres were set up and some special primary schools were given the form of School cum-Community Centres. Under this scheme, 116 Modern Community Centres and 454 School-cum-Community Centres were created, in addition to which many libraries, rural libraries, service centres and public colleges came to be established.

Second Plan : During the second plan, the National Fundamental Education Centre was set up with the assistance of UNESCO. Its objectives were the following:

(i) Training workers of noteworthy importance for social education, for example, district social education organisation.

(ii) Conducting research.

(iii) Creating audio-visual aids and teaching materials.

(iv) Performing the functions of an information centre.

At the same time, the Social Education Institute was established at Indore. New literature was produced for the neo-literates and literary camps were organised. The Delhi University and the National Book Trust undertook the task of training librarians to man public libraries.

Third Plan : By the third plan, literacy had risen from 16.6% to 24.0%. In different states, different kinds of programmes of social education were implemented. In addition to the public or Janata colleges, six Vidyapeeth institutions were set up in Mysore State. A social education department was set up in Rajasthan University. 205 district libraries were created in 13 States, and States also gave financial aid for distributing books in rural areas.

Fourth Plan : The three preceding plans had not given requisite importance to social education. In the fourth plan, a sum of Rs. 3.6 crores was allocated by the Central government for this purpose. The sum was invested on the following activities:-

(a) Organising and strengthening the social education administration.

(b) Establishing labour Vidyapeeth institutions.

(c) Creating suitable literature for the neo-literates.

(d) Developing and expanding the library service in Delhi.

(e) Developing a central institute of library science.

(f) Training librarians.

(g) Implementing other services related to libraries.

(h) Giving aid to voluntary educational institutions.

(i) Initiating practical schemes, setting up Janata colleges, and organising continuous education and adult schools.

(j) Developing social education institutions for the workers.

New literature was got prepared for the neo-literates with the assistance of UNESCO. 419 books were given awards, and an adult encyclopaedia was published under the title *'Gyansarovar'*. A book entitled *'Hindi Vishwabharati'* was published in ten volumes. Workshops were organised as a part of literary camps. Among the non-governmental organisations which do praiseworthy work in the sphere to social education are Indian Adult Education Association, Social Adult Education Committee, and the State Adult Education Council.

The Central Education Advisory Council, at its 31st meeting, laid down the following standard or criterion for adult education:-

(i) Recognition of about 350 words.

(ii) Ability to write numerals upto 100.

(iii) Ability to read simple charts, posters, etc.

(iv) Knowledge of objects of daily utility.

(v) Ability to write simple sentences and names.

Fifth Plan : Again, relatively less importance was attached to social education in the fifth plan. The movement that was initiated in 1937 for the total eradication of illiteracy among the masses remained a failure then, and because of this, adult education came to be modernised in the form of social education.

This programme was implemented throughout the country through the medium of community development programmes, but, for a variety of reasons, even this programme remained ineffective. As a consequence, the social education programme continued to function primarily through local institutions, with the assistance received from the State and Central governments. However, many important ideas and schemes came to light. The Vidyapeeth of Mysore, the Gram Shiksha Mohim of Maharashtra, the Bombay City Social Education Committee, the Literacy House of Lucknow, and the Rural Library Movement of Lucknow, etc., are the main forums of social education.

The Farmers' Education and Creative Literacy Movement initiated in 1961 has proved of great significance. By the end of the fourth plan period, it was expected that ten lakh farmers in 100 districts should have benefited from this movement. In addition, departments of adult education were set up in some universities for giving impetus to continuing education.

Through social education, efforts were made to provide information about the various aspects of life through programmes concerned with agricultural extension, handicraft training, family planning, child and family welfare, nutrition programmes, etc. However, the total impact of these programmes has not succeeded in bringing us near to the national goal of eradicating illiteracy.

With the expansion of primary education, the percentage of literacy, which was 24 in 1961, rose to 29.6, but the equally bitter truth was the fact that the number of illiterates rose from 333.6 million in 1961 to 386.7 million in 1971, which was obviously due to the rise in population. However, if the age groups 15 to 25 years or 25 to 45 years are taken into account while considering the above statistics, the situation appears to be a little better.

Continuing education is that form of adult education, or social education in which educational opportunities are provided to those who have given up education prematurely. In the sphere of higher education, continuing education is required most in the sphere of technical education, a fact indicated by the surveys and conclusions of the Scientific Manpower Committee (1949), Engineering Personnel Committee (1956), the Working Group on Technical Education and Vocational Training (1960), and the Technical Manpower Assessment Committee (1966), etc.

Technical education points to the path for the future plans. Hence, it becomes necessary to provide opportunities for education through correspondence courses, part-time courses or self study courses so that abilities may be developed and people may remain in touch with the latest addition to human knowledge. For this purpose, it is desirable to formulate a general policy.

For the fifth plan, the allocation of funds for adult education is illustrated in the following table:-

Adult Education Plan

	Plan	*Expenditure Rs. in Crores*
1.	State Adult Education Council	1.00
2.	Literature for adults	2.00
3.	Functional Literacy	4.00
4.	Aid to Voluntary agencies	1.00
5.	Research and Experiments	2.00
6.	Capable Schemes	10.00
7.	Continuing Education	30.00
	Total	50.00

Considerable thought was given to bringing adult education into the list of the nation's priorities. In the first place, social justice cannot be made available, and democracy cannot succeed in the absence of training in productive techniques, knowledge of fundamental economics and creation of the right attitudes. And, the success of democracy and social justice were the foundation stones of the fifth five year plan. And it was generally accepted that even the success of such a vital programme as the Green Revolution depended upon the success of adult education.

The various experiments conducted so far in social education have brought to light many important activities and ideas. All such programmes must have the in-built quality of attracting adults towards themselves. There is necessarily an intimate relationship between the adult's routine activity and social education. It should be closely related to introductory education, expansion of agriculture, cooperation, etc. Social education must be linked with the national service scheme, and even the predetermined curriculum will have to be linked to national as well as local requirements. It is also inseparably related to research and the creation of suitable literature. We must lay down a variable network of libraries in rural areas, and our aim should be to make illiteracy a thing of the past within the next few years.

1. Linking creative literacy with such nationwide and productive programmes as the extension of agriculture, animal husbandry, reclamation of land, irrigation and drinking water schemes.
2. Linking creative literacy with such important national programmes as family planning, child and family welfare programmes, etc.
3. Initiating programmes for health and nutrition, literacy, recreation, social organisations, etc., wherever the density of population is high.
4. Laying stress on the programmes that proved successful in the past ; organising adult schools and polytechnics, etc.

Of the allocated sum of Rs. 28,750 crores for social education, 20 per cent was spent upon these programmes. Rs. 580 crores were to be spent upon the training of employees. According to the plan, the States and the Centre could make provisions for Rs.100 crores, while Rs. 20 crores were set aside for setting up departments of continuing education in various universities. At the same time it was also true, that, of the total educational budget of Rs. 2,200 crores not even Rs.120 crores could be set aside for social education, and hence a provision of only Rs. 50 crores was made for this purpose.

Sixth Plan : Adult education has been given national importance in the blue-print of the sixth five year plan. In India, about 20 crore people are illiterate. In addition, about 70% of the children opt out of schools by the time they reach the fifth class, and so they also fall within the categories of illiterates or semi-literates. For this reason, the sixth plan lays special emphasis upon the eradication of illiteracy, and creation of universal primary education and industry-centered education. There is a scheme for introducing a nation-wide educational programme for the illiterates in the 15 to 35 years age group. For this, it is intended to seek the cooperation of universities, labour unions, public service planners and voluntary organisations. It is hoped that the scheme will benefit 10 crore individuals.

Under this plan, importance has been given to the speeding up of earlier programmes, which include - (i) creative literacy of farmers in rural areas, (ii) setting up of labour schools and multipurpose adult education centres in urban areas, (iii) search for adult education centres in universities, setting up of Nehru Youth Centres, (iv) national service scheme. The plan aims at activating all these schemes, and it is hoped that literacy will be brought to 15 lakh people in the first year, 45 lakhs in the second year 90 lakhs in the third year, 180 lakhs in the fourth year, and 320 lakhs in the fifth and final year of the plan. This objective can obviously be achieved only through a powerful, effective and committed administrative mechanism. Some of the special features of this plan are as follows:

Attention to Weaker Sections : The plan provides for the education of the weaker sections in rural as well as urban areas, with special attention to providing literacy to the people in the 15 to 35 age-group. Special attention will also be given to women, Scheduled Tribes, landless labourers, farm labourers and other weaker sections of society.

Society and National Development : The plan envisages that special efforts should be made to ensure that the poor and illiterate individuals develop the necessary awareness about themselves, become conscious of the social reality surrounding them, organise themselves to overcome the difficulties of daily life and become partners in the process of social and national development. Apart from literacy, attention will also be paid to the fact that mixed programmes catering to the needs of the poor are initiated, comprising of general education, health education, family planning, development of vocational skills, science in relation to daily life, knowledge of technology, physical education and cultural activities.

Inspiration to Adults : The success of the adult literacy programme depends upon the motivation of the adults, and for this purpose particular attention is to be devoted to the selection and training of workers, production of good quality teaching materials, introducing developed methods of learning through the medium of doing and living, surveys and facilities for guidance.

Cooperation of Voluntary Organisations : In order to make the plan a success, the cooperation of voluntary organisations, youth and others interested in social service activities as well as organisations engaged in commercial activities will be sought. Labour unions, retired teachers and those engaged in formal education will also be made use of as far as possible, and adult education will, again as far as possible, be linked with other developmental activities envisaged in the plan.

Stress on Decentralisation : In order to make adult education a success, emphasis has been placed on decentralisation in the sixth plan. A National Board of Central Education has been established at the centre, and it is planned that similar agencies will be created at the state, district, block and local community levels.

Programme : In the sixth plan, the programme for adult education is spread over the entire plan period. The first year is to be devoted to preparation. It is hoped that this programme can be given suitable momentum by making schemes at the block and district level after consulting all related agencies, motivating voluntary youth workers, retired employees, other agencies, the adults themselves, establishing resource centres in every region, preparing suitable curricula, preparation of teaching materials, devising methods and materials for training, training of instructional personnel at the district and project level, etc. All these activities can be regarded as preparation for the programme.

Cooperation Schemes : In this programme attention has also been paid to the state agencies, centres for national development, industry, service planners, entrepreneurs, labour organisations, and the specific qualities of particular areas and groups. The programme has been kept free from the formal modalities of the department of education. In order to achieve the desired progress, the administration, cooperative units and the inspection machinery have also been mobilised.

Finance for Adult Education : In view of the national importance of the problem of adult education, a sum of Rs. 200 crores has been allocated to it. This amounts to 10% of the education budget, whereas in the fifth plan, the allocation for adult education amounted to only Rs. 18 crores, or 1% of the education budget. This budgetary provision is only one source, and it is planned that other resources will also be exploited for this purpose. For example, the various service planners and project officers will provide finance for their own adult education programmes. In the tribal regions adult education will also be financed from the budget for the agricultural and rural development, there will be provisions for providing functional literacy to the agriculturist. Thus, the provisions for adult education within the total educational budget is only one of the provisions. Once the scheme is implemented and experience gained, more funds will be made available, as need arises.

General Difficulties

The National Education Commission has opined that education does not end in the school. It is a life long process. The adult today seriously needs to understand the rapidly changing world and the increasing complexities of social life. Even those who have obtained considerable education should start learning once again because its alternative is isolation from the present reality. The objective of reconstructing our nation can be fulfilled only when each individual continues to receive the latest education so that he may use his intellect skillfully and determinedly in order to bring about economic development, social change and social security. The Education Commission has rightly pointed out that the farmer who turns over the soil or the worker who manipulates machines must understand the nature of the soil or the machine. He must be aware of the scientific process inherent in productive activity so that he may be able to make full use of new achievements and bring about progress.

Maulana Abul Kalam Azad expressed his views on the importance and function of social education by saying that social education means total human education. It grants the individual literacy so that the knowledge of the world may be available to him. It teaches him how to adapt himself to his environment. This implies giving him education in advanced skills and modes of production so that he may achieve the highest economic level. Its purpose is also to give knowledge of the basic principles of hygiene so that our domestic life may be healthy and prosperous. This will benefit the individual as well as society. Through this education, we should impart to him the lesson of citizenship so that he may obtain some knowledge of the world and also be enabled to participate in those decisions of the government which are conducive to peace and progress. However, the path to adult and social education is littered with many concomitant problems, that is, those problems which always raise obstacles in the path of social education. These problems are described in the following paragraphs.

Vague Policy on Adult Education : Ever since the achievement of independence, our policy on adult education and the programmes formulated for it have invariably been vague and undefined. An effort was made to achieve clarity in the community development programme, but even that was partial or biased, since it was intended only for rural adults. It has no provisions for adults in urban areas.

Lack of Finance : The finance so far invested in adult education has proved inadequate, with the result that this programme, which should have been given the highest priority in national development, fell behind. At least Rs. 27 crores should be spent annually upon this programme.

Absence of a Comprehensive Plan : This programme was accepted in principle, but it was never implemented in a suitably comprehensive manner. Had this been done, the problem would have been over come a long time ago. Dr. Frank went as far as to say categorically that if one literate Indian makes another Indian literate, the problem will be overcome within five years.

Problem of Curriculum : The curriculum of adult education has itself proved a problem, because adults were imparted a certain amount of literacy, but no knowledge of anything else, though this can be done. The method adopted for adults is the same as the one used for teaching children, though the needs, attitudes and abilities of adults are completely different. The curricula designed for them must necessarily take into account their particular needs.

Methods of Teaching : The curriculum should fulfill the needs of adults while the methods of teaching should be such that they help in the achievement of this goal. For the spread of literacy, sentence-charts, diagrams, stories, simple words, radio, television, libraries and the drama stage, etc., can be used successfully. But, in reality, because of a paucity of resources, the techniques of adult education are not brought into use in our country to any noticeable extent.

Problem of Teachers : The problem of teachers for adult education has existed from the very beginning. Under these circumstances, an experiment was made by using teachers of primary schools for this purpose, but it proved a failure because the additional allowance given to the teachers was too nominal. In addition, the extension officers, social educators and rural service workers exhibited complete indifference.

Problem of Continuing Education : Continuing education obviously refers to an educational process which always goes on, and in the sphere of adult education, it refers to the education imparted after literacy has been achieved. If facilities for such education are available after literacy has been imparted, some benefit can be derived from it.

The Agencies of Social Education : Apart from the official agencies involved in social education, some voluntary agencies, are also usually, engaged in this programme, but in India, there is a dearth of such agencies. However, the Literacy House in Lucknow and the Adult Education Council in Delhi are doing this work. These institutions aim at producing trained social educators. Only when there is a growth in the number of such agencies can we hope that social education will make rapid progress.

Administration : Social education has a very vast field and there is no uniformity in administration. The various ministries of the government of India have made efforts to train and educate their employees. The Central Education Advisory Committee has organised conferences and seminars from time to time.

Social Education Institutions : Institutions engaged in social education do not get help at the right time and consequently their enthusiasm dies out prematurely.

Training of Workers : There has also been, in general, a dearth of trained workers in the sphere of social education, because of which the Education Advisory Committee has recommended that such workers be trained.

Post Social Education : It is necessary to make arrangements for further education of adults after making them literate.

The Education Ministry of the government of India has suggested the following measures for overcoming the difficulties:-

(i) For individuals of 13 or 14 years of age, primary schools should arrange classes of two hours each at least three or four times a week. This work should be apart from the regular teaching programme of these schools.

(ii) Teachers should be trained for imparting education to the 14-15 age group. The following programmes should be taken up simultaneously:-

  (a) Regular classes should be arranged for men and women over a five month period.

  (b) The Neighbouring Group Method should be adopted, under which the teacher should educate groups of people in his neighbourhood. Experience has shown that adults show laziness and unwillingness in coming to teaching centres, and hence, it may be more practicable for the teacher to go to their centres instead.

  (c) A Home Class movement must be initiated for the education of women, which can be made an integral part of the Rural Education Programme. Students and teachers should offer their cooperation.

  (d) Teacher training establishments should formulate and implement programmes of adult education in their respective communities.

  (e) Voluntary organisation should organise adult education schemes.

In the opinion of the Indian Adult Education Committee, the important work of literacy must not be lost sight of in the broader perspective of social education. Literacy should remain an important element in social education because, through the written and spoken work, it affords the adult a powerful medium for becoming educated.

What is needed today is that the various programmes of social education must be organised and harmonised. The objective, should be clear, and the adults must be strongly motivated to receive social education. Success in this endeavour depends upon local leadership and local agencies.

Programme with Four Points : Gandhiji said that illiteracy was a blot upon India's fair name. This blot must be wiped out with all expediency. The objective of adult education is not merely literacy, it must be linked with the daily life of adults. From this viewpoint, the literacy programme must have three elements- (i) it should be based on work so that it may impart skills to the learner, (ii) illiterate individuals should be able to think about the nation's problem, and (iii) adequate skills in reading, writing and mathematics should be developed so that informal education can then be continued indefinitely.

The Four Point Programme for social education is as follows-

Literacy Classes : By 1953, 400,000 individuals were made literate through 40,000 classes. By 1955, 7,000 classes provided literacy to 89,000 individuals. In community development centres, 85,000 classes helped to make 600,000 individuals literate.

Community Centres : Community centres perform the functions of providing literacy, recreation and information.

Youth Clubs : Youth clubs have been organised in villages with the result that village protection groups, youth welfare centres and other such units work for social education have come into existence.

Women's Committees : In each development centre, women's welfare groups and women's councils should be set up so that women can be given information about and involved in hymn singing, social discussion groups, use of smokeless stoves, knitting, stitching, nutrition and balanced diet, domestic skills, general health care, domestic economics, home decoration, literacy, etc.

The following means or instruments are employed in social education- (a) the common audio-visual aids, (b) black-boards and chalks, (c) charts and flash cards, (d) flannel and other materials, (e) other audio-visual materials, (f) films, (g) radio, (h) television.

The Education Commission has expressed the views that every possible effort should be made to overcome these obstacles, even though 20 years may pass in the process. It has suggested that- (1) For the 6-11 year age group, universal education must be achieved in 5 years. (2) Arrangements must be made for part time education. (3) Arrangements must be made for vocational education.

Various Approaches

The Commission has suggested that the following two methods should be adopted for this purpose-

Selective Approach : In this context, those groups are included which can be controlled easily, it also includes vocational training, in which industrial and commercial enterprise, large industrial enterprises and the government itself can take up budgets against illiteracy. In this method, the following fields can be comprehended (a) Most workers in industrial establishments are illiterate, and hence such establishments can be required to make arrangements for the education of their own employees. (b) The state should make arrangements for the education of their own employees. (c) The state should make arrangements for the education of all illiterate classes concerned with social and economic growth, since the number of such individuals is very large. (d) Programmes for imparting literacy should be an invariable part of every scheme of social education.

Mass Approach : This is concerned with developing a general method of public or mass education in which advantage will be taken of all educated men and women for eradicating the illiteracy of their brothers and sisters. Voluntary organisations can take effective steps in this direction. Existing schools can be converted into community centres. Regarding this approach, the Kothari Commission has argued that a movement for collective or community literacy depends largely upon the voluntary services of all educated individuals, including governmental as well as non-governmental employees and other sections of society. It has suggested that students of the primary, secondary, undergraduate students and students of vocational schools should be engaged in the teaching of adults as a part of the National Service Scheme.

This Commission has made the following suggestions for accelerating the literacy movement:-

(A) Organising a curriculum for adult women through the central social welfare board, with 'rural sisters' teaching women in the rural areas with the help of the community.

(B) Generating social skills.

(C) Adopting education as a dynamic process.

(D) Running ad hoc courses.

(E) Training through units which should be for teachers and common people. In this, students should be given suitable opportunities, and use should also be made of radio and television.

(F) Generating a suitable atmosphere before initiating the programme.

(G) Preparing the adults psychologically to make them receptive.

(H) Making use of such means as radio, television, films, lectures, etc., so as to make teaching suitable.

(I) Making schemes for literacy in accord with local circumstances.

(J) Making the programmes attractive.

(K) Seeking the full cooperation of universities, industries, etc.

(L) Organising an effective administration.

Research and Experiments

The field of social education presents vast opportunities for educating the public. Various kinds of efforts have been made for educating people all over the world, and for this purpose various experiments were conducted. The USA and USSR despite the fundamental differences in their political and economic structure, both accept and understand the importance of kind of education. There, the schools, colleges, clubs and institutes and other institutions which work for improving the standards of the fore mentioned have been provided with extensive cultural facilities. In India, too, various experiments have been conducted in the sphere of social education. These are -

Organisation of Tours and Camps : In such schemes, adults are sent to camps for completing a predetermined course of study which aims at teaching them reading, writing and healthy citizenship. K.G. Saiyadain has laid special emphasis upon the utility of such organisations, because in camps, the atmosphere generated is suitable for the growth of brotherhood as well as leadership. However, it must also be kept in mind that the organisers of tours and camps should have adequate knowledge of mass psychology. These camps can prove to be the nerve-centres of social education, and so they should be managed with sympathy and understanding.

Janata (Public) Colleges : Like the 'folk schools' of Denmark, Janata or public colleges were established in India, too. After observing their work, one observer commented that the most important element was not the quantum of knowledge obtained by the students but the fact that their thoughts and sentiments were stimulated. It is conceivable that they would forget much of what they had learnt, after they left school, but after leaving school, they appear to be completely changed. By that time, they have learnt to listen, observe, think and make the best possible use of their abilities.

According to Pyare Lal Rawat, the foundation stone for a public and cooperative life will be laid in the social centres in rural society. Janata colleges have been set up to produce educated and trained workers for such social centres. Leadership will take birth in these colleges. They will not have the form and structure of the ordinary colleges because their purpose is to train young men and women to perform activities of social, cultural and educational value among the rural people so that they may be able to provide leadership to the rural areas. In other words, their purpose is to generate knowledge and education among the rural people, to teach the rural people better ways of living so that they may lead a better and more contented life. The objective of these colleges will be to make Indian rural people responsible citizens of a democratic society by arousing their civic, social and cultural awareness.

Community Centres : Community centres were set up in rural areas to provide education, sociability, recreation as well as education in good citizenship. These centres were set up in the village squares (chaupals), panchayat houses and schools, and provided with such materials as carpets, furniture, books, radios, newspapers, periodicals, sports goods, etc.

Intensive Libraries : Where community centres have not been established, intensive libraries have been set up. These libraries contain literature suitable for the adults, as well as books on agriculture, cottage industries, cooperative societies, health and other such subjects of utility.

Educational Caravans : Educational caravans were put into use in the rural areas around Delhi. These caravans are equipped with film projectors, health materials, libraries and other teaching materials. This caravan sets up camp at one place, and then its workers spread all round, making arrangements for adult education.

Adult Education Departments in Universities : The Rajasthan university has made adequate efforts towards adult education by setting up a department, which has also initiated a number of schemes for continuing education. Other universities should imitate Rajasthan in this respect. Universities can make their contribution to social education through postal courses, short-term education, extension services, post education contact programmes, etc.

Mass Education Movement : 20 years ago, the 'Parichaya' (acquaintance) trust was set up for the spread of mass education for the Gujarati speaking people. So far, this trust has published as many as three hundred books on various subjects. This movement was strengthened by the activities of Wadilal Dagli (Editor, *Commerce*) and Yashwant Joshi (Editor, 'Parichaya' trust publications). Dagli was inspired in this endeavour by the Chicago University pamphlets; which he saw at Berkeley (California). He thought of spreading mass education in his mother tongue. The work began with only Rs. 500. Each pamphlet was priced at 0.40 paise. In the first year, the organisation enrolled six hundred members. The publication was based on the principle of giving 10% royalty to authors and Commission to the middle men.

This movement brought about a social revolution, and also provided the illiterate people with a ray of hope. So far, the trust has published 300 pamphlets, thus providing the neo-literates with reading material on a variety of subjects. The trust now plans to publish similar literature for neo-literates in other languages also.

Informal Education : In the fifth plan, one important experiment in the sphere of social education was that of informal education. In this context, the Central Education Advisory Council has prepared a scheme for linking social education with national development. The scheme envisages providing further opportunities for education to those who were compelled to abandon their education too early, Correspondence courses, evening classes, etc.; are part of this scheme. It will provide free and informal opportunities of education for everyone.

Village Education Muhim : This experiment was carried out in Maharashtra. Some social workers conducted adult education classes. In. Vidharabha, some enthusiastic workers were given training and the number of adult education centres was thus increased. This movement was based on the declaration of the workers that they would maintain their own literacy, send their children regularly to school, maintain unity in the village and seek to fulfil the goal of integral development of the village.

Now, this programme is being conducted by District Councils. It has three objectives:-

(i) Putting an end to illiteracy among adults (14-50 age group)

(ii) Granting neo-literates opportunities to remain in constant contact with education.

(iii) Bringing about the comprehensive development of villages through social education centres.

Village Vidyapeeth : This experiment was initiated in Mysore. Through it, the spread of education in economics, agricultural education, etc., was achieved. The project received inspiration from the Danish folk high schools. In these institutions, a class has to remain at the school for 5 or 6 months for studies. This helps to develop a harmonious community life.

Punjab Literacy Project : Mrs. Helen Butt developed an intensive literacy method (Hindi) in the Neelokheri block of Karnal. After its initiation by Mrs. Butt, the project continued with the help of 20 teachers, 7 lady teachers (planning and panchayat department), and 4 supervisors. Its success is proved by the fact that 36 classes for men and 11 classes for women were started. 1000 adults attended these classes. Each full time teacher taught two classes on alternate days. Classes were held on three days a week basis over a period of six months.

The learners were taught to read and write Hindi. In addition to literacy, a programme of continuing education was also conducted over 3 months. A short nine-day programme for training teachers was also conducted. Besides, literacy was spread through the Immediate Learning Method. When the project was introduced at the state level, the farmers showed exceptional enthusiasm for it, proved by the fact that attendance in the classes was as much as 19.4%. Mrs. Helen Butt has said after her experience of this project that the total expenditure on adult literacy scheme should be borne by the education department and the institutions (panchayats) which stand to benefit from them.

Adult Education Department Rajasthan University Jaipur : In 1965, the Rajasthan University at Jaipur set up a department of adult education in order to explore the possibilities of adult education by spreading continuing education. This department organises conferences and seminars at regular intervals. It also organises a variety of short-term courses for the neo-literates as well as-the semi-literates. This department has done the following kinds of work with the assistance of the government, the university and voluntary organisations- (i) studies in the philosophy and concept of adult education. (ii) education in literacy- social, economic development and literacy, adult literacy and the methods of teaching, teacher training, village education muhim, (iii) portable audio visual materials, library, conferences, discussions, (iv) liberal education, (v) public cooperation, (vi) training in leadership (Mysore Vidyapeeth), (vii) the sphere of continuing education industrial and vocational development, (viii) education of adult women, (ix) agencies and organisation. This department continues to think upon and discuss such issues as the university and social responsibility, the work done in foreign countries on adult education, the educational requirements of community, continuing education,-vocations, agriculture, training, liberal teaching, evening colleges, correspondence courses, adult education and related disciplines, etc.

Commission for Educational Development

Adult education is one of those aspects of education on which the Kothari Commission has thought at length. The Education has expanded the scope of adult education, and for its success and spread, it has suggested the following six-point programme (1) eradication of illiteracy, (2) continuing education, (3) correspondence courses, (4) libraries, (5) role of universities in adult education, (6) the organisation and administration of adult education. We will now consider the recommendations of the Commission in the light of its programme.

Illiteracy Elimination

The Education Commission has pointed out that as compared to the situation in 1951, there were 26 million more illiterate people in 1961. As compared to 1951, there were 20 million more illiterates, despite the fact that literacy had increased from 16.6% to 28.5%. It also accepted the fact that the nation was paying a heavy price for this illiteracy, because illiterate persons are not really independent and complete citizens. Besides, illiteracy acts as an obstacle in economic, social and political development, control of population, creation of security, etc.

The Commission has suggested that any programme for the eradication of illiteracy should have the following bases - (i) As far as possible, adult education should be based on work, and it should aim at change of attitude, creation of interests and skill. The information given should bring about an increase in the learner's skill. (ii) Adult education should stimulate the learner's interests in national problems and also make a powerful and effective contribution to the nation's social and political life. (iii) It should make adults capable of reading, writing and calculation. If the learner's wish they can ensure their own improvement through informal knowledge.

It is evident from these three bases that the literacy drive will have three stages - (a) in the initial stage, the adult should be taught reading, writing and calculation, and also given information about citizenship and national problems. Besides, information about his vocation should also be imparted to the learner. (b) In the second stage, the knowledge obtained in the initial stage should be reinforced and the skills developed further. Adults should be enabled to understand and face their personal problems. (c) The third stage should help the adult to participate in continuing education.

A useful programme of adult education depends upon the acceptance of certain basic facts. We must see such programmes in the light of industralisation and modern agricultural progress, as making illiterates useful instrument in the country's general as well as economic development, as turning them into an effective work force. For this, the following facts should be considered:

Targets : The success of adult education depends upon successful planning. There should be a proper time schedule for programmes for the people, preparation of resources, training of workers and provision of other needs. The Commission has recommended that the programme should not be prepared for the whole nation, instead, state-wise planning should be adopted. The progress of adult education depends upon the educational facilities, public cooperation and existing organisation in each region. The Education Commission has expressed the hope that, on the basis of proper planning and implementation, 60% illiteracy can be eradicated by 1971 and 80% by 1976. Consequently, the Commission has recommended that every effort should be made to eradicate illiteracy. It has hoped that within 20 years, no part of the country should remain backward.

Programmes for Eradication of Illiteracy : The Commission has suggested the following programmes (i) Providing for compulsory education of at least five years for the 6-11 years age-group. (ii) Providing for part-time education of the children in the 11-14 age-group who had to give up their education for some reasons. (iii) Making arrangements for the part-time general as 'well as vocational education for individuals in the 15-30 age group. This group will include individuals who have received education partially.

Strategy of Approach : The Commission has rightly argued that every effort must be made to overcome obstacles to adult education. We must consider the population in our country and determine our strategy accordingly. According to the Census of 1961, there were 1 million illiterates in the 15 + age-group. Literacy in urban areas was 47%, while in rural areas, it was 17%. The distribution of literacy also depends upon the region. While in Delhi it was 52.7%, in NEFA it was as low as 1.8%. Besides, there was considerable differences between the literacy among men and women. Social groupings, caste and class and the nature of the community have always hindered adult education. Besides, the differences in the nature of a region lead to different levels of motivation towards adult learning. The Commission has felt the need for the acceptance and observation of certain general principles, and so it has suggested two approaches for success in this endeavour- (i) Selective approach, and (ii) Mass approach. Programmes based on both approaches should run simultaneously.

A Remedial Measure

According to the Commission, the selective approach is suitable for the group which can be identified easily and also kept under control with relative ease. Such a group can be effectively motivated to obtain education. Such a group can be made useful and the literacy programme can achieve success. Even vocational training can be given to such groups. Under this approach, the following programmes can be formulated :

1. Almost 4% illiterate people are employed in industrial and professional organisation. Hence, the Commission has recommended that large firms, trading and industrial organisations and institutions may be legally made responsible for the adult education of their employees. They should be made literate within three years. The owners of such organisations must bear the entire responsibility of making their employees literate. The government should bear all expenses related to education, such as supply of teachers, teaching materials, books and other tools. The Commission is convinced that the owners themselves will, in the long run, benefit from the education of their employees.
2. The Commission has suggested that large organisations managed by the administration must give primacy to the important programme of adult literacy.
3. The humanitarian attitude is necessarily linked with all programmes for social and economic progress. They include a large number of people who have never even seen a school. Hence, it appears logical to argue that provisions must be made for the education and training of all workers in the schemes for industrial, agricultural, and trading development or improvement in health and education.
4. The Indian government has implemented numerous schemes for social welfare and economic development. These include such schemes as the creation of the Khadi and Village Industries Commission, community

development schemes, child welfare schemes, etc. The Commission's view is that adult education should be made an integral part of all such programmes.

In order to put an end to illiteracy, it is necessary to mobilize all literate people in society. This approach is unorthodox, and it has not yet been adopted in practice in India. Russia has achieved spectacular successes in adult education through this approach. In India, Maharashtra has achieved notable success through its Village Education Muhim. In this approach, the workers seek the cooperation of the community and make schemes for mass education. The only difficulty in this approach is the laxity in follow-up, but this can be taken care of. Such a programme possesses the following characteristics:

1. This approach depends more upon political and social institutions rather than administrative educational institutions.
2. Adult education, by its very nature, is voluntary, and the drive behind it is the individual's own motivation. Hence, national unity and security, health and social welfare should be implicit in adult education, a fact which must never be lost sight of by educational planners, administrators or workers.
3. This approach depends upon the voluntary services contributed by such educated individuals in society as doctors, lawyers, teachers, students, engineers and other individuals, though, of course, the brunt of the responsibility falls upon the teachers and students. It is for this reason that the Commission has recommended that adult education should be propagated, through compulsory national service at every level of education.
4. *New Responsibility of the School :* In connection with adult education, a new responsibility should fall upon the schools. This will also help to modify the attitude of the school. This approach comprehends not only the student in the school, but the entire community. It provides an important sphere for extension service.

A programme of adult education cannot be run successfully as long as a proper plan is not formulated. For the success of such a programme, the following points must be considered:-

1. Before the implementation of the programme, the government, and all social and political leaders should arouse the interest of the community and bring about mobilisation.
2. The individual adults taken into the scheme should be psychologically motivated in a suitable manner. They should become aware of the importance of literacy.
3. All means of mass communication, such as radio, television, films, slides, drama and literary organisations should be made use of in such programmes.
4. Whenever the programme is to be implemented, the necessary teaching aids such as books, charts, graphs, guide-books, etc., must be prepared before-hand.
5. In planning for literacy local, needs and conditions should be kept in mind.
6. The literacy programme should also have provision for the continuing education of neo-literates. Follow-up programmes should also be organised.
7. The adult education programme cannot be left entirely and exclusively to the teachers. They must be offered the cooperation and assistance of the following- (i) extension services, agricultural and industrial departments, (ii) the use of mass media instruments, such as the All India Radio.
8. Libraries should also extend their cooperation to this programme.
9. Training in leadership should also be part of this programme.
10. Students, teachers and others interested in the spread of adult literacy should be given suitable training.
11. A powerful administrative and supervisory mechanism must be evolved.

12. In this progamme, schemes should be devised for bringing people into contact with each other through study groups, committees, clubs, recreation groups etc.
13. The public, too, should recognise and appreciate such programmes.
14. *Literacy for Women.* The percentage of illiteracy among women is greater than among men. In the urban areas, 34.5% women are literate while in the rural areas this percentage is 8.9, a situation similar to that found existing in the whole world. Hence, as many lady teachers as possible should be appointed to speed up the education of women.
15. *Follow-up :* The success of any activity depends upon the follow-up action given to it. Hence, for adult literacy also, properly planned programmes of follow-up action should be devised.

Continuing the Studies

Adult education occupies the most important place in our country's educational set-up. In the rapidly changing circumstances of today, life as a whole should be conceived of as a continuing process of learning. It is now being generally accepted that the modern method of education does not provide extensive education for one's entire life. Hence, to complement it, full-time, part-time or in-service educational programmes are devised for those who have left school and reached adulthood: Generally, the system of continuing education is devised for two classes:-

(i) Those people who participate in part-time education along with other individuals. Individuals of this class increase their qualifications by receiving part-time education in schools and colleges.

(ii) Those persons who can study only at home, but who need some assistance in getting official recognition for their study.

Continuing education is meant for persons who want to complete the education left incomplete by their leaving school.

Individuals working in institutions also need opportunities for improving their qualifications and abilities. There are also some individuals who wish to study literature, language or some special subject merely for the pleasure of it. Adult education seeks to bring education within the grasp of every kind of person by catering to his special needs.

Hence, the Education Commission has suggested the following steps for developing continuing education- (1) For part-time education, a parallel system must be developed within the educational structure. Just as degrees, diplomas and certificates are granted to full time students, similar recognition should be available for part-time curricula and courses also. (2) Education institutions should provide the necessary leadership in this process ; they should understand the individual's problems, solve them and help them in obtaining knowledge as well as the necessary help. (3) Through special part-time courses and mixed programmes, efforts should be made to improve the mental horizon of workers and employees ; their knowledge and skills should be improved and a sense of responsibility engendered in them. (4) Specialised institutions should be established, for example, the Central Women's Welfare Council, Vidyapeeths, etc.

Courses of Correspondence

For millions of those people who have to stand upon their own feet very early in life and struggle for livelihood and survival, correspondence courses provide a means by which they can satisfy their ambition for education, which would otherwise remain unfulfilled. Such courses are very much in use in foreign countries, such as the USA, Sweden, Japan, the USSR, Australia, etc. In India, too, experiments have been conducted in this form of education by the Delhi, Meerut and Himachal Universities. Although this method does not provide any immediate and direct contact between the students and the teachers, the relations between the two can become quite intimate through exchange of correspondence. Besides, it is also to be noted that there has generally been a dearth of teachers who can inspire students through direct contact.

Correspondence courses should be designed to encourage an exchange of views, and they should not restrict themselves merely to the exchange of written information. Individuals who wish to study science through the correspondence courses should be allowed to make use of laboratories during vacations. Even in education as a subject, there should be arrangements for correspondence curricula through Programmed Learning, a method which has been productive of good results.

The correspondence system of education should also get the assistance of radio and television, which can be used for the expression of fundamental and emotional ideas. Courses of this kind should be designed not only to enable students to obtain degrees, but also to give information and knowledge to individuals engaged in agriculture, industry and other productive activities. These courses should be organised through the extension departments.

The following are the recommendations of the Education Commission for the development of correspondence courses:

1. Those individuals who can take part in courses or curricula should receive education through correspondence courses. For this, extensive correspondence courses should be organised.
2. Students studying through the correspondence system should be given opportunities to meet the teachers at regular intervals. As far as possible, they should also be allowed to avail of library facilities existing in schools and colleges.
3. Correspondence courses should be assisted by the radio and television network.
4. Correspondence courses should also be organised for those individuals who wish to develop their literacy or aesthetic values.
5. Correspondence courses should not limit themselves to helping students merely to obtain university degrees. Instead, they should also contain courses which may lead to increased production in agriculture and industry.

6. Through correspondence courses, school teachers should come into contact with fresh knowledge, new methods of teaching, etc.
7. The education ministry, with the assistance of other ministries, should set up a National Council of Home Studies. Its functions would be to evaluate the correspondence courses, the agencies involved in such education, and the identification of spheres in which correspondence courses can be introduced.
8. Those individuals who wish to appear at examinations conducted by Boards or universities, on the basis of self-study, should be allowed to do so.

Libraries' Role

Libraries have always played a leading role in the growth of knowledge. In their absence, the possibilities of developing the habit of reading are very few, especially in rural areas. The Commission has suggested that, for the spread of mass education, school libraries should be utilised as public libraries. It has suggested that:

1. The suggestions of the advisory committee on libraries should be accepted, and on its basis, a network of libraries should be spread over the entire country.
2. School libraries should be organised and structured as public libraries.
3. Libraries should be dynamic; they should attract adults towards themselves.

The importance of libraries is reflected in the following statement from UNESCO. It says that in the whole world, and especially in developing countries, there is great need for the expansion of free libraries as a part of the educational programme. Libraries satisfy the needs of the prevailing educational system and help the teachers in their work. In the absence of public libraries, many adults and young men gradually sink towards illiteracy on leaving the school.

Universities' Role

Commenting upon the importance of universities, the Education Commission has declared that the image of a university is that of an intellectual, 'closed' community which gives rise to knowledge, spreads and preserves it, but this is the traditional image. The walls which divide 'town and town' no longer exist. There has come about a revolution in the life of the university, with the revolutionary idea that the community can be linked to the university for the mutual benefit of both.

The Delhi University introduced the correspondence courses and soon found that the demand for them was growing rapidly. In the same manner, the Rajasthan University set up a department of adult education, which was widely applauded. The idea was widely appreciated in Meerut University also.

The function of the university is to bring about a growth and improvement in the social, economic, educational and cultural spheres, and through special agencies it can have a profound impact upon these spheres. Universities should organise effective and powerful programmes for various vocations. It is their duty to ensure that their teachers are constantly in touch with the latest editions to knowledge. In the context of adult education, the Education Commission has made the following recommendations regarding the role of universities:-

1. Indian universities should shoulder a heavier burden in educating the adults in the country. This can be done in the following ways- (a) departments similar to the Rajasthan University's department of adult education should be set up in other universities. (b) Universities must contribute to social and economic growth. (c) They must nourish community life and cultural values.
2. A Board of Adult Education should be constituted by taking representatives from the various departments involved in making the adult literacy programme a success.
3. Universities should be given financial aid for the proper implementation of the adult education programme.

Organisation and Administration

The Commission has clearly felt that the basic weakness in the efforts being made by governmental, non-governmental and voluntary agencies towards the spread of adult education lies in the absence of proper planning and cooperation. Hence, it has suggested the establishment of a National Board of Adult Education to overcome this shortcoming. The council should have representatives from all related ministries. It should have the following functions:-

1. Advising the central and state governments on informal adult education, offering for consideration blueprints for teaching and training.
2. Wherever necessary, setting up institutions, helping in the preparation of literature, teaching materials and necessary teaching programmes.
3. Creating harmony between the efforts of various departments and governmental as well as non-governmental agencies.
4. Evaluating the achievements from time to time and making suggestions for future improvements.
5. Encouraging research, evaluation and survey activities.

Similar organisations should be established at the state level also. At the district level committees should be set up to function as integral parts of the district councils. They should be assisted by village and block committees. They should also be in intimate contact with extension programmes in the spheres of agriculture, cooperatives, health, community development, etc.,

On the question of administration, the Commission's view is that a separate department within the ministry of education should organise this work. The government must accept full responsibility, and every department of the government should be cognizant of the importance of adult education. In addition, every department should help in implementing this programme. Undoubtedly, adult education is the concern of the department of education, but it is also true that, in order to achieve success, it will be necessary to depend upon some particular mode of action.

As far as the question of voluntary agencies is concerned, they should be given financial and technical assistance. Adult education is a sphere in which such agencies can work freely. Besides, the nature of the work is such that its progress and mobility provides a necessary background for the success of all our planning for national development.

Equality and Equity in society are the constitutional provisions in India. Socialism has been viewed variously. In India, method of socialism are based upon parliamentary democracy using gradualist evolutionary processes. Goals of education in India in relation to socialism have been determined taking into consideration Indian democratic system and problems of Indian society.

The present chapter deals briefly, the meaning of socialism, sociology, goals of socialism, goals of socialism in relation to education, problems in the development of egalitarian Indian social order through education, meaning and importance of sociology of education, role of education in achieving goals of socialism and programmes for achieving goals of socialism.

Socialism Meaning : According to Webster's Comprehensive Dictionary, meaning of the concept socialism in different contexts is reproduced here to pick up the meaning with specific reference to meaning of the concept socialism in terms of Indian Socialistic Republic:

1. Public collective ownership or control of the basic means of production, distribution, and exchange, with the avowed aim of operating for use rather than for profit, and of assuring to each member of society an equitable share of goods, services, and welfare benefits; as a system of social and economic organisation planned, attempted or achieved through various methods for examples

Methods in Utopian or Christian Socialism : Methods involve cooperative communal groups holding all things in common.

Methods in Guild Socialism : Methods based upon organisation of producer groups and the professions in syndicalist guilds to be represented in a federal legislative body.

Methods in Fabian or British Labour Party Socialism : Methods are based upon parliamentary democracy using gradualist evolutionary processes.

Methods in Marxist-Leninist State Socialism : Methods are based upon revolution, expropriation, and dictatorship of the so called proletariat, in short, communism.

Creeping Socialism : Methods are based upon anything considered as a gradual or piecemeal encroachment upon the system of private property and free enterprise through state action: used as an epithet.

Concept of Sociology

1. Webster's Comprehensive Dictionary: Sociology is the science that treats of the origin and evaluation of human society and social phenomenon, the progress of civilization and the laws controlling institutions and functions.
2. Auguste Comte a French philosopher, used the word "Sociology in 1837. He used this word to designate the application of the scientific method to the study of human nature and society. According to Comte, Sociology is a fundamental science because it had a method of exact investigation. Comte placed Sociology in the hierarchy of sciences at the end: Mathematics, Astronomy, Physics, Chemistry, Biology, Psychology and Sociology. Comte held that Sociology dealt with social phenomena, which he thought, were complex and difficult to describe.
3. Frederic Le play a contemporary of Comte followed scientific and objective approach to the study of social problems.
4. Herbert Spencer published his book entitled "Principles of Sociology" in 1876. He considered that human individual was like a cell and society was like an organism. Individuals perform different functions as cells in the organism perform different functions. Cells function in relation to other cells and the total organism. Similarly, individuals function in relations to other individuals and total society. Individuals

in advanced societies are more differentiated as compared to those of less advanced societies.

5. Moore and Cole considered sociology as the study of plural behaviour. Plural behaviour is the behaviour in relation to others - the behaviour of man in relation to other men and in relation to the groups or associations. Social interaction is the central theme of sociology. It includes the interaction with culture and other institutionalised interaction patterns such as the family, the play group, religions, economic and educational institutions i.e. every form of group living.
6. *Duncan:* The scientific study of the processes of interactions of persons and the patterns these form in relation to biological, psychological and cultural influences. The views of Duncan highlight that interactions are influenced by biological, psychological and cultural Factors.
7. *Merril and Eldridge:* Sociology is the study of human relationships. The studies include the way human beings interact with other human beings; study of customs and traditions that grow out of these interactions; study of institutions that crystallise these basic human interests and the change that occur in these institutions; study of changes in the light of human welfare; study on the effects of changes on the behaviour and personality development of the individual.
8. *Ginsberg :* Sociology is the study of society, that is, of the web or tissue of human interaction and interrelations. Sociology may also be defined as study of human interactions and interrelations, their conditions and consequences.
9. *Robbins :* Sociology deals with the whole man in relation to all the social, cultural and biophysical backgrounds. Sociology studies man in his total social relationship which include all aspects such as political, economic, psychological, religious, etc. The main focus is on social

relationship. Sociology studies culture, religions and other institutions as these throw light on social relationships.

10. *Alex Inkles* : Sociology is the study of social order which is the underlying regularity of human social behaviour.
11. *Max-Weber* : Sociology is a science which interprets social behaviour with the aim of arriving at causal explanation of human behaviour.

Scope

1. Sociology explains interpersonal and group behaviour. Every individual is a member of a group by birth or choice. Groups play a continuous and effective roles in developing the personality of an individual and at— explains the causes of the behaviour of the individual.
2. Sociology explains nature of social groups such as the family, the community, the occupational groups, religious groups, racial groups, and the notion of the state.
3. Sociology explains various social changes that are taking place within a group life.
4. Sociology explains various processes of interaction (competition, conflict, cooperation, accommodation and assimilation) and their results such as acculturation and socialisation.
5. Sociology studies social change and social control.
6. Sociology studies the concepts of civilization and culture.
7. Sociology studies social problems such as crime, juvenile delinquency, poverty and their possible solutions.

Goals and Objectives : To quote Preamble of Indian Constitution;

"We, the people of India, having solemnly resolved to constitute India into a sovereign, democratic and socialist republic and to secure to all its citizens Justice (social, economical and political), liberty of thought, expression, belief and worship, and equality of status and opportunity and to promote among them all fraternity assuring the dignity of the individual and unity of the nation."

To quote Indian Constitution:

> "The development of India as a great cooperative common wealth necessarily meant equality of opportunity and social justice for all. Any narrow communalism or provincialism must, therefore, be repressed and the evil of the caste rooted out."

The constitution's provisions are for the development of egalitarian Indian social order. Education is an instrument to achieve these constitutional provisions.

According to Dr. M.S. Sachdeva, characteristics of socialistic pattern of Indian society are as follows:

1. Principal means of production in the Indian society should be under the social ownership of control.
2. Rate of production should increase through required steps.
3. The national wealth should be distributed equally i.e. principle of equality in distribution should be followed.

Education and Socialism

Egalitarian Social Order

1. Provision of universal education.
2. Equality in educational opportunity.
3. Spelling out the social aim of education in line of spirit of socialistic pattern in India or social skills development.
4. Curriculum development for social development of Indian citizens.
5. Strategies of teaching for development of social skills in the learners; Examples: Socialised recitation methods Project method Team teaching. Large group teaching techniques e.g. seminar, conference, panel discussion etc.
6. Discipline concept and socialism

Developmental Problems

1. Sex
2. Colour

3. Race
4. Language
5. Caste
6. Religion
7. Politicial opinion
8. Social origin
9. Economic condition
10. Birth
11. Illiteracy
12. Poverty
13. Unemployment
14. No emphasis on national unity.

All the above factors have no place in the concept of equality and equity in education. Education can help to tackle these problems and developing egalitarian Indian social order.

The Significance

Meaning : Sociology of education is an analysis of sociological processes involved in the educational institutions. This area of study has evolved out of the field of Educational Sociology which is defined as the application of general principles and findings of sociology to the administration and for process of education.

According to Vipula Chaturvedi (quoted by Pandey 1983), Sociology of Education is concerned with educational aims, methods, institutions, curricula and administration in relation to political, religious, social and cultural forces of society. It endeavours to examine the influence of social life and social relationship on the development of personality of an individual.

According to Ottaway, Sociology of Education focusses upon the social relations by which the individual gains experiences.

Importance

1. The aims of education are determined in the context of development of social behaviour of the learners.
2. Curricula are developed according to social aims of education. These serve as means with the help of which social behaviour of individuals can be developed.
3. Methods of teaching are determined in line with social aims and curricula.
4. Social discipline can be developed among individual. Individuals behave in a manner keeping in view the interests of other people also. Individual interests are not only taken into consideration.
5. Educational institutions are considered as social system or a sub-social system of the social system. Such concept of the educational institution helps in the development of desirable social behaviour in an individual.
6. The teacher education programmes (aims, curricula, methods, institutions) should be oriented in the light of development of social behaviours among teachers so that they may play their roles for bringing desirable social values and attitudes among students.
7. Educational administrators are oriented in the light of social aims of education.

Achieving Goals through Education

Aims of Education : Studies are done regarding determination of social aims with the changing times.

Curriculum : Studies on development of curricula are based upon sociological principles with the changing times.

Methods of Teaching : Methods of teaching are identified for development of desirable social behaviour of learners. Project method, problem-solving methods, small group methods (seminar, workshop, etc.) are already in use for achieving desired social aims.

Learning Resources : Studies on the programmes and provision of learning resources are done in line with social aims of education.

Teacher Education : Studies on teacher education programmes and educational administrators/managers are done in light of social aims of education.

Factors of Social change : Studies on the influence of forces (political, religious, social and cultural) are done that influence the social life and social relationship of every individual or a group of individuals.

Education as Instrument of Social Change : Studies are being done on the role of education as an instrument of socialisation.

Transmission of Values : Studies on the role of education as a means of transmission of cultural values are being carried out.

Social Change : Studies on the role of education for bringing desirable social change by bringing change in the attitude and value system of learners.

Various Educational Programmes

1. Common School System.
2. Neighbourhood schools.
3. Navodaya Vidyalayas.
4. Universalisation of primary education.
5. Formal and non-formal programmes for secondary education.
6. Women education at all levels of education: primary, secondary and tertiary.
7. Education of scheduled castes and tribes at all levels.
8. Education of the handicapped, Physical & Mental.
9. Adult education for all sections at all levels of education.
10. Distance education for all citizens at all levels of education.
11. Sanskritisation & Westernisation and modernisation strategies for social development.

Functions in Future

1. Discuss the meaning and scope of Sociology.
2. Comment upon the following:
   (a) Varied views on the concept of Sociology.
   (b) Scope of Sociology.
   (c) Auguste Comte and Sociology.
3. Give a comparative account of meaning and scope of Sociology and Sociology of Education.
4. What do you mean by Sociology of Education. Discuss its need, importance and scope.
5. Define Sociology of Education. Write about its scope.
6. Give a comparative account of Sociology and Sociology of Education.
7. Comment upon the following:
   (a) Meaning of Sociology and Sociology of Education.
   (b) Scope of Sociology and Sociology of Education.

3

Moral Problems

The development of morality is an important aspect for the formation of good character. Today, there is deterioration of morality in society. The moral aspect has been neglected not only at the social level but at the national level also. In the educational programmes only moral development has been neglected.

The Motives

In the modern age, the aim of education is all-around development of personality. In the present education system, provision has not been made for intellectual education by giving importance to intellectual development. Thus to successful life, important human qualities such as sympathy, cooperation, mercy, compassion, love, truth, sincerity etc., have been ignored. The development of such human qualities along with intellectual development should be the aim of moral education.

Formation of Character

Character is very important in life. "Nothing is lost when wealth is lost, something is lost when health is lost but everything is lost when character is lost. "Thus character is the most important aspect of personality.

Character is related to morality. The definition of man of character is very wide. Generally, only that man is a man of character whose feelings are human and are directed towards the good and happiness of others. Such a personality can be developed by moral education. For the formation of character of future citizens, moral education should be given from their childhood. The method of moral education has to be different from that of intellectual education. It cannot be given only through lectures. Children by nature like to imitate. So for moral education, it is necessary that the teachers are of good characters.

Religious Relations

The ideal of character formation is kept in the background of all religions. Religion is specially important in moral education from this point of view. All the religion teach us to adopt truth, non-violence, compassion, and pity. But today, religion has taken the form of groupism and communalism which is harmful for character development. No religion prevailing today can be called human religion. In the present circumstances, moral education can only be related to human religion. So in the absence of suitable conditions, the teachers should adopt a religion which is based on the principles of humanity and this alone should be made the basis and medium of moral education.

Behaviour and Morality

Good behaviour is a significant part and powerful medium of moral education. The practical aspect of the teaching of good manners is very gradual. It begins with the first stage of the development of life. Being imitative by nature the children can learn many things of good manners in their family. The parents can make their children cultured by paying attention to their behaviour and by telling them many other things about it gradually. Thus, children can become familiar with the methods and techniques of dealing properly with other people. So the parents and guardians should be fully cultured. Good manners can form background of moral education but for this teachers should be well mannered in order that they may be ideals and worth imitating for children.

Different Stages

Attention is paid to the student's age, intelligence capacity and mental level while determining educational programmes. Similarly, for moral education also programmes should be designed to suit the students of different levels.

Primary Stage : At primary stage, due attention should be paid to the interest of students. The educational programmes should be sufficiently interesting. For this, poems, stories and songs etc., may be very suitable. Considering the understanding level at the primary level, the curriculum should be brief and teaching methods should be easy. Education in obedience to parents, keeping of love and sympathy amongst brother's can be given through quotations from Ramayan. Story of Eklavya from the Mahabharat will teach lessons of devotedness and faith in the teacher.

Moral education can easily be given by selecting stories from ancient Indian books like Vedas, Puranas and Panchatantra etc., Shravan, Prahlad, Dhruv and Harish Chandra in ancient Indian religious books and such other characters in medieval works may be guiding examples for moral education.

The children may be made familiar with the different religions and societies of today in order to develop an international understanding.

Secondary Stage : At the secondary stage, the mental level of students becomes so much mature that more concrete programmes for character formation may be started. In order to make the youth successful in future life, the programmes at this stage should be of various kinds.

At the secondary stage, students should be given opportunities to work for the welfare of man and society and efforts should be made to inculcate in them ethical virtues. For the formation of character, illustrations and stories may be cited according to need.

But care should be taken to safeguard the personal feelings of the students, as up to this age sentiments and discretion develops in them.

College and Higher Stage : At the college and higher stage, the students prepare themselves for future life. So at this stage, the programme of moral education should be wide. A man of character, rising above the consideration of nation, community, class, religion and group, etc. is full of human sentiments. He considers the entire world as his home and others as members of his family. At this stage, the teacher holds an important position for moral education and he may place his character as mirror from which the students will imbibe in their ideals.

The problem of religious education is one of the most burning problems of the country. There have been divergent views of scholars about the religious education. Some are of the opinion that religious education should be included in the curriculum while others feel that in a secular democracy, religious, education is not essential. Even western scholars have different opinion. Ryburn is of the opinion that for the all-around development of the student, religious education is most essential. Ross says that religious education should be included in the curriculum. He writes, "It is through religions that the feet of youth can be set on the road to the absolute values, truth, beauty and goodness".

It is only through religious education that the feelings of universal brotherhood can be developed amongst the masses. An eminent Indian philosopher Dr. Radhakrishnan has written, 'The troubles in the whole world including India are due to the fact that education has become a mere intellectual exercise and not the acquisition of moral and spiritual values." The moral and spiritual values can be achieved only through the religious education. We are also of the opinion that some kind of religious education is essential in our country.

The Nature : Now, the question arises that in a secular democracy like India what should be the nature of religious education. Since ancient times religious education has been the part and parcel of the curriculum of education in our country. In ancient days the basis of education was the religion and the ultimate goal of education was to acquire 'Moksha'. In medieval times also, religious education was imparted. Mosques were the centres of education in which the religious education was imparted. It is only during the British period that the importance of religious education was not felt. In free India also there is in fact, no provision for the religious education but as we have already said that for the all-around development of child and removing the chaos prevailing in the Indian society religious education should be included in the curriculum.

India is a country in which believers of different religions live together. Under these circumstances, the education should not be according to the beliefs of one or the other religion but the basic principles of all the religions should be taught. In fact, our religious education should be a moral or ethical education. There is no need to teach the deep principles of Hindu or Muslim religion but those principles must be taught which are concerned with the development of character.

Our religious education should not only be theoretical but it should be practical. The teacher should put up the examples of moral values before the students. The students should be taught in such a way that religious education may develop in them the feeling of nationalism and internationalism. Those who are against the religious education say that religious education is impractical and unpsychological. It develops hatred among the people . But they are wrong. If we go deeply into the matter we find that all these evils develop only when we are narrow-minded. When we only talk of one religion or the other, one sect of the other, the feeling of communalism develop. Our submission is that religious education is in fact the moral education.

The students should be taught in such a way that feelings of communalism may not develop. Ethical values should be encouraged in our teaching. Good points of all the religions, which are for the development of our character, fellow-feeling of nationalism should be taught to the students. The aim of our education should be the universal brotherhood. Only then the real purpose will be served and we shall be able to achieve our goal of human welfare.

Problems of Indiscipline

Causes of Growing Indiscipline

In our educational system the indiscipline is common. After independence, we have hardly been successful in minimising the gravity of this problem in our educational institutions. The Secondary Education Commission has observed, "No amount of improvement and reconstruction in education will bear much fruit if the schools themselves undermine the indiscipline." Prof. Humayan Kabir is of the opinion, "Failure to take effective steps at this stage can so aggravate the problem that may shake the very foundation of national life." A number of factors are responsible for the growing indiscipline in our educational institutions. The mistake lies partly with the present social, economic and political conditions, partly with the conditions of our homes and partly with the party politics in our institutions. Professor Humayan Kabir in his small treatise 'Student Indiscipline' has diagnosed the following four causes of indiscipline :

1. The loss of leadership by teachers.
2. Growth of economic difficulties.
3. Defects in the existing system of education.
4. General loss of idealism.

Here, we will deal with all of them and also discuss the opinion of eminent educationists in this regard:

Loss of Leadership by Teachers : The teachers of today are not the Gurus of the olden days. Their prestige has gone down. They are not better than the labourers in the eyes of students. They are the spiritual parents of olden days. There are numerous reasons which act as handicaps in teacher's attempt to act as the leader of students and society. Sweeping criticism of the present system of education, inadequate salaries, and the consequent frustration, entry of such persons in the profession who are the teachers by compulsion and not by choice are the reasons for this state of affairs. Some other factors responsible for this are the control of the politicians over the educational institutions and the acceptance of tuition by the teachers on almost commercial basis and the strained relations between the authorities and the teachers, etc. The Secondary Education Commission has observed, "Discipline among students can only be promoted if there is discipline among the staff both within the school and in organizations connected with the teaching profession."

Growth of Economic Difficulties : Education in India is absolutely unprofitable. Problem of unemployment is the greatest problem that we are facing. Our education system does not ensure any betterment of financial condition. The present day education does not enable youths to earn their livelihood. Have a look upon the records of employment exchanges of India and you will be shocked to know that educated class is starving. When such is the condition, how can the indiscipline be removed from the educational institutions.

A young man studying in university knows that it will be difficult for him to get a job, even if he passes bis B.A. or M.A. His mind is always worried and tense. This creates feeling of insecurity in him which leads to indiscipline. In educational institutions, the gap between the poor and the rich students is too wide. This leads to discontentment with the existing order and gradually the students become indisciplined.

Defects in the Existing System : Our existing system of education is quite defective. It is purely indifferent to the development of character among pupils. Our young men are mostly, at present, ill-equipped youth, filled with a robust optimism in the beginning of their educational career. The present system of education does not create the thirst for knowledge, the zeal to work hard and ambition to be high in wisdom. Our examination system is also defective. According to Francis W. Parker, "The fundamental reason the children do not act is because they do not have the conditions of right action. Maulana Azad had said, "I am convinced that if the young are at tune restless and turbulent, it is not due to any intrinsic defect in them. The restlessness is largely due to the fact that they do not have enough channels for the expression of their youthful urges."

Most of the educational institutions, running on the commercial lines, fail to establish spiritual and moral links between the teachers and the students. This creates indiscipline. The money-minded authorities do not care for the welfare of the children, there is no provision for personal contact between the students and teachers, as the classes are being kept overcrowded. Untrained and unqualified teachers are appointed on lesser salaries. Too much talk of self discipline has also done some harm. There is no check on the students. This loud talk reveals that there are no rules for them. They are the cruel kings of their society and can do whatever they like.

General Loss of Idealism : The standard of morality is falling day by day in every walk of life. Idealism, morality goodness, truth and beauty are merely on paper and not in actual practice. The all-around deterioration of ideals, virtues and morality is a potent cause for growing indiscipline amongst our students.

The youth festival held at Delhi analyzed the following causes of indiscipline:

(a) Economic difficulties, (b) Bad home atmosphere; (c) Faulty system of education; (d) Unemployment among educated youths; (e) Corrupt social influences; (f) Overcrowded classes and larger enrolments; (g) Politics; (h) Lack of proper attention to problems of students.

Indiscipline and Politics : Active politics is one of the important causes of indiscipline. Mahatma Gandhi was of the opinion that politics and religion are synonymous, indicating the same truth. But now-a-days-politics has nothing to do with religion.

It is prevalent in its most corrupt form and our students are the victim of this dirty politics which has resulted in indiscipline in every walk of life. A Commission under the chairmanship of Mr. Harish Chandra, former judge of the Allahabad High Court, was set up. The Commission recommended, "Political parties should not carry their politics and rivalries into the campus of educational institutions and should avoid uncalled for interference with their working. There should, however, be no objection to students establishing clubs of their own where they may discuss and debate the ideologies, thoughts and principles of the various political parties in the country from academic standpoint. "

Late Maulana Azad also remarked, "A student must have knowledge of political movements, but should acquire that knowledge as a student. This is not a stage of plunging into politics and there can be no greater disservice to the country than to allow the students to be swept away by political passions. The growing unrest and indiscipline among students is not the result of certain errors from the side of students but is also a responsibility of those who have not been able to channelise their energies in the right direction."

In Nut-shell : In a nut-shell, we can say that there are several factors of indiscipline in schools. They are personal, social, political, educational and psychological.

Personal Factors : (a) Physical and mental deformity, (b) intellectual inferiority or superiority, (c) stonny age of adolescence and (d) bad habits.

Social Factors : (a) disturbed state of society, (b) bad home environment, (c) lack of parent's education and (d) evils of society.

Political Factors : (a) mistaken belief of Swaraj or Freedom, (b) bad influence of political parties and (c) mistaken concept of democracy and secularism.

Educational Causes : (a) no proper aim of education, (b) frequent changes in curriculum, (c) organisational , (d) lack of moral education, (c) lack of healthy and attractive school surrounding, (f) dearth of zealous teachers and (g) lack of right type of co-curricular activities in schools.

The main psychological causes of indiscipline in schools are:

(a) repression of student's instincts, (b) weakness of parents and teachers and (c) unpsychological handling of pupils.

Kinds of Indiscipline : Indiscipline is of two kinds, viz. (i) Group indiscipline, (ii) Individual Indiscipline. It is difficult to deal with group indiscipline; some of the typical acts of group indiscipline are; (a) Strikes and gang-behaviour, (b) Aggressive fighting and quarrelling; (c) Rowdyism. Individual Indiscipline is comparatively easier one to tackle. Some of the acts of individual indiscipline are: (a) Truance and late coming (b) Cheating and telling a lie; (c) Stealing; (d) Scabbing.

Conflicts of Indiscipline : It is essential to point out various internal causes of tussle between the students and the authorities. They are :

(a) Demand for removal of a teacher on the grounds of inefficiency from the point of view of the students.

(b) Retention of the teacher whom management wants to transfer or retire.

(c) Refusal of the authorities to permit some students to appear in the examination, due to the shortage of attendance or unsatisfactory work.

(d) Demand for any type of holiday.

(e) Demand for the change of the dates of the examination or stiffness of the examination papers.

(f) Demand for the establishment of students union.

(g) Demand for the remission of fine or fines and enhancement of funds.

General Nature

The common forms of indiscipline prevalent in the schools are: (i) Disrespect for authorities and college rules and regulations, (ii) Disrespect for teachers, i.e. disobedience, (iii) Late coming, (iv) Not doing home work, (v) Unruly behaviour in the class, i.e. making noise, (vi) Damaging and spoiling the college property, (vii) Writing indecent and abusive Language upon the walls and other parts of the college building, (viii) Making uncalled for remarks for the fair sex, (ix) Forming gangs and organising strikes, (x) Using unfair means in the examination, (xi) Delay in paying the fees, (xii) Dishonest dealing, *i.e.* stealing, (xiii) Aggressive behaviour, i.e. bullying, teasing, beating, etc.

Preventive Measures

The remedies of school indiscipline may be classified under two heads, viz.; (a) positive, (b) Negative.

Positive Remedies : Under positive checks, we may have the following remedies: (a) Pupil self-Government, (b) Restoration of the lost leadership to the students, (c) Improvement in the economic lot of the students, (d) Parent-Teacher relationship, (e) Reform in the system of education, (f) School environment- tradition, law and regulation, (g) Material conditions of work, (h) Corporate life of the school, (i) Games and co-curricular activities, (j) Revival of the sense of values, (k) Rewards, (1) Control over external influences.

Negative Checks : Under negative type of checks, following measures are generally adopted in the institutions in order to maintain discipline, law and order, 1. Corporal punishment, 2. Extra work given as a punishment, 3. Fine 4. Work other than class work given as punishment, 5. Isolation, 6. Moral punishment, 7. Suspension and expulsion.

Steps Desirable : So far as possible only positive types of checks should be enforced. Negative types of checks should be rarely used, when there is no alternative . Negative checks do not change the feeling of the students while positive checks are capable of that. By negative checks, the students get frustrated. They do not commit the acts of indiscipline before the teachers but in the absence of a teacher they become most indisciplined. Our aim is to achieve self discipline and positive types of checks will be helpful in our task. Self disciplined students are the real builders of the nation and are the real guards of democracy and this kind of discipline can only be achieved by positive type of checks.

The Disintegration

There are many reasons for this decline in the standard of our education. Following are some of the main causes which are responsible for the decline of standard of education in India.

Growing at Pace

The development of education in India is taking place rapidly. The number of students receiving education is constantly increasing and it is likely to increase more in the near future. Although the number of students is rapidly increasing yet it has not been possible to provide them necessary facilities. The number of able teachers is also not increasing with the same proportion.

Suggestions : In order to solve the above mentioned problem Kothari Commission has recommended that selective system of admissions should be adopted in the universities. The number of students in the educational institutions should be determined keeping in view the facilities available in the institutions concerned and the number of teachers. The university should prescribe necessary qualification for admission and the best students should be selected from among those desiring to seek admission in the universities. The new and modern methods should be adopted while selecting the students. Until these methods are fully developed, the percentage of marks secured by the students in pre-university examination should be made the basis of their admission. Each university should establish a Board of University Admission. In order to help the students to select different subjects of higher education, the University Grants Commission should establish Central Testing Organisation.

Facilities Required

Another reason for the low standard of education in our institutions is that the students do not have the same faculties which are provided to the students of the universities in other countries of the world. The libraries of universities are not properly equipped and are not able to make available all the necessary books to the students. Due to the lack of books the students are not able to study properly. The environment and the conditions in which our universities are imparting education are likely to lower the standard of education. In many degree colleges, there is not even proper seating arrangements for the students. There are thousands of such degree colleges, which do not possess even playgrounds. In such conditions, the lowering of the standard of education is quite natural.

Suggestions : A high committee should be appointed for providing necessary facilities to the students. The Government of India and the State Governments have been making every possible endeavour to provide grants in order to remove the difficulties of the students and equip properly the libraries etc. But it may be made clear here that only the Government's efforts alone will not solve this problem. The non-Government institutions should also come forward and make as much contribution as possible in this field. It is the sacred duty of the rich class of the society to spend as much as possible to raise the standard of higher education. In progressive countries life America, non-government institutions contribute a lot in the field of higher education. The rich class and the non-government institutions of India should also emulate the example of America.

Teacher's Poor Conditions

The conditions of the teachers teaching at the university stage is also not up to the mark. It is true that new U.G.C. scales are quite charming but to some of the states teachers are not paid according to them. The accommodation facilities are also not proper and most of the teachers teachings at the higher stage live outside the university or college campus.

Suggestions : All the states should immediately implement the U.G.C. scales. In addition, the teachers should be given proper places for living and studying. It is the duty of the Government to see that university teachers are very highly paid so that brilliant students may like to choose teaching profession instead of other services.

Teacher's work Atmosphere

Another reason for the low standard of education is that the teachers have been burdened with too much work. The conditions of working of the teachers are such that they are not able to perform the teaching work properly. At the university stage where prominence is given to the research work, it is completely improper to burden them with too much work.

Suggestions : In order to remove the above-mentioned defects, it is necessary to reduce the hours of working of the teachers. Besides this, they should be encouraged to devote their utmost time in the research work. Each teacher should be given one year leave with salary within a period of 5 years of service for increasing his knowledge and for travelling to foreign countries. They should also be provided with concessional tickets. They should have complete freedom in performing the teaching functions. Only teaching work should be taken from them. It is very bad practice to burden the teachers with administrative and other works of educational institutions. The suggestions made by Kothari Commission in respect of the promotion of the teachers, improvement in the condition of their service and work etc. are very important and should be implemented with immediate effect.

Another reason for the decline in the standard of higher education is that there is a wide gulf between the teachers and the students. While in western countries the students and the teachers work together like a family and perform some type of functions in their interest. In India, it appears that the interests of the students and teachers are separate from each other.

Suggestions : In order to establish close contact between the teachers and the students, it is necessary to adopt tutorial system. Besides reducing the number of students in each class, at different hours 4 or 5 students should meet a teacher and hold discussions with him. Debates and discussions should be organised. These debates and discussions help to establish close relations between the teachers and the students. They are able to increase their knowledge with the help of the teachers.

Improper Examination System

Defective examination system is also one of the chief causes leading to the decline in the standard of university education. It was pointed out by Radha Krishnan Commission that only one suggestion is made to reform university education, it would be in respect of present examination system. Too much importance is given to the essay type of examinations. Consequently, the students think that they will achieve success by studying some selective questions and so they do not devote their full heart and soul into the studies throughout the year. Most of the students study only selected questions and hence the standard of education is constantly declining. Besides this, the number of pass marks is so low that they secure them very easily.

Suggestions : To reform the present examination system, it is necessary to give less prominence to the essay-type examination and give emphasis on internal assessment or evaluation. In place of essay-type examination, objective tests would be more useful. So far students securing 60 per cent; 45 per cent or 48 per cent and 33 per cent marks are awarded first, second and third divisions respectively. The above mentioned percentage of marks should be increased to 70, 55 and 40 respectively.

Party-Politics : The prevalence of cheap party-politics is yet another cause which is responsible for the decline in the standard of education in Indian universities. Different political guides endeavour to make their influence in the universities. In every province, there are some particular persons who are ever eager to establish their control over universities. Consequently, because of party politics such teachers are appointed who are not properly suitable for teaching work. The groupism of the teachers also lowers the standard of teaching. The teachers remain busy in group party-politics and they do not get sufficient time to throw themselves heart and soul into the teaching work.

Suggestions : The need for keeping the college and universities away from party-politics need not be over-emphasised. All the political parties and scholars should consider this problem seriously. We should think that the future of our country depends upon the progress of higher education. If the standard of higher education goes on constantly declining, we cannot make progress in any field. A conference should be organised for keeping the universities away from party-politics. There should be free discussion in this conference over this problem. Thereafter, a date should be fixed, on which the suggestions should be submitted in this connection. Government should implement the suggestions of the said Committee. As far as possible the politicians should not be appointed in the universities. The Vice-Chancellors should be appointed from among the prominent educationists of the country and they should keep themselves away from party politics and the influence of prominent politicians.

The Indiscipline

Last but not the least, the growing indiscipline among the students is also one of the chief causes responsible for the decline in the standards of higher education. This indiscipline can be of many types and there are many causes for it. The prominent among these causes are the social and economic difficulties; growing unemployment; non-availability of educational facilities, group party politics; lack of interesting subjects in the curriculum etc.

Suggestions : Kothari Commission has suggested that not only the teachers but also the students, parents, guardians; society, Government and political parties should work together to solve this problem. Such type of programmes should be organised in colleges and universities as may keep the students busy in constructive work and keep them away from party politics. Every possible endeavour should be made to solve the problem of unemployment. Unless and until the problem of indiscipline is satisfactorily solved in the colleges and universities, it would be wishful thinking to hope for an improvement in the standard of our higher education.

It is clear from the above discussions, that there are many reasons which are responsible for the decline in the standard of higher education. It is not only necessary but also expedient to check the decline in the standard of teaching and every possible effort should be made to improve the existing standard of higher education. If we intend to come at par with other advanced countries of the world, it should be our sacred task to work sincerely to raise the standard of higher education.

4

Population Problems

The population explosion is the most potent cause of the crisis which the world is facing. This explosion has come about through a natural and automatic process, but it has been implicit in its very far-reaching consequences. The increase in material resources and every individual's right to live have created an upheaval in the world of education. When we forget the international arena, and think of this problem in the context of India, we find the situation even more pitiable and disheartening. In every five year period, the addition to our population is more than the existing population of England, and if this situation continues, there can be no reason to doubt that problem of foodgrains will assume truly alarming proportions.

Meaning and Definition

The notion of remaining constantly aware of the increase in population and its future consequences arose in 1960. Efforts were then made to define and clarify the concept to relate it to education. Stressing the importance of this, Philip M. Hauser remarked that "It is about time for twentieth century school curricula to comprehend and understand twentieth century demographic findings in the context of their 20th century implications."

In India, it was Prof. Sloan Wayland of Columbia University, who gave concrete shape to the notion of population education. According to him, irrespective of the nomenclature, we are concerned with the fact that the public policy on family planning, nation and family, the desirability of family planning, etc., should be comprehended under the counselling system in formal education.

At the same time, studies should be conducted into the economic and social development of education, size of the family, and the dynamism of the qualities of a nuclear family. Hence, it is necessary to develop a special method of education at the school level under the linguistic provisions in a particular society.

Burleson has conceived of population education as population awareness. In his view, the increase in population brings about an increase in the already increasing expenditure on education. Education can modify the problem by arousing a population awareness among teachers and students. Population education is the awareness of knowledge relating to population. It has two objectives (1) Educationists and others concerned with them should understand the importance of population, the disadvantages of its nature. (2) Teachers and students should understand the nature of their own tendencies.

Aims and Objectives

Population education is essential for the reconstruction or restructuring of our modern, rapidly changing society. The NCERT has set up a special wing entitled Population Education. It has set out the following objectives of population education:

1. Orientation of the school teachers towards preparing training units on which students will obtain information about the increasing population and the problems created by it and also take interest in finding solution to the problem.
2. Conducting experiments in extracurricular courses in selected schools, and implementing similar experiments on a larger scale if successful.

3. Preparation of suitable teaching material for population education in schools.
4. Making provisions for research and study concerning population education in schools and making the programme more effective.
5. Evaluating the productiveness of students covered by the programme and developing the necessary skills.

It is evident from these objectives that in the programme of population education, it is necessary to keep in mind the ecological complex. According to Duncan, Ecological complexes are built up out of changes in the environment, changes in the structure of population measures for fighting the problem of population and the mutuality of factors, and an account of these complexes amounts to population education.

In the same way, Chauls has expressed the following opinion on population education. He says that population education should comprehend the culture of the students, the population situation of their society, their own views about the existing situation, their logical, reasoned and organised ideas on the situation of the population and its effects.

The UNESCO workshop defined population education in the following terms- "Population education is our educational programme which provides for a study of the population situation in family, community, nation and world with the purpose of developing in the students rational and responsible attitudes and behaviour towards coping with the situation."

Need and Significance

It is only natural to ask why we should have population education. The answer is very obvious. Today, population is increasing at such an alarming rate that material resources have completely failed to keep pace with it. There is a complete imbalance between material resources (food, clothing, housing and the size of the population. The existing situation naturally encourages exploitation and misery, thus leading to increasing social injustice.

In order to face and overcome these conditions, educationists and demographers have come to feel that the problem must be given the form of a revolution in ideas. This implies that the problem of population must be given the form of a revolution in ideas. This implies that the problem of population must be integrated with education. In India, the task of educating people about the problems of population is being done by the governmental agency, NCERT, and the informal agencies-Family Planning Association, All India Federation of Education Association, etc. These programmes are directed at - (1) schools, colleges and other educational institutions, (2) those who have left school or have not received any education, (3) those imparting training to teachers, teachers themselves and those who impart education through training, counselling and guidance.

Indian Scenario

In India, the concept of progress means industrialisation, exploitation of resources, improvement in the standards of living through material progress, and acceptance of education as the medium of the foregoing. Population is the focal point of the fulfilment of these objectives. The cooperation of all possible agencies is essential for understanding the problems likely to arise in the future and for promoting this programme of population education.

Educational Scheme

The Family Planning Association of India has prepared the following for population education -

Fundamental Reason

1. Family and the individual focal points of population education at these levels, determination of scope and syllabus.
2. Nation
3. The World

The following elements will be comprehended under these objectives-

Population, Factors and Results : (Rates of birth, death, life and increase).

Human, Situation and Environment : (Population, reduction in consumption and production).

Social, Economic and Development Aspects : Production, national production, health, education, housing employment.

Family Life and the Individual Aspect : (Family and social institutions, education for family life, sex education, position of women).

Fundamental Values and Qualities of Life : Objectives of society, techniques, a consumer's society, utilisation of resources.

These programmes will be implemented through studies, discourses, regional schemes and research.

Introduction and Sensitivity of Groups

1. The objectives outlined above will be achieved with the help of the ministries of education and health and other ministries, administrators; educationists, principals and teachers.
2. Arrangements will be made for discourses, contact with the people, publication, guidance cells, training syllabi, etc.

Plans for Future

(Syllabi, extracurricular activities, etc., in village/city).

1. This programme will be implemented through the medium of schools, colleges, social education classes, adult education classes and classes for the employed.
2. For this purpose, arrangements for reading class units, context books, hand-books, audiovisual material, information centres and library facilities will be made.

Study and Research

1. Studies into marriages in villages and cities, sex, family life, population problem, awareness of the population problem and the attitudes towards it.

2. A survey of guardians of school-going children for an understanding of begetting of children, sex, family life, population awareness and study of problem.
3. A study of the knowledge of teachers with a view to introducing population awareness, marriage, family life, sex relations, begetting of progeny, etc., into the syllabus.
4. A study of the leaders of education in the contexts outlined above.
5. Active research into teaching methods and techniques, pertaining to sex, family planning, population education, problems, etc.

For all these programmes, close contacts will be established with educational research institutions, teachers' training institutions, social welfare institutions and voluntary agencies so as to impart speed to the programme.

At present, the Population Education Department has taken the following steps under the Fore mentioned programme- (1) preparation of context books, hand-books and publications, (2) preparation of teaching material, (3) publication of a monthly magazine, (4) establishment of libraries and information centres, (5) issue of teaching materials to schools at low prices, and (6) preparation of kits for population education.

At present, all of us are being swept onwards by the inexorable flow of an ever-increasing population, but we must try to escape from this flood and also forestall it for the sake of our own existence. Today, the crowds in universities are growing larger, colleges lack even an inch of spare space. Our population annually increases by 13 millions, which is equal to the entire population of Australia. In the next twenty-five years, our population will double itself. In order to solve the problem of the future, we should adopt the following programmes:

1. Departments of education should make arrangements for in-service training, research and programme implementation.
2. Various departments of universities should conduct research and prepare desirable literature.

3. Departments of science should conduct factual experiments into the evil consequences of rise in population.
4. Various programmes of population education should be implemented through seminars, discourses, exhibitions, etc.
5. This programme should be made a part of education at every level.
6. The United Nations Fund for Population Studies has been set up at Bombay with the cooperation of the World Health Organisation and the United Nations for the purpose of combating the problem of education at the international level.

It is hoped that through the implementation of this programme, the increasing population will be brought under check, and our future generation will be freed from the spectre of a gigantic problem.

5

Dropout Problems

Stagnation and Wastage

Definition and the Meaning : At different stages there different term of education. Any student who receives education at any stage is expected to complete his education within that prescribed period. In practice, we find that many students who join the schools or colleges very enthusiastically, leave education after some time. Such type of students do not complete the study of their curriculum and consequently the time, money and energy spent on such students proves to be mere wastage. It is rightly remarked:

> "The most popular use of the word 'Wastage' in education means, the wastage of time, effort and money after those students who do not successfully complete the course of study undertaken by them."

While clarifying the meaning of the word 'Wastage' Hartog Committee remarked the following:

> "By wastage we mean premature withdrawal of children from schools at any stage before completion of the primary Courses."

As stated earlier there is a definite term for the education of curriculum at every stage. The students at every stage of education are excepted to pass the examination after studying their whole curriculum but it has been found in general practice that many students are not able to pass the examination in one class or in more than one class within the prescribed period. In other words we may say that they do not pass every year in that class. Thus, they stagnate in the same class whereas their other colleagues pass that class and study in the next class. This process has been called the process of stagnation. Thus, by stagnation we mean the stay of students in a particular class for more than one year. According to the Report of the Hartog Committee:

"By stagnation we mean the retention of a child in a lower class for the period of more than one year".

Problem with Education System : It was the Hartog Committee that for the first time pointed out the 'Wastage' and 'Stagnation' taking place in Primary Education.

The meaning and definition of the word 'Wastage' and 'Stagnation' given by the Hartog Committee have already been mentioned earlier. It was pointed out by the Hartog Committee, "Primary Education is ineffective, unless it atleast produces literacy ."On the average, no child who has not completed primary course of at least 4 years will not become permanently literate. The Hartog Committee also devoted its attention, to the wastage and stagnation that was taking place in the secondary education. As in the case of primary education, the wastage and stagnation were eating the vitals of the secondary education also.

A Committee of the educationalists set-up in the year 1983 was of the opinion that out of 100 students taking admission in class 1 only 41 reach up to class V and 26 up to class VI. The average percentage of H.S. and equivalent examinations in different years was 45.8

Wastage and Stagnation in University Education : The problems of wastage and stagnation exist probably in a greater degree at the stage of University Education. In this connection, the University Education Commission has remarked that great wastage of public money is taking place every year but what is still more regrettable is the fact that there is the indifference towards the serious loss of public money as there is for the wastage of time, money and energy of the students and their parents or guardians and their ambition and aspiration. Dr. Kamath and Dr. Deshmukh in their paper on the wastage at university level wrote that even in an eminent collage, Furgusson College, Poona, it is prevalent. In this college, out of 408 students admitted in the faculty of arts, 193 left the studies without completing their courses. In the faculty of Science out of 1423 students 594 left the studies without completing their course.

Grounds for Stagnation and Wastage

Faulty Administration : Our educational system cannot said to be completely free from any defects. There are very few schools which can claim to be successful in making the mental, physical and moral development of the child. In most of the classes and colleges, the standard of teaching is low, there is lack of trained teachers, lack of educational implements or aims is a special feature and there is a great lack of educational buildings built in healthy environment. In such conditions, neither the students are able to throw themselves heart and soul into the scared task of acquiring and learning of Knowledge nor the teachers are able to do their teaching work with complete enthusiasm and skill. Secondly, both the teacher as well as the students are burdened with the task of receiving education and imparting education respectively, just pass their time.

Reform in Administration : In order to solve the problem of 'Wastage' and 'Stagnation' the teaching standard of the educational institutions should be raised; teachers should be trained, necessary educational implements should be provided, educational buildings should be built in healthy environment; schools and colleges should be made more attractive and proper provision should be made for the entertainment and sports and games of the students.

Vicious Environment : Ordinarily the students have to pass their time in vicious environment in schools as well as out side the schools. In each class there are a number of such boys whose habits and behaviour, method of conversation, etc. are deplorable. Such type of students never sincerely aim to pass their classes every year and other students by coming in contact with them start ignoring their studies.

The environment outside the schools and colleges, specially in the cities, has become very vicious. Obscene songs played on loudspeakers, exciting advertisements of films, dirty processions, films, etc., are proving great obstacles in the study of the students. If these conditions persist, it will not be astonishing if the problems of wastage and stagnation assume even more serious form and nature in a near future.

Improvement in Environment : It is necessary to change and improve the environment in which the students pass their times in the schools and outside the schools. It can be done only with the joint efforts of the Government, the people and the teachers, it is the sacred duty of the Government to inculcate qualities of social reform, sanitation, health and co operation, etc. in the parents and guardians of the students and should make provision for general health entertainment and adult education. The government should by law ban the playing on of obscene songs on loudspeakers, the exhibition of exiting advertisement of the films and the boys and girls up to the age of 18 years should be prohibited to enter the cinema houses. Dirty films and advertisement on television should be stopped. So for as teachers are concerned they should perform their duties by building a healthy environment in the schools.

Ineffective Method of Teaching : The teaching methods which are prevalent in most of the educational institutions do not make the desired effects upon the students. Incompetent and untrained teachers, lack of proper aims and implements of teaching, lack of space, excessive number of students in classes etc. are some of the main defects of the present educational system. Because of the existence of these defects in the present teaching methods, the method of teaching has become at present dull and consequently the prevalent teaching methods fail to create a desire in the students towards their lessons.

Psychological Methods of Teaching : In order to solve satisfactorily the problem of 'Wastage' and 'Stagnation' at different stages of education, it is necessary that new and psychological methods of teaching should be adopted. Trained teachers, necessary implements of education, good educational buildings built unhealthy environment, etc. are necessary for improving the prevalent teaching methods.

Defective Curriculum : Yet another cause of 'Wastage' and 'Stagnation' in education is the prevalence of defective curriculum. The present curriculum is rigid and one-track and it includes a large number of subjects. The children of the cities as well as of the village have to study the same curriculum, no matter whether their interest is towards it or not. Besides this, no endeavour has been made to make the curriculum interesting by including some handicrafts or other such subjects.

Reform in Curriculum : In order to solve the problem of 'Wastage and Stagnation' reform in curriculum has become necessary and expedient. Any curriculum cannot be regarded as appropriate and suitable for an indefinite period. It is necessary to change it in accordance with needs and circumstances on the basis of experience and experiments. Consequently, the curriculum of the schools should be modified and if necessary completely reorganised keeping in view the local environment and needs. Separate curricula should be prepared for the students of the rural and urban areas and subjects should be by keeping in mind the interest and needs of the boys and girls. Utmost endeavour should be made to make the curriculum simple, interesting and practical. It should also include some handicrafts which should fulfil the local needs.

Defective Examination System : Another cause which is responsible for 'Wastage' and 'Stagnation' in education is the defective examination system. Nearly 50 per cent of the students fail in different examinations every year. This large number of failure of students is because of the defective examination system.

Change in Examination System : The present system of examinations is full of many defects and it should be changed and reorganised as soon as possible. The students should be awarded marks on the basis of works done by them in classes throughout the whole year and not on the basis of annual examination only. According to R.V. Panuekar, "Schools are established in order that children may be taught, not that they may be foiled." This statement must be given serious consideration and efforts should be made to make the necessary provision so that the wastage caused by the large number of failure of students every year may be minimized as much as possible.

Pupil's Health : It has been observed for several years the physical conditions of the students has been deteriorating. It is because of the lack of edible things, lack of nourishing food and because of the increase of different diseases. Because of being weak and ill, majority of Indian students are not able to devote themselves properly to their studies and consequently they are not able to complete their course within the prescribed period.

Improvement in Pupil's Health : The Government should pay special attention towards the improvement in the health of the students. It is the responsibility of the Government to make proper provision of health and nourishing diet for all the students. In all the progressive countries, food or other type of provision is made for the nourishing diet for the students. Our Government should also give special attention to solve this problem.

Illiteracy of Guardians : A survey made in the: state of Maharashtra revealed that "Wastage and Stagnation' is comparatively more in the children of backward class. The main cause of this is that guardians of the children are illiterate. Being themselves as illiterate, they fail to understand the cultural and social importance of the education to their children. Consequently, even if they admit their children in some schools, they take them out of those schools sometime because from their point of view the time thus proves to be a wastage. What is true of the guardians of these backward classes, is attitude of most of the Indian people because the majority of our population continues to be illiterate.

Eduction of Guardians : The guardians of children will understand the importance of education of their children only when they themselves are educated. In order to educate the illiterate guardians night schools, adult schools and part-time schools should be established in a large number.

Financial Handicaps : The financial handicaps are also responsible for 'Wastage' and 'Stagnation'. It is true that 60 percent of the wastage caused in primary education is because of the financial handicaps. The financial condition of the Indian people is so miserable that when provision has been made for free education of their children they find themselves unable to meet other expenses connected with the education. Besides, they have always before them the question as to whether they should send their children to schools or to a place, where they may earn something to contribute to their major income.

So far as the education of girls is concerned, they are taken out of the school only after providing the knowledge of alphabets, etc. It is because of the fact that girls do not get in return any financial help from the education of the girls.

Increase in Individual Income and Control on Prices : In order to check the 'Wastage' and 'Stagnation' in education, it is necessary to improve the financial condition of the guardians. Our Government is very conscious of this gross situation and have been making every possible endeavour to improve the financial conditions of their people. The country is moving rapidly on the path of industrialisation and every possible effort is being made to increase the production of food grains and other agricultural commodities. The efforts that have been made so for to improve the financial condition of the people, have resulted in the increase in per capita income of the Indian people.

Undoubtedly, the increase, in per capita income may solve much of the financial difficulties of the people but yet another serious thing which needs proper consideration is the Question as whether this increase will be sufficient keeping in view the constant soaring of prices of essential commodities. There has been much increase in the paces of our commodities. The experience of last few years clearly indicates that the economic conditions of the middle and lower classes have deteriorated. Unless these problems are satisfactorily solved, it would be futile to hope that the problems of 'Stagnation and Wastage' in education will be solved in the near future.

Social Evils : Yet another cause which is responsible for 'Wastage' and Stagnation' in education is prevalence of many social evil in Indian society. Coeducation of girls and boy is still looked with suspicion. Consequently, if at one place there is no separate provision for the education of girls then they remain deprived of education and in case they are fortunate to get admission in some schools, then they are forced on account of certain circumstances to leave education after a few years because of the prevalence of social evils of early marriages. Many girls and boys leave their studies at a premature age. This and many other social evils are responsible to a great extent for the prevalent 'Wastage and Stagnation', that is taking place in the field of education at different stage.

Suggestions : The evil cannot be remedied by taking certain concrete steps. In our society the roots of feelings of opposition to coeducation, early marriages have gone so deep that unless they are rooted out completely, it is not possible to check the 'Wastage and Stagnation' in education in the near future.

There can be only two ways to solve the prevalent feelings and viewpoints. Either the society should be completely changed through revolution or the defects of the society should be removed slowly and gradually. The second way seems to be more poetical and proper but its responsibility lies upon the shoulders of young men and women of the country. If they throw themselves heart and soul into this work, they can develop a new consciousness among the people and they can form a new era of science and technology in the country.

6

Environmental Problems

Bharat H. Desai rightly points out in an article "We are in the midst of a deepening environmental crisis triggered off by unprecedented growth and development of the human race. The unbroken history of rapacious exploitation of natural resources and the continued neglect of the need for regeneration and conservation have begun to boomerang", observes a High Powered Commission in its report submitted to the Government of Gujarat recently.

The twelve-member High Powered Commission (HPC) headed by R. Parthasarathy, Chairman of Vadodara Urban Development Authority (VUDA), was constituted "to study the problems of people affected by large undertakings in Gujarat". However, the findings reached and the recommendations made by the Parathsarathy Commission have wider ramifications, meriting attention for environmental protection in India as a whole especially its recommendation to set up a statutory environment protection agency.

In the post-independence era, urbanisation in the wake of large-scale industrialisation has brought about widespread environmental degradation. Industries sprang up all over Gujarat in the sixties in an unplanned fashion which uprooted hundreds of small and marginal farmers following land acquisition. "The plight of the land losers", according to the HPC, "has been aggravated partly by inadequate negligible compensation and partly by the failure of existing policies and programmes to rehabilitate them adequately, economically and socially." Apart from this, most of the villages affected by land acquisition are suffering from inadequate or near absence of basic minimum needs. The rapid felling of trees, disappearance of greenery, destruction of village forests, indiscriminate disposal of solid and semi-solid wastes by industries in and around affected villages are leading to serious health hazards for the people. "There has been nearly no rehabilitation worth the name of the land losers' families", laments the HPC.

The world is facing or rather passing through many crises but the most dangerous crisis is that of gross and constantly increasing pollution of the environment. Needless to say that if immediate attention is not paid, ways are not rooted out; plans are not implemented in their right direction to put a check on the growing hazards of pollution, the entire humanity may be in the grip of destruction, devastation and it maybe a sign of doom and loom for all of us. For this, proper environmental education is inevitable if we are to attack the problem, not only at the roots but also with a view to have a final solution to our growing gigantic problems of the devilish pollution.

Let us, first of all, see as to what is meant by Environment. In an article-Crisis of Environment-Environment is explained as under:

> Environment refers to surroundings - those natural things around us, from the essentials which sustain human life, such as the earth's atmosphere or healthy air or drinkable water, to the non-essentials that nevertheless make life sustainable, such as wild animals, clean places or human living space.

Thus, the environment is not just pretty trees and tigers, threatened species of birds, animals and plants and the ecosystems.

It includes the entire entity on which we live and on which our agricultural and industrial development depends. Saving or preservation of the essential ingredients of life and of the rich natural diversity of the planet is consequently necessary for healthy existence.

The compulsions and complexities of life sometimes require us to make a dent into natural wealth; but everyone now agrees that the fewer such dents human beings make, the better for them and for the coming generations. Certain actions become inevitable, but several others are advisable for man. Continuous destruction of the vital environment certainly robs us, and also the succeeding generations, of variety and beauty in nature.

Undeniably, the environment has become the world's common problem. The environmental health of a country is in fact an indicator of the quality of life of the people. The need for an environmental ethic is now universally accepted. The environment is in grave danger, but it can certainly be saved. Conservation has necessarily to be adopted as a long-term strategy : it must be made a mode of life.

We need air, water and adequate land of sufficient quality to sustain life. Continuous research and monitoring have to be done to ensure that these precious resources are preserved. The importance of their preservation is apparent from the fact that air, water and land are finite, limited sources, and can be exhausted. To use a Term of economics, air, water and land must be regarded as capital, not as income. Even the Vatican and the Holy Sect, representing the Pope, said: "Stewardship of the resources of the physical world has always been a key concern of religion."

Besides this, it will be worthwhile to note that broadly speaking atmosphere that implies both-natural as well as social-in natural atmosphere generally, air, water, trees, vegetables are included. Again it is divided in two parts-biological and non-biological. There may be further sub division-such roots of bio-atmosphere in the forms of generator, consumer and destroyer. Under natural atmosphere all the living beings fall under the head of consumer.

The second atmosphere takes into its compass —social, economic, political and family relations.

The Components

Balanced use of Natural Resources : There has been a prevalent misconceived notion that more use we make of available natural resources, more the progress of the world. Actually there becomes an imbalance in the nature if there is an unrestricted exploitation of available natural resources. Y. Nondumma is right when she points out that this mis-conceived notion of the exploitation of the natural resources under the pretext that they are meant only for exploitation by and for human being, will take the entire humanity to a point of destruction. As it will lead to the entire change in the environment.

Control over the Waste Material : In every industry there is left enough material which is nothing but waste. This waste is either thrown into the water or somewhere on the ground. In both the cases the atmosphere becomes polluted either through water or through air. To have a control over such a waste material is inevitable if we want to preserve the environment or face pollution.

Check on Industrial Development : Industrial development brings with it environmental degradation and may be a menace for the humanity if no check in the right direction is made on this. Industrial development adversely affects the community and surrounding atmosphere all around.

Proper Utilization of Natural Resources : Nature has given us coal, gas, oil and many other minerals, etc. As there is no limit to the greedy nature of the human being, he has started extracting every thing mercilessly and putting the same at his disposal without caring for its proper utility and the limit to which the same should be exploited, according to need and limit. The result is explicitly clear. At certain places there is drought while at other place there are heavy rains and floods. It brings untold miseries but man has still not learnt a lesson to make a balanced use of natural resources.

Pollution : A Worldwide Problem : The United Nations has repeatedly expressed deep anxiety over the ceaseless pollution all over the world and the innumerable problems it creates. In the initial discussions on environment there were wide differences on the issue. The UN Conference on Environment, held in Stockholm in 1972, became known for controversial approach. Two leading US environmentalists openly contradicted each other over whether too many people or too few resources were responsible for the world's deepening ecological crisis.

The Eastern bloc, led by the Soviet Union kept aloof because the UN had not fully recognised the German Democratic Republic. The Third World accused the industralised nations of using the "pollution problems" as an excuse to keep it underdeveloped ; and well-known anthropologist Margaret Mead warned of the need for a "Copernican Revolution" in thinking if we were not to irreversibly damage the natural world.

Since the Stockholm session there have been the UN Habitat Conference on Human Settlements in Vancouver in 1975 and the UN Desertification Conference in Nairobi in 1977. In 1972 only 10 nations had environment programmes ; today the number is nearly 100. Third World attitudes have changed dramatically. As the concern has mounted, so has the Doomsday syndrome.

Scientific agencies issue urgent warnings to emphasise the gravity of the population crisis-four births and two deaths every second; 10,000 new chemicals a year are being introduced into the world some deserts are encroaching at the rate of 30 kilometres annually; a century ago 96 per cent of all energy used was either human or animal and now the figure is 1 per cent ; the oceans are dying and the earth's protective ozone layer is being broken up by aerosols and supersonic aeroplanes. The list of disastrous deeds is endless.

The need to teach people about the environment has become increasingly obvious. In October, 1977, nearly 400 delegates from 74 countries gathered in Soviet Georgia for a major intergovernmental conference on environmental education organised by UNESCO in collaboration with the UN Environment

Programme (UNEP). They heard UNEP Executive Directors' blunt warning: "Environmental education is now a matter of life and death." Dr. Amadou Mahtar M'Bow, UNESCO's Director-General, cautioned that the problems of the environment were "jeopardising the development of mankind."

There is a growing number of hopeful examples : 15 out of 18 nations surrounding the Mediterranean signed a "Save the Mediterranean" agreement ; Tanzania had invited international environmental experts to advise on the design of the country's new capital; the USA and Canada were cooperating to revive the Great Lakes. The Chinese have been conserving energy by the widespread use of bio-gas collectors, which produce gas for cooking and generators, and the Soviet Union is minimising the effluence from the pulp plants around Lake Baikal, which contains one-tenth of the world's entire fresh water supply.

An international conference to consider the question of saving trees and forests was held in Paris in January, 1986. The meeting was convened by President Mitterand and brought together for the first time Heads of States and senior government leaders from 36 nations to discuss forestry issues.

Because the pollution envelops the entire world and as such no country- remains aloof from its evil effects, there is an awakening throughout the world to save it from the fatal clutches, of the fearful dragon of pollution.

Pollution Causes

Y. Naidumna has rightly stated that the unlimited exploitation of the natural resources has lead to dangerous consequences and now there are only two ways left before the entire human race for its existence-one is to make the environment useful keeping the needs of life while the other is to put a check on waste material along with the use of natural resources. Following are causes of pollution:

Rapid Rate of Development : The editor of *Competition Master* rightly says :

> "The irony of the situation is that the more the economic and industrial development in the world, the more the danger to the environment". At many places, "development" has acquired a sinister dimension—pollution. It threatens forests and farms, human health and aquatic life. Disposal of hazardous wastes is another allied problem.

The United Nations Economic and Social Commission for Asia and the Pacific (ESCAP) warned early in February, 1985, that the Asian environment, already in a critical state, is likely to be burdened with additional load resulting from development activities. Statistical data compiled by this U.N. agency indicated that from 1970 to 2000, the volume of-solid wastes will increase five times- dissolved solids, pesticides, biochemical oxygen demand, and particulates.

These statistics mean that every environment has what is termed "carrying capacity", or the amount of pollution or damage an environment can sustain or "carry" without further degradation. A lake that is ten times larger than another one can carry roughly ten times the pollution load. If the loads are not minimised or the environment upgraded to an extent that it will be able to carry them, the environmental degradation will inevitably worsen. As for the size of the expected future loads, solid wastes refer mostly to garbage, there is hardly any Asian city where garbage collection is efficient enough to avoid piles of refuse on the streets.

Biochemical oxygen demand (BOD) is a measure of the quality of oxygen required in the natural decomposition and recycling process. BOD is expected to increase four times by 2000, but there are no more sets of clean rivers, lakes and seas to accommodate the additional waste. Many Asian water resources are already at, or past, their carrying capacities.

Chemical Pollution : The editor again throws light on the evil effects of chemical pollution- "There are even more dangerous chemicals in use in India than MIC which caused havoc in Bhopal in the world's worst disaster of this kind. The plastic industry uses a chemical closely related to MIC known as toluene di-isocynate

(TDI) to make polyurethane foam. TDI is used more extensively than MIC and is far more dangerous to human beings.

"A group of chemicals called polychlorinated biphenyis (PCBs) are highly toxic. These are widely used in the electronics industry and there is no control on PCB use in India. But only when these chemicals are discharged into water can the Water Pollution Act apply to them.

"There are other equally hazardous chemicals which are being manufactured, sold and used in India, and about which there is no information at all.

"Oddly enough, there is no law in India authorising the Government to collect information on the number of chemicals imported or produced in the country. In terms of tonnage at least 70 per cent of the pesticides used in the country have been classified as highly toxic or hazardous by WHO. Protection and improvement of the environment became a priority issue only in the Fifth Five Year Plan (1974-79)".

Acid Rains : Out of the smoke and other waste material a by product of mills and factories, there is a lot of acid rain which not only damages the outer surface of earth but gives birth to many fatal diseases -amongst human beings and life on this earth.

"Acid rain", which contains 65 per cent sulphuric acid, 30 per cent nitric acid and 5 per cent hydrochloric acid, is caused by pollutants which fossil fuel-based industries emit. It has destroyed considerable vegetation. Sweden and Canada are the worst victims of acid rain which is no respecter of national boundaries.

Disturbing the Nature : The pollution caused by machines, motor vehicles, mills, factories, petroleum products, etc., the felling of trees, the digging of the hills and such other fearful devices have given birth to a lot of problems such as soil erosion, the presence of dangerous gases and compounds the layers of smoke and dust prevalent all around are some of the major problems we are facing under its impact.

Population Pressure : In 2000 A.D. there will be 3.4 billion people to feed instead only of 2.6 billion in the early eighties. It is clear, therefore, that if current tends are allowed to persist, Asians will face a grim future-not just zero development, but regression. Undeniably, population pressure is the root cause of virtually all pollution and environmental damage. A realistic national timetable for population stabilisation is clearly indicated.

Problem of Pollution

As discussed in an article in *Competition Master*

"Surveys have revealed that India has suffered greater havoc by destruction of natural wealth and pollution of the environment than other countries. India as a whole is adding about 4 million tonnes of sulphur dioxide, 7 million tonnes of particulates, one million tonnes of carbon monoxide, besides nitrogen oxide, hydrocarbons and several other toxic substances. Bombay illustrates the catastrophic dimensions of air pollution in the country: With all its industries, it emits daily 1000 to 1700 tonnes of pollutants. In Calcutta about 1300 tonnes of pollutants are discharged every day.

Because of the three thermal power stations and massive burning of domestic fuel, Delhi has suspended particulate matter as high as 640-1000 microgram per cubic metre one of the highest in the world. Delhi is a topper in respiratory diseases. The other badly affected towns are Kanpur, Ahmedabad and Coimbatore.

Dr. S. Dhillon Riply, an eminent environmentalist from Smithsonian Institute, said at a seminar in Delhi last year that in India "massive exposure of land, the soil and water and the air to the fruits of technological advance and development without regard for essential biological precepts can only hasten the degradation of what has been a fair land and a marvellous one for all manner of life."

Grim evidence of this came through the well-documented World Conservation Strategy prepared by the International Union for Conservation of Nature and Natural Resources in cooperation with the United Nations, Environment Programme and the World Wildlife Fund. This revealed that more than half of India suffers some form of soil degradation.

A recent study of the Doon Valley indicates that the once beautiful area is fast becoming an ecological disaster. The region's 2000 mm rainfall has percolated into its limestone belt-a vital cog in the ecological cycle of hills. Thoughtless limestone mining over the past 20 years has resulted in a 50 per cent drop in agriculture productivity and the drying up of several perennial streams which once watered the land. Very few commercial concerns have benefitted from the "rape of the land", but thousands of residents continue to suffer.

Life and Death Issue : An even more ominous warning was given in November, 1985, through the Second Citizens, Report on the State of India's Environment (1984-85) released by the New Delhi based Centre for Science and Environment (C.S.E.). The C.S.E. has a high reputation. Its first report in 1982 was hailed by the United Nations Environment Programme as "a model for other countries to follow."

The rapid pace of environmental destruction in India through soil erosion, deforestation, pollution and urban decay is already affecting the lives of millions of poor people ; the country faces social, economic and ecological disaster if its environment is not properly managed. The report seeks to establish a link between environmental destruction in rural areas and urban decay. Many slum and pavement dwellers in India's cities are 'ecological refugees'.

A five-year study of air pollution in Bangalore city has shown that pollution due to automobile emissions and domestic firewood consumption (cars and kitchens) pose a greater danger than industries.

The construction of dams and power stations, the growth of the mining industry and the destruction of forests and grazing land have displaced large numbers of people. The World Bank financed Narmada Valley Project involving the construction of 329 large dams at a cost of 3.5 billion will displace a million people.

The report is not merely a catalogue of catastrophes. It points out that, proper environmental management can provide India with opportunities to tackle poverty. Government-controlled wasteland, which covers between one-third and half of the country, has enormous agricultural potential. But where wasteland development is taking place, few attempts are being made to involve the landless. Most afforestation schemes, for example, are designed solely to meet the industrial requirements of paper mills and fibre manufacturers.

In a signed statement at the end of the report, the authors call for a new 'social order' for resource management. Government policies have served to create' a strong sense of'alienation' among village communities which should be left to manage forests, grazing lands, rivers and lakes themselves.

'Environmental activism' has increased dramatically in India. The building of two dams has already been stopped as a result of public protests-the Silent Valley Project in Kerala and the Bedthi project in Karnataka. The Munda people of Chhotanagpur are fighting against a third project-the massive Koel Karo Scheme in Bihar. A coordination committee and the participation of local leaders of various political parties from probably the strongest popular anti-dam movement in India."

Many dangerous chemicals are used in India. The Plastic Industry uses chemicals Toluene-diiso-Cynate which is closely related to MIC which caused havoc in Bhopal Gas tragedy in 1984. Needless to say that this (TDI) is more fatal for life. Similarly a group of chemicals called Polychlorinated biphenyis (PCB) which are highly toxic are widely used in electronic industry. Besides this there are other hazardous chemicals which are being manufactured sold and used in India. In terms of tonnage at least 70 percent of the pesticides used in the country have been classified as highly toxic or hazardous by WHO.

Education's Role

Before we discuss the role of education in the eradication of pollution let us keep in mind a few things like its impact on health, the radio active waves, rise in respiratory and eye diseases, the growth in diseases caused by virus, the gastroenteritis diseases, various diseases relating to noise resulting in deafness, and other diseases of lungs and heart. The growing adverse effect on all types of vegetation cannot be ignored.

Now it shall be worthwhile to discuss the role of education in the eradication of pollution. Following are the measures if adopted in letter and spirit in the right earnest, may bear fruitful results.

1. New ways of looking at the environment so that its value can be reflected in the national accounts, better planning and legislation, more careful and wider use of existing and new environmental technologies, including the all-important environmental impact assessment-a way of appraising the effect of any proposed project on the environment before it is launched.
2. The new Environment (Protection) Act, 1986, is far better in approach than the earlier laws. The Water (Prevention and Control of Pollution) Act, 1974, and the Air (Prevention and Control of Pollution) Act, 1981, were weak and merely regulatory in character.
3. The aim of the new measure is stated to be: 'To provide for the protection and improvement of environment and for matters connected therewith.' The Act contains provisions for tackling the inter-relationship between nature and human beings and the diverse kinds of pollutants. Section 6 (b) empowers the Central Government to make rules for 'the maximum allowable limits of concentration of various environmental pollutants (including noise) for different areas'.
4. There is a section on hazardous industries and environmental disasters. Thus, hazardous industrial pollution is also covered. A hazardous substance is defined as "any substance or preparation which, by reason of its chemical or physio-chemical properties or handling, is liable to cause harm to human beings, other living creatures, plants, micro-organisms, property or the environment: (Section 2 (e).

5. There are stringent measures to check hazardous pollution. Section 8 of the Act states clearly: 'No person shall handle or cause to be handled any hazardous substance except in accordance with such procedure and after complying with such safeguards as may be prescribed.' Section 6 (f) empowers the Central Government to make rules for 'the procedures and safeguards for the prevention of accidents which may cause environmental pollution and for providing remedial measures for such accidents.' Moreover, it is now mandatory for a person responsible for the discharge of any hazardous substance in excess of the prescribed norms to immediately inform the concerned authorities and to render all possible assistance. Earlier there was no such responsibility.
6. Vigilant citizens can initiate proceedings against an establishment that is polluting the water supply or otherwise ruining the environment. The penalties for defaulters have been made more stringent. The Water Act provided for a maximum imprisonment of six years and/or a fine upto a total of Rs. 5000 ; in the Air Act the limits were a maximum imprisonment upto three months and/or fine upto a total of Rs. 5000. The new Act provides for imprisonment of defaulters for upto a total of seven years and/or a fine which may extend upto Rs. 1 lakh.
7. However, there are some flaws even in the new Act. One, all power and authority is vested in the hands of the Central Government.
8. (i) There is no provision relating to forests, even though it is open knowledge that in India about 50 per cent of the energy consumed is non-commercial or collected from fields, trees and bushes.

   (ii) Secondly, supplementary legislation in respect of enhanced penalties and for tightening the enforcement of the provisions has yet to be brought up. Nor is it clear whether the new Act supersedes or supplants the two earlier laws. The enhanced punishments may or may not be deemed applicable to cases which fall under the purview of the other Acts. The areas of jurisdiction have not been clearly demarcated.

(iii) Thirdly, there is no clear provision for public participation which is vital for preserving the environment. The relevant issues are left to official bodies (Air and Pollution Control Boards) and other regulatory agencies. Any individual can file a complaint with the Government against a factory management, but it requires the complainant to give 60 days' notice, which permits the offending management to bring its emissions within control. The role of the public, especially voluntary bodies, needs to be enhanced considerably under the Act.

9. Section 6 (e) of the Act empowers the Government to make rules for "the prohibition, restrictions on the location of industries and the carrying on of processes and operations in different areas". But there is no mandatory provision for the industry to prepare and submit to the concerned authorities a suitable environmental impact assessment report before the location is approved. The US National Environmental Policy Act, 1969, requires that an environmental impact assessment must be prepared prior to any federally financed project. In India all that a government-financed industrial unit needs is a simple "no objection" certificate from the concerned Pollution Control Board.

10. *Stress on Ecological Balance :* Addressing the first meeting of the National Land Use and Wastelands Development Council on February 6, 1986, Prime Minister Rajiv Gandhi called for a nationwide "people movement" to protect the country's ecological balance. He suggested a time bound land reclamation and afforestation programme. The approach to this problem could not be departmentalised or compartmentalised but had to "respond to the differing needs of every section."

An integrated approach, not hemmed in by internal contradictions, would ensure sufficient food, maintain nutrition levels, meet fuel and fodder needs and raw material requirements of industry and help preserve natural habits. 'We will have to mobilise not just the Government, but we will have to mobilise absolutely everyone. Stressing the need for decentralisation of nurseries, tree growers' cooperatives, he called for the involvement of farmers, youth and women in the programme. The landless and the marginal and small farmers should be the key elements in the programme.

11. *Strategy Needed* : Having experienced the ill effects of industrial development, it is high time a long-term strategy for environmental protection is evolved. In this respect, the Parthasarathy Commission has strongly pleaded for a Regional Development Strategy and a National Urban Development Policy with a view to contain metropolitan chaos, for developing secondary cities and to ensure development of existing small and medium towns as well as establishing new ones, as part of a regional strategy generating employment and promoting decentralised urbanisation. In addition, a clear industrial location policy will ensure setting up of specific large industries at specific locations with a predetermined time-frame. It will ensure not only systematic industrial growth but also facilitate in taking measures for environmental protection economically and in a coherent manner.

12. All State governments, semi-government bodies and municipalities as well as social organisations have been propagating "grow more trees" campaign. To boost the idea of growing more and more trees, the government has taken up the project of "social forestry" on a large scale. The project aims at planting trees singly or in groups wherever they can be grown.

13. Apart from increasing the forest wealth, the programme generates additional earnings to the Panchayats, more

employment to labour, and it provides cheap fuel to the village poor. In Dhanoli, a village in Valsad district of Gujarat, social forestry has achieved remarkable progress. By adopting the scheme of raising village forests in only four hectares of land a net income of over Rs. 43000 was generated.

14. Social forestry not only prevents felling of trees but also tries to distribute the produce of the project directly to the people of the area. The scheme also aims at growing more trees and forests on unused land and promotes research in the science of trees and their varieties.

15. Community lands in villages are wasted and used only for grazing village cattle. This unproductive use of land yields the village panchayats hardly Rs. 4000 to Rs. 5000. But the same land, if utilised for a cluster of trees for which the Government provides free seedlings, can fetch a much higher income to the Panchayats. The Gujarat Government has decided to give 50 per cent of the net profit realised from the sale of village wood-lot to the Panchayat. Crores of trees are required to strengthen and support agricultural and animal husbandry, to combat pollution and to attract adequate rains and also to stop erosion of fertile soil.

16. But social forestry, especially the growing plantations of eucalyptus, has been criticised by several ecologists, sociologists and economists. The environmentalists claim that social forestry is encouraging monoculture, and in particular the plantation of eucalyptus, which makes up 80 to 90 per cent of all the trees planted so far under these programmes: Eucalyptus, it is contended, degrades the soil and permits nothing to grow beneath it. It is a heavy consumer of water and lowers the water table.

17. *The Ganga Plan :* The Government of India has launched a Rs. 292-crore project to clean up the mighty Ganga, which has been greatly polluted as a result of the inflow of effluents and dirt from various sources. There are about

100 cities situated along the banks of the river, in the States of U.P, Bihar and Bengal. Nearly 4200 small and medium units are responsible for polluting the holy river. The Ganga Project is the largest and most ambitious of all the environmental protection plans launched in the country.

18. The cleaning up work began at Rishikesh and Hardwar in September, 1985. Cleaning the Ganga is also in progress at Varanasi waterfront, which is heavily polluted. A Central Ganga Authority had been constituted under the chairmanship of the Prime Minister himself.

19. The wanton destruction of natural wealth, including forests, and the indiscriminate setting up of chemical industries endangers the lives of both human beings and animals. The greed for personal gain, the general decline in values, the knowledge that one can flout the laws with a vengeance and get away with it, or at worst to pay a small fine, have cumulatively rendered ineffective the agencies entrusted with the duty of protecting the environment. There are poachers galore, but it is only rare that legal action is taken against such offenders.

20. Besides, there are wide variations between official data and the actual position. For instance, the Forest Departments in the States have been spending crores of rupees during the past 30 years and claiming that a large area has been brought under forest cover. The Union Minister of State for Environment and Forests Mr. Z.R. Ansari, said in the Lok Sabha that only 13 per cent of the country's geographical area is under "forest cover" according to satellite pictures, whereas the revenue records show the area to be 22.7 per cent.

21. In February, 1986 the Supreme Court directed the Union Government to examine the possibility of setting up environment courts. The court judgement in the Shriram Foods and Fertiliser Industries case may well provide a basis for action by the Government to safeguard the

environment in areas where potentially hazardous industries are located. The court has in fact set out a framework for appropriate governmental action. It has also set up a monitoring committee to ensure that the expert bodies recommendations are implemented. Even more significant is the suggestion that measures should be taken to educate the workers and provide early warning systems for the public.

Analytical Appraisal

While the increasing awareness and rethinking about the importance of preserving all aspects of the environment, including forests, clean air, and wild life is welcome, there is an urgent need for earnest implementation of declared policies. So far, the implementation has been poor and, consequently, the environment has been deteriorating; forests, in particular, are disappearing at a disconcerting pace. It is time to recall the farsighted Chanakya's observation in the 4th century B.C. that "the stability of an empire depends on the stability of its environment:" Strong and committed machinery is needed and it must have sufficient resources.

Ecology also has some effect on poverty. Undeniably, an ecologically and scientifically sound afforestation programme can provide a solution to the problem of India's poverty, if it is not based on the profit motive alone. More research is undoubtedly needed to evaluate the costs of monoculture based social forestry. Unless afforestation programmes are linked with the basic needs of the rural poor, they will prove economically counter-productive and ecologically disastrous.

Obviously, the plunder of what nature has built over billions of years has to be stopped. We need a new life-style with environmental ethics as an integral part of it, not only for this generation but also for the future generations to live and enjoy the freedom of this planet and beyond. It is important in this regard to reduce the rate of population growth to one per cent from the present 2.2 per cent, as China has done. Industries generating high pollution should be moved out of the perimeters of cities.

Environmental education should be made compulsory at every level of learning.

For the rapid protection of environment the following measures should be adopted:

1. Aesthetic sense among the citizens be developed.
2. Attitude towards cleanliness be evolved.
3. Civic sense must be prevailed.
4. Social forestry be adopted.
5. Religious attitudes towards trees be scientifically developed.
6. Eco club be established.
7. Research in Environmental Studies in every subject be promoted.

7

Problems of Integration

People's life style is the replica of different social values. As is the society, so are the life styles. There have been variations in life styles from time to time. In an age of autocracy, the life styles become too much limited. In democratic times, when everybody has his own way of life, it is but natural that there will be good many life styles becoming popular. At the time of independence of the country, it was a fully integrated and combined type of society. But with the passage of time, there has been some sort of disintegration. So much so that today it has become a popular trend of life. Perhaps, it is coming out as a fashion of life. Only a few individuals advocate it, but majority of people have their disliking for it. There is disintegration in the personality of an individual. Equally, there is disintegration in the member of a family.

It is seen that in a family, different religious beliefs are cropping up. Likings and dislikings also vary from one individual to another in the family. One member of the family wants to have one type of breakfast, another wants a different type and the third one has his own peculiar taste. All this shows a socially disintegrating small unit of a family. Similar is the case of society, the state and the nation when we review the different aspects of life from various angles.

Disintegration is becoming a trend of life. There is disintegration because of different beliefs, customs, traditions, cultures and values of life. Questions arise - Was it so in the past ? Was it so before the independence of the country ? Was it so at the time of independence of the country ? Perhaps, no. Not at all in that spirit as it is now.

Need of the hour in our country is national unity and integrity. Education can play a very significant role. In the words of Dr. Radhakrishnan, "If India is to remain free, united and democratic, education should train people for unity and not localism, for democracy and not dictatorship."

In the same context, Pt. Jawahar Lal Nehru remarked, "We should not become parochial, narrow-minded, provincial, communal and caste-minded, because we have a great mission to perform. Let us, the citizens of the Republic of India, bring out the integration of the Indian people. We have to build up this great country into a mighty nation, mighty not in the ordinary sense of the word, but mighty in action, mighty in culture and mighty in its peaceful service of humanity."

Meaning and Nature

As per Advanced Learners Dictionary of Current English, nationalism is strong devotion to one's nation; patriotic feelings. It is loyalty, love and devotion towards one's nation. A person who possesses the sentiments and feelings of nationalism is called a nationalist. Mrs. Indira Gandhi said, "Even if I die in the service of nation, I would be proud of it. Every drop of my blood, I am sure, will contribute to the growth of this nation and make it strong and dynamic." So feeling of love towards the country, devotion and spirit of self-sacrifice is nationalism. A true nationalist stands far above party politics and is ever-ready to serve the nation and safeguard it from any type of outer dangers. The fundamentals of national unity are coexistence, tolerance, cooperation and unity.

The Concept

Brubacher says, "Nationalism ordinarily indicates a wider scope of loyalty than patriotism in addition to ties of place. Nationality is evidenced by such other ties as race, language, history, culture and tradition."

According to Humayun Kabir, "Nationalism is that which depends on we-feeling towards the nation."

According to Education Commission Report, (1964-66) "National integration includes a confidence in nation's future, a continuous rise in the standard of living, development of feeling of values and duties, a good and impartial administrative system and mutual understanding."

Dorothy Thompson's view, "National integration is a feeling that binds the citizens of a country."

National Integration Conference Report, 1961. "National integration is a psychological and educational process involving the development of a feeling of unity, solidarity and cohesion in the hearts of people, a sense of common citizenship and a feeling of loyalty to the nation,"

Narrow Concept **:** Some people talk of nationalism in the limited sense. They are heard saying-my country and not bothering about others or the country of others. When people limit their views to their own limited sphere, to their own nation only in this age of internationalism, that creates hatred, jealousy, conflicts and that leads to destruction of peace and war.

Hitler's views, Hitler used to say that the Germans have been born to rule over the world and others to be ruled. The concept 'My country flood or bad, should be dear to me' is wrong. This narrow concept destroyed the humanity.

According to Bertrand Russell, "The boys and girls are given the education that their greatest worship or devotion is for that country of which they are citizens and the creed of that worship of the country that whatever the government does is desirable. Therefore, they are taught false History, Political Science and Economics so that they may criticise the lesson of worship of countries of other persons."

Mudaliar Commission says, "There is no more dangerous maxim in the world of today than 'My Country right or wrong' the whole world is now so intimately interconnected that no nation can or dare live alone and the development of a sense of world citizenship has become just as important as that of national citizenship."

Pt. Jawahar Lal Nehru said, "Nationalism is such a strange element which while it instills life, development, energy and integration, at the same time makes it narrow because on account of it a person thinks about his own country as separate from other countries of the world."

Nationalism and patriotism are not synonymous. Patriotism is old and nationalism and internationalism are modern. Brubacher rightly remarks, "Nationalism ordinarily indicates a wider scope of loyalty than patriotism."

Broader Concept : True or pure nationalism means love and devotion for one's country but not at the cost of hatred for others. A true nationalist is a well wisher of everyone and he strongly believes in world peace. In fact, the spirit of true nationalism in a person tends to make him a lover of internationalism.

Present Condition

It becomes an important study to find out the real causes of the present fast deteriorating social situations. There is more and more of disintegration with the advent of life. The following seem to be the causes:

Frustration : In the society we find that there is too much of frustration seen almost in everybody. Nobody seems to be satisfied with his lot. Of course, the degree of frustration varies from person to person, and from family to family. The businessman has his own frustration, the employee has his own, the teacher has his own frustration, the Head of an institution has his own, the teachers and the students have their own reasons of frustrations. Whatever may be the cause of frustration but all this makes them lovers of loneliness and seclusion. They dislike sharing their views with others and they find it difficult to have belief in others.

Corruption : The corruption in society is rampant. We may take up any circle, social, political, economic, there is favouritism and disfavouritism. Justice to one and all is rather disappearing. Corruption from the top to the lower levels is spreading various type of ills in the society. Naturally it has its disintegrating effect on the growing and developing personalities of the children.

Lack of Good Leadership : The society of today has no shortage of leaders but surely there is dearth of good leaders. A good leader is replete with truth, honesty, goodness and sincerity. Such a person is a true leader, is the true path shower but the society of today is devoid of any such leadership. The educational institutions are generally headed by the most unfit type of leaders. Many teachers don't possess the qualities of leadership and they fail to imbibe such qualities among the students under their control. In political circles also, there are no good leaders. These so-called leaders come to the people at the time of elections only and then they are never seen before the next elections. They are only the mongers of votes who come for their own selfish motives only. In the capacity of political leaders in a circle or a region whatever is expected out of them, they fail to do any such thing. They even fail to hold the reins of the country truly. Whatever they do and whatever they stand for, their own selfish interests are involved. In the society, the real leaders, social workers etc., who are ever ready to serve others in times of difficulty, are also very much limited. Day by day their number is decreasing.

Public Clashes : Public life mostly stands disturbed. Every now and then, various types of communal clashes are seen. Whenever such clashes are noticed, they present a very gloomy picture of the whole society. The commonness of such incidents in the present day life is having an increasing effect on the students community. Whatever happened in the social circles is now very often seen in the centres of learning. Groups of students are seen fighting leading to confusion and chaos.

Lack of Patriotism : Patriotic feelings showing the oneness of the people for the country are fading. People are becoming more and more selfish and their thoughts and ideas are mostly of self-centered type. Perhaps they have forgotten the sacrifices made by the great heroes of the country for the glory of the nation.

The Significance

The greatest need of the country is to strengthen itself through national unity. National unity is essential for any country at any time. It is doubly so for India in view of varied compositions of her population, the vast distance that separates her different parts, the vastly varying climate and physical features that condition the daily fives and occupations of the people and above all, because of the period of rapid change-social, political, economic and technological -through which she is passing to discover her bearings in the modern world. We should have full faith in nationalism and national understanding. Varied views on need and importance are given below:

Pt. Nehru gave a call to Indian people saying: "The time has surely come when every Indian must look within and ask for himself whether he is with the nation or with a particular group. This is the challenge of our time that every man, woman and child must face."

Kothari Commission : According to the Kothari Education Commission Report, national understanding (national integration) implies:

1. A confidence in the nation's future.
2. A continuous rise in the standard of living for the masses which included reduction in unemployment.
3. A deep sense of values and obligations of citizenship and growing identification of the people, not with national loyalties but with nation as a whole.
4. Assurance of good and impartial administration, equal treatment for every citizen.
5. Mutual understanding and respect for the culture, tradition, and ways of life among different sections of the

people. Only a united nation can stand firmly like pillars to shoulder without any type of outer or inner threats to its existence. The present situations that prevail all around further necessitate to have a strong united nation. Then and then only it will be able to exist prosperously in the teeth of any type of oppositions or threats. The following points show clearly that national integration is the only way out to overcome the different type of deteriorations going on in the country:

A Democratic Country : At the time of independence, the national leaders accepted the country as a democratic republic. Now that has to be maintained. For this, proper education about the democratic values has to be imparted to all the citizens of the country. Misunderstandings of any type in the understanding of the democracy will have to be ended.

A Secular Country : India accepted secularism though there exist people who have faith in different type of religions. Everybody has his firm convictions in his own religion. It is the process of education which helps them understand that the basis of all religions is the same and the ultimate goals are also the same. Only the way of life which is actually very temporary, is different. Thus people will be enabled to have full faith in secularism. Naturally then, they will have all regards for each and every religion.

Unity in Diversity : In India there are people of different cultures. In many cases, it is seen that there are too many variations among the different cultures. In the absence of conscious efforts uniting them, they will remain separated and will not perhaps share their living together with others. So some type of intercultural ties have to be thought of and implemented.

Geographical Features

India is a vast country which is spreading far and wide. If we see to the geographical placement of different religions, the South and the North are the two extremes with lot of divergences and variations. People of one region have different ways of life, traditions, conventions which "have hardly any similarity with the ones being maintained in the other region. There is need of making them understand that they are Indian nationals. Their progress and prosperity depend upon their beliefs in true national values.

Linguistic Differences

Different people living in India use different languages for their communication purposes. There is so much of difference that one can hardly be understood properly by the other. It is rather difficult to give equal recognition and status to all the languages. A useful way out has been arrived at through the process of education. The three language formula surely helps in this regard when everybody accepts Hindi as the national language and learns it. It unifies all the people of the country to some extent. Then, English as an international language further strengthens the contacts of the people with one another. The importance of mother tongue remains because it is given the status of first language.

Dr. Radhakrishinan. It the words of Dr. Radhakrishnan, "If India is to remain free, united and democratic, education should train people for unity and not localism, for democracy and not dictatorship."

Pt. Jawahar Lal Nehru beautifully remarked, "We should not become parochial, narrow-minded, provincial, communal and caste-minded, because we have a great mission to perform. Let us, the citizens of the Republic of India, bring about the integration of Indian people. We have to build up this great country into a mighty nation, mighty not in the ordinary sense of the word, but mighty in action, mighty, in culture and mighty in its peaceful service of humanity."

National Integration

National Integration Through Emotional Integration : National integration is not a mechanical process, it is rather a psychological process. In fact, emotional integration is the basis of national integration. Emotional attachment links people and persons firmly and strongly.

Humayun Kabir's view, "National integration does not depend on race or language or religion or geography, singly or collectively, though they help, but on the feeling of belonging to one nation."

Pandit Nehru's view: "Let us, the citizens of the Republic of India stand up with straight backs and look up at the skies, keeping our feet firmly planted on the ground and bring about the synthesis, the integration of the Indian people.

Political integration has already taken place, but what I am after is something deeper than that, an emotional integration of the Indian people so that we may be welded into one strong national unit, maintaining at the same time all our wonderful diversity."

Efforts at the National Level : Following steps have been taken at the national level to foster national integration:

1. Formation of National Integration committee under the Chairmanship of Smt. Indira Gandhi.
2. Appointment of Emotional Integration in Committee under the Chairmanship of Dr. Sampurnanand.
3. Periodical Conference of Chief Ministers to discuss the problem of national integration.
4. Establishment of National Integration Council.
5. Conference of the Vice-Chancellors to tackle the problem of national integration.
6. Setting up of an organising committee by the standing committee of National Integration Council to conduct organised campaign against communication in the country at a massive scale, with which all the political parties, eminent sociologists and educationists would be associated and so on.

Role of Education : Education plays an important role in bringing about national integration. Ever since India's independence, many efforts have been made in this direction. There have been commendable achievements, but much more need to be done. Let us visualise the efforts and the achievements.

The Success

1. A national system of education (10+2+3) has been accepted almost in every state of the country. Earlier there were different systems of education in different states. It is a very favourable step in the direction of national integration.
2. The same system of education implies the same curriculum. The textbooks prescribed for different school classes have been nationalised. Now NCERT syllabus or CBSE syllabus is prescribed. All school textbooks have been published by NCERT. Those books have been adopted or adapted in different states of the country.
3. Language problem has also been solved to a great extent. Three language formula has been accepted. Regional languages, mother tongue, national language of the country and international languages have been accepted. This is another step in the direction of national integration.
4. Efforts have been made to have the same pay scales for the employees all over the country. It has successfully been done in the case of college and university lecturers. More efforts are being made to have same pay scales for other categories of employees all over the country.

Thus we find that something has always been done at various levels in the interest of national integration. Education can still play a more crucial role in the attainment of objectives leading to national integration.

The Kothari Commission Report observed that one of the basic objectives of education should be to accelerate the process of social and national integration.

The Gajendra Gadkar Committee of the National Integration Council observed that education from primary to postgraduate stage should be reoriented to:

1. serve the purpose of creating a sense of Indianness, unity and solidarity;
2. inculcate faith in the postulation of democracy and

3. help the nation to create a modern society out of the traditional one.

The latest in this regard are the observations made in the National Policy on Education 1986. While indicating the essence and role of education, it states:

"Education has an accelerating role. It refines sensitiveness and perceptions that contribute to national cohesion, a scientific temper and independence of mind and spirit thus furthering the goals of socialism, secularism and democracy enshrined in our Constitution."

Suggestive Ways

Here below are suggested some ways and means:

> Promotion of national integration must be an important aspect of school curriculum at different stages. The whole school climate should be conducive for inculcating different values related to national integration. Lectures or sermonisations do not help much. The teacher himself should be a living symbol of national integration. A really good teacher is able to effect the students in desired ways.

Dr. Radhakrishnan remarked, "National integration cannot be built by bricks and mortar. It cannot be built by chisel or hammer. It has to grow silently in the minds and hearts of men. The only process is the process of education.'

Teacher's Role

1. The teacher of language should talk about not only the languages that he is teaching but also some other languages in his teaching, he can draw comparisons with other languages. His knowledge of other languages will imbibe in the learners love and regard for different languages.
2. In the teaching of History, the teacher can draw the attention of the students to the achievements of mankind.

They learn how to appreciate the works and deeds of bravery of others. The history of India's struggle for freedom reminds the students about the sacrifices made by others. They will learn many things and value their hard earned freedom.

3. Through teaching Civics, the teacher can explain the rights and duties of the citizen. The students will be able to understand the Constitution. The topics such as fundamental rights, duties, system of government, etc. emphasize the unity of the government.
4. In Geography, the teacher explains to the students about the location of different regions, raw materials produced in there and thus their use in the factories which are located there or somewhere else. The teaching of this subject thus highlights the interdependence of various regions and areas. The policy of give and take between different regions helps in bringing the people together.
5. Through the study of Science, the students become logical and rational. They tend to have a scientific temperament. Generally, people quarrel over trifles or other petty issues which don't have any scientific basis. When the students are able to think logically, they are then not prejudiced just for nothing. Thus, the study of Science helps in inculcating the ideals of national integration.

Principal and Teachers

The Head of the institution and his team of teachers can plan many things for national integration. These can be put to practice to achieve the goal of national integration. Here below are explained some ways and means:

1. The head of the institution and his whole staff should present a unique example of united whole.

   The Head should ensure that there is one team of the whole staff and not a team divided into groups. It will stand reflected formally or informally. It will have its effects on the student community.

2. The schools should celebrate days which are of national importance. Instead of declaring a holiday, the school should celebrate the Republic Day, Teachers Day Childrens Day. It will have a very good effect on the minds of the young learners.
3. Festivals of different communities from which the students come may be organised. The celebration of one festival may be for one house which may have students from different communities. This will increase mutual understanding and also add to national integration.
4. Respect and love for national flag, national anthem, patriotic songs, etc. should be maintained. The students should be encouraged to recall such songs.
5. Intra-school and inter-school essay writing competitions, declamation contests on themes related to national integration may be organised from time to time. Prizes may be given to the students having outstanding performances.
6. Extension lectures by persons of eminence who worked for the nation, may be arranged. The students will be able to learn many things from their experiences of life. They should be asked to confine their speeches to the themes of national integration or emotional integration.
7. Inter-state matches for different games, inter-state youth festivals for different cultural items may be organised. It will increase mutual understanding among students of different cultures and social groups. It will naturally help in national integration.
8. Tours and trips to different places may be organised with the sole educational purpose of better mutual understanding. It will improve upon feelings of unity.

National integration is the need of the hour in the present day social set-up of life. Education is the main instrument which can help in achieving the desired goal. There is need of using education in its right perspectives. In the words of National Integration

Committee, "Education should, therefore, be reoriented and made more broad based. It should aim at:

1. Equipping students with intimate knowledge of the different aspects of this country including the events that had led to the freedom.

2. Encouraging all studies and activities which lead to greater understanding between communities and states, thus fostering a feeling that the country and its sources leading to the citizen who thereby acquires certain rights and privileges alongwith corresponding duties and responsibilities."

According to National Integration Committee, "Reading material provided to boys and girls in schools and colleges should be properly examined. Textbook Committee should receive definite guidance in this particular matter. If possible, model books should be prepared by the centre. There are some Dont's which can be kept in mind while preparing textbooks. The Centre should appoint a Committee for this purpose. Popular books on regional Indian heroes known for their national outlook should be prepared."

1. What do you mean by national integration ? How should educational places and programmes be geared to the task of national integration?
2. Why is national integration important for us ? How far can we achieve it through education?
3. 'National integration without emotional integration is a myth.' Explain and give illustration.
4. As a headmaster of high school what programmes would you start in your school for propagating national integration?
5. What is national integration ? How does it differ from emotional integration ? How can education promote both?
6. 'Education should be for nationalism'. Suggest ways and means for making it all successful.

Problems of Integration

There are some tendencies at work in our country which are hindering our national integration. Different languages, states, classes and castes, political parties, tendency of ignoring national interest for personal ones, regionalism, poverty and different communities are some such elements which are challenging our national unity. We have adopted a democratic system of government. Hence, diversities prevailing in the country have to be recognised. It is not necessary that individual differences often enrich our national life. But these diversities should not take such a shape as to endanger our national security and unity. Today, the diversities widespread in the country have threatened our national security. Some humiliating incidents have happened in our country in the name of language and regionalism. Boundary disputes between two states, quarrel between two states for a particular city, and communal riots and fighting in some places, are blots on the good name of our country.

This shows that we are not following the right course. Some people demand a separate state on the basis of regions. Today, the unprincipled behaviour of some political parties and their internal groupism are likely to strangulate the nation. Most of the political parties seem to be affected by personality cult instead of following some principles. The division of Congress and other parties is not so much a quarrel of principles as it is show of personalities or for personal interest by dancing at the tune of some individuals. All these conditions are against the development of a healthy democratic system. Therefore, national integration has become a problem and is one of the main problems of our education. Hence, we shall try to find out its solutions.

Political Harmony

Today, there are some persons of confused mind in our country who doubt the political unity of the country. It is true that several kings ruled over this country and there had been many independent kingdoms from time to time. But at the same time, it is to be noted that a current has always been flowing throughout the country which kept the country united. Our places of pilgrimage are not centralised within a particular region. They are spread throughout the country, Rameshwaram, Dwarika, Jagannathpuri and Badrinath are the glaring examples. It was a wonderful wisdom of our religious leaders that they established places of pilgrimage in the four corners of the country in order that people from one corner may go to the other and may visit the whole country, may know each other and consider themselves of this vast land with a feeling of oneness. Since the beginning of Indian Civilization and culture, our countrymen have been anxious to go on pilgrimage and they have been visiting different places of pilgrimage. People from north to south, south to north, east to west and west to east, have been going from one part of the country to the other. Thus there has been cultural exchange since older days and people have been considering themselves as citizens of one country.

Different rivers of our country have been considered sacred and adorable. Such rivers do not belong to one region alone. Krishna, Kaveri and Godavari of the South, Sindhu of West, Ganga, Yamuna, Sarayu and Gomti of North and Brahmputra of east have been considered holy and worth worship. Similarly, mountains of different regions in the country have been considered sacred. Different cities of the country have been recognised as places of pilgrimage and centres of cultures. Thus, it is clear that our great men have always tried to unite the country with a cultural thread and they have always been successful in their efforts.

This feeling of cultural unity inspired our religious leaders and social reformers to inculcate the feeling of common citizenship in our countrymen. It is because of this feeling that whenever our great leaders have raised their voice on any issue, the whole country has followed them. It was because of this that all the groups in the country fought the struggle for freedom under the banner of Indian National Congress, forgetting their religion, caste or community and consequently won independence. The unity shown by the people for winning freedom was not artificial, but something natural. In fact, that was the voice of country's conscience. Gandhiji's 'Dandi March' and 'Quit India Movement' had shaken the country so much that even the British Empire had begun to doubt its permanency. Many such examples and incidents may be cited to prove when on incident in one corner of the country moved the whole nation. This is a glaring example of our unshakable national unity. Chinese invasion in 1962 and Indo-Pak war of 1965 had united the whole country and it was evidenced that same feeling was running the views of the whole nation: The period of Ashoka the Great and the Great Emperor Akbar gave us a glimpse of this kind of unity. The rebellion of 1857 supports our feeling of oneness. Needless to say that we should make our political and national unity durable and should not encourage deceptive forces.

Emotional Harmony

Emotional unity of our countrymen is essential for our national integration. So long as our countrymen do not consider themselves as one and do not realize that first and foremost they are citizen of this country and their personal, sectarian, social and religious interests are secondary, there can be no national integration. They must be made to feel that from historical, geographical point of view, India has always been one country and one nation and will always remain so. They should be convinced that ours is a culture which every person should be proud of. In foreign country whenever is a talk of Indian culture before any Indian living abroad; he is over-joyed and feels a natural pride.

When we see bay of Bengal, Kumari Antreep of Indian Ocean in the South, Gulf of Kutch in the west and Himalayas in the north, an emotional current runs within us and this current fills us with reverence to India. The same feeling is created when we stand on the banks of Ganga, Yamuna, Sindhu, Krishna, Kaveri, Godavari or Brahmaputra. Whenever we remember our sacred rivers, our heart is filled with joy and then we think of these saints and great men who created new chapters of our culture from time to time and tried to unite us. Our rivers and mountains are not only geographical units, but different constituents of our culture have been produced in their vicinity.

Our Indian culture has been created by the thinkers, living close to the jungles, valleys and rivers, so our culture does not have that artificiality which is found in industrial cultures. We have to make this emotional unity stronger. Education is a powerful means for the fulfillment of this aim. The poets and authors of our country should praise our mountains, rivers and oceans in such a way that attracted by praise the people are lost in them. We should attract the attention of our people to this through education. By doing so all will be emotionally integrated and will rise above their personal interests for good of the country.

Social Harmony

In our country different groups based on community, religion, caste, poverty and wealth are found. These groups remain indifferent to each other and there is lack of national unity. They are wanting the feeling of brotherhood. There is influence of caste in some religion, sectarian feeling in the other and some particular religion in another. In fact, the situation is very pitiable. For national integration, it is necessary that people of different classes and communities are brought to each other and feeling of unity is infused in them.

For this, some collective programmes should be arranged and people of all classes, communities and different religions should be invited. Every community should be made to feel that the interest of their community lies in the interest of the country which is the first and foremost than anything else. So, no class or community can make progress by ignoring the interest of the nation. Needless to say that we have to forego communalism, religionism and regionalism for social unity. This does not, however, mean that we should have no love for our community, religion or region and should forsake them.

It only means that we should first think of the country and after that of anything. We have to inculcate the feeling of 'Nation first, anything afterwards'. It was only due to this feeling that people coming from different countries of Europe were able to establish a nation in America. Similarly, there are followers of several languages, regions and religions in Russia. But these elements never proved a hinderance for the unity of the country because the people there kept national good over all. Religionism, casteism, regionalism and linguism have been encouraged by some of the political parties in our country and these parties have acted against national unity. All of us know very well that at the time of elections different political parties plead for religion, class, caste and region and want to secure votes on the basis of these slogans. A candidate is selected from that caste or religion which dominates a particular area. Such an action is just a misuse of caste for political interest and it creates conditions for national disintegration. All such policies will have to be changed for the sake of national Integration.

Inter-caste and Inter-state Marriage

Some people are of the opinion that for national integration, inter-caste and inter-state marriages should be encouraged. This means that people should marry in to other castes and religions, forgetting their own caste and religion. Similarly, persons of different regions north, south, east and west should not hesitate in natural marriages. The children born of such marriages will be above caste, religion and regionalism. They will consider themselves Indians first and anything else afterwards. In support of this argument, people cite the example of U.S.A. and Japan. The Spanish, German, French and British people who settled in America after migrating from different countries of Europe, accepted inter-caste marriages.

The off-spring of these people consider themselves an American first and take pride in calling themselves as such. Similarly, in Japan also followers of different religions are found in one family and their off-spring call themselves Japanese first and not of this or that religion or caste. Thus, national and integration in America and Japan has been very much encouraged. In our country, this process should be adopted voluntarily and anyone who is desirous of intercaste marriage should be encouraged and should be given special social recognition. But we should bear it in mind that in the context of social situation in our country, it will not be wise to arouse a countrywide current for intercaste marriages. But whenever such examples are found, due importance should be given to them, because such step is a good means for national integration.

Economic Harmony

The economic inequalities pervading the country are weakening her. Some have a wealth of lakhs and crores and some are dying for want of two square-meals in a day. These inequalities will have to be removed for the sake of national integration and so that no specific class or community remains backward. For this, it is necessary that minorities and backward persons are given special help. They should be given special facilities of education, houses and government services. If the backward classes are satisfied and feel comfortable, they will contribute to the national integration.

Language of the Nation

The question of national language has become very important for us. According to the Constitution, Hindi in the Devnagri Script has been accepted as state language and in 1965 Hindi was to occupy the place of national language of the country. But in 1965 when this place was accorded to Hindi, riots broke out in South and in Calcutta and these are, in fact, a blot on the nation. Although majority of people in different regions of the country are prepared to accept Hindi as national language but they were forced to follow so slow policy regarding Hindi due to riots and disturbances in January and February of 1965.

If we want to encourage national integration, we should not be in a haste for Hindi. So long as people of non-Hindi speaking areas do not agree to accept 'Hindi', the clause of the Constitution regarding Hindi should be kept in abeyance. We should prepare the non-Hindi People for accepting Hindi with national love. Although it is time that we can not continue a foreign language as link language for ever. Our general Indian public cannot learn English. Some say we shall have to accept some Indian language. This does not mean that knowledge of English is not useful for us. In order to take benefit from international culture and knowledge, the knowledge of English is very necessary. So the subject of English should not only be available in our schools, colleges and universities but it should be compulsory at degree stage. Inspite of all this we have to adopt our own language, and so far that language is Hindi. So long as the related clauses of the Constitution are not changed, we should strive for the acceptance of Hindi as a national language in such a way that one day the whole country may be prepared to accept it gladly. But as long as non-Hindi people do not show their willingness to accept it, Hindi should not be imposed on them as it will be against national integration.

Therefore, we should remember that our national language Hindi is helpful in national integration rather than an obstruction. Evidently, we have to work in this direction cautiously, affectionately, sympathetically and with wise entreaty.

Educating the Masses

We have indicated in previous pages that in education is a powerful means for national integration. Through education we can inspire the future citizens for it. So the aim of national integration is to be kept supreme over all while organising the different components of education.

In framing the curriculum, the classroom teaching, in educational centres, cultural activities, in the organisation of co-curricular activities, in the management of schools, in the various stage of education (schools, colleges or universities), in the appointment of teachers, in the distribution of educational facilities, in the composition of textbooks we should follow such policies as will encourage national integration rather helping the tendencies of class, community, religion etc.

In the existing situation of the country and the international context, the need for unity should be emphasized more. We have to be careful that no disruptive forces flourish against national integration, if we follow the suggestions given in previous pages, we shall be successful in maintaining national unity.

The spirit of a country is inherent in its culture. The chief function of education has always been to transmit the culture of the country to future generations. Different countries have different cultures. Hence, different countries try to transmit their cultures to the children and youth of country through their specific systems of education. After the British rule becoming well established in our country in the nineteenth century, the education system was shaped according to the British deals. Hence the education system always remained aloof from the Indian background, but after the achievement of freedom in 1947, the problem of removing the education system from this serious defect has become very important for us. Now we want to Indianise our education. In this chapter, we will discuss this problem.

Spirit of Indianisation

Different persons have given different views regarding the meaning of Indianisation. The meaning of Indianisation was considered to be the following of Indian methods in place of British methods in the Indian national life. This was a narrow meaning of Indianisation. According to the wider meaning of Indianisation, it is to include the foreign elements in the Indian Public life that it is made richer while maintaining its national and good points of our culture, characteristics. This meaning also includes the inculcation of the feeling of Social and National responsibility in the public life of the country. It is to be remembered that we have to overcome the tendency of Hindunisation, purported by some narrow-minded persons in our effort for Indianisation. In fact, we have to keep Muslims, Christians and other countrymen with us in the sequence of indianisation, otherwise Indianisation will be meaningless.

Indianisation does not mean making it governmental. Its aim is the development of the feeling of proper social and national responsibility in the people. National feeling should not be interpreted in the political context alone. The national feeling goes further by including political sincerity in it attachment to the country, feeling of pride for our cultural heritage, respect for national language, national flag, great men of the nation, national anthem and national beliefs are all included in it. Those foreigners who come upto our expectations in these various contests, can also be considered fully mixed up in this national feeling. For example, Smt. Annie Besant and Mr. Stocks, though they were not born in India, will always remain a part of our national life since they proved true to our expectations. Contrary to this many persons who were born in India, can never come in the purview of our definition of Indianisation, if they have declared themselves deadly against our country. The national feeling of a person is his inner inclination his religion, caste, language or political party have very little influence on it. By Indianisation we mean this favourable inner inclination of an Indian though he may belong to any religion, language or political faith.

The Indianisation of education means that education has got to be geared to the needs and aspirations of the country. For this adjustment we have to continue to move with the ever changing nature of Indian culture. To make education capable of fulfilling the demand of the country and to make it according to the means and functions needed at a particular time, will be called Indianisation of Indian education.

After the winning of freedom in 1947, new needs and aspirations have arised in the Indian public life. Consequently, the unsuitability of education continuing since the British times disturbed our minds. So, the rulers of the country made several efforts to bring the needed changes in the educational system of the country. In these efforts generally the following three main characteristics may be noticed:

Efforts of Reinclusion of the Basic Elements of Ancient Education : The establishment of D.A.V. Colleges and some Gurukuls on the basis on the views of Swami Dayanand is a symbol of such an effort. Some educational centres established by Ram Krishna Mission and Shantiniketan established by Ravindra Nath Tagore are other examples of such an effort.

Efforts of Making the Education of the Country Modern : Education policy framers and the rulers of our country have realised it well that education can be capable of preparing worthy citizens according to the present day needs only when modern western knowledge and science are adequately included in our education.

Basic Education : The educational system initiated by Mahatma Gandhi was a praiseworthy effort of inculcating self-reliance, constructive skill and practical knowledge in our students. Being dissatisfied with the then prevailing education, Mahatma Gandhi advised to implement this scheme. It was a revolutionary step for a change in the very base of our education system i.e. at the stage of primary education. This revolutionary step had the following main points:-

(1) The child will be the centre of education.

(2) He will learn while working.

(3) The work alone by the child during the process of learning will be productive.

(4) Some craft will be the pivot of education.

(5) Children will imbibe the feeling of dignity of manual labour.

(6) The medium of education shall be the mother tongue.

(7) The various subjects will be taught by co-relating them with the selected craft.

(8) The teachers and student will do their work based on the ideals of truth and non-violence.

(9) The teachers and students, both will work for social upliftment.

Evidently, the above ideals were placed before us to provide a strong base for education and prepare worthy citizens. But basic education did not succeed according to its ideals because of several reasons, although it was accepted as a national policy of education for primary level. We have mentioned the causes for the failure of basic education in a separate chapter earlier. However, it is true that basic education has not been able to achieve its proposed objectives so far, but it must be admitted that basic education has been a revolutionary effort in the direction of Indianisation.

University Commission of 1948-49, Secondary Education Commission of 1952-53 and Acharya Narendra Deo Committees of 1939, 1952-53 the university and Secondary Education Commissions established by the Indian Government and Acharya Narendra Deo Committees appointed by the Government of U.P., have made efforts of Indianisation and modernisation of University and Secondary education in their specific contexts. It is not necessary for him at the recommendations of these Commissions here, because they have already been discussed under separate chapters earlier.

Kothari Commission 1966 : This Commission appointed by the Indian Government is yet another revolutionary effort for the Indianisation of education. We nave already discussed some of the main recommendations of this Commission in a separate chapter. It is not necessary to repeat them here again. However, the essence of these recommendations is briefly given below, as it fits in with the needs of Indianisation of our education.

(1) The development of the social, moral, and spiritual beliefs of Indians should be made possible through education.

(2) The development of democratic ideals should be done through education.

(3) Increase in production is possible only through education.

(4) Modernisation of the country can be done through education alone.

(5) Education should help in the development of social and national integration.

National Policy on Education

In July 1968, our Government announced National Education Policy on the basis of the recommendations of Kothari Commission. This declaration is a symbol of our efforts of Indianisation. The following are some of the main elements of this declaration:

(1) To bring education close to public life.

(2) To make efforts for the qualitative improvement at all the stages of education.

For bringing education close to the public life; the following programmes should be adopted.

(a) To develop new moral and social beliefs.

(b) To make special attention to science and industry at every stage of education as far as possible.

In order to achieve the above objects, the Indian Government has decided to work according to the following principles in the field of education.

Increase in the Salary and Allowances of Teachers : In this regard, the government has decided that it will continue to strive to achieve the above objectives. It must be remembered that the State Government are trying to improve the status of the teachers through all possible means with the help and aspiration of the Central Government and University Grants Commission. A glowing example of this effort are the new scales of pay of the teachers at various levels, implemented by the U. P Government and some other states in the country.

Encouragement of All Indian Languages : In order to improve the culture, literature and philosophy and public life, the government has decided to develop all Indian languages, the national language and culture. Along with it, for expansion of knowledge, it has stressed the need of encouraging the study of English and some other international languages.

National Service and Work Experience : The aim of national service and work experience is to be achieved according to the capacity of the students at every stage of education.

Equality of Education Opportunity : Equal opportunities of education are to be provided to the children of various regions, such as, hill areas, sea beach and barren lands and to backward and disabled children, children of tribal areas and gifted children.

Science Education and Research : In order to make the country prosperous, science education should be emphasised and new Research should be conducted in this fixed programme.

Development of Talent : Talent (meritorious persons) in the country should be discovered and developed.

Education in Agriculture and Industry : Special attention should be paid to the development of agriculture and different industries in order to make the country self-sufficient.

Preparation of Books : Various original books on science and knowledge should be prepared and the gifted authors should be rewarded for the work.

Reforms in the Defective Examination System : For the proper evaluation of students achievement, the examination system should be reformed.

Necessary Changes in Secondary Education : Secondary Education should be extended to those areas where it has not been provided so far. Facilities for technical and vocational education should be available at the secondary stage.

University Education

(i) Technical and vocational educational should be extended to the University stage.

(ii) Laboratories, libraries and other necessary material-aid should be arranged for this stage.

(iii) New Universities should be established cautiously.

(iv) Improvements in Research, Training and Postgraduate curriculum should be brought about.

(v) Some model research centres should be established.

(vi) Short-term education and correspondence education plan should be started.

(vii) Literacy and adult education should be extended.

(viii) Proper attention should be paid on the educational structure. This structure should be uniform for the whole country.

(ix) Necessary resources be developed for the games and sports of students.

(x) Secondary Education up to 10 years, higher secondary education for two years and Graduate education for three years, that is, the pattern of 10+2+3 should be implemented throughout the country.

In fact, our leaders in the sphere of education have no interest as to how to Indianise education. However, whatever has been discussed in the different pages of this chapter, there can be no doubt, in fact, that our national government is looking towards Indianisation.

Issue of Languages

Language problem has been prevalent in our country in one form or the other since ancient periods. Earlier Sanskrit was the main language of our country but at that time there too was a conflict between Sanskrit, Prakrit and Pali. In the Muslim period, Arabic and the Persian were the official languages but Urdu and Hindi were also adopted. In 1835, Lord Macauly gave great emphasis to the English language and since then all out efforts were made to make English the medium of instruction. During the British period, medium of instruction was English. After independence the question was that which language should be adopted as the medium of instruction. Language problem can be seen in two forms: (1) Problem of the medium of the teaching; and (2) Problem of study of different languages at different stages.

Teaching Medium

As we have already said that in Ancient India, Sanskrit was the medium of instructions. Later on Pali and Prakrit took place of Sanskrit During the middle ages, Arabic and Persian were the medium of instruction. During the reign of Akbar, Hindi and Urdu were also given great importance. After the arrival of Britishers in India, there was a visit change in the educational policy. In 1935 Lord Macauly emphasised that English should be the medium of instruction and it remained the medium of instruction for more than hundred years.

After the independence, controversy of the medium of instruction arose. Different scholars put forward the different views regarding medium of instruction. Some of the scholars were of the opinion that English should remain the medium of teaching while others were in favour of state language Hindi. Some pleaded for the regional languages. Radhakrishnan Commission recommended that Indian Languages should be the medium of instruction in place of English. Mudaliar Commission recommended that up to the Secondary stage, Mother tongue or the regional language should be the medium of instruction, the Commission was of the view that English should be replaced by Hindi and it should be compulsory in all universities.

In 1955 the languages Commission also recommended that Hindi should be the medium of instruction, and university examination should be held in Hindi. Kothari commission was of the view that the regional languages should be the medium of instruction up to the primary and secondary stage. Even at the higher stage of study, regional languages should be the medium of instruction. English should be replaced by Hindi.

From the above discussion, we come to the conclusion that the problem of medium of instruction is very tedious. The only solution of the problem is that English should be replaced by the regional languages and State language Hindi. Hindi should be compulsory in all the universities of the country.

Language Study

In Ancient India there was no such problem. Sanskrit was the main language which was studied from one corner of the country to other corner of the country. In addition to Sanskrit, Prakrit, and Pali were also studied. During the Muslim period the study of Arabic and Persian was compulsory. In addition, Urdu and Hindi were also studied. During British period, three stages of education became clear Primary, secondary and higher. At all stages of study, study of English was compulsory. In addition, Urdu and Hindi were also studied. Facilities for the study of Hindi, Urdu and regional languages were also provided. Up to the secondary stage and higher stage of study, English was compulsory. In the Constitution of independent India, it was provided that English shall be replaced by Hindi during 15 Years. Radhakrishnan Commission was of the opinion that at secondary stages and University stage, study of three languages should be compulsory.

(1) Mother tongue, (2) State language, (3) Hindi in almost all the institutions of the country. Mudaliar Commission recommended that Hindi should be integral part of the curriculum of all the universities. English should be replaced by Hindi Kothari Commission recommended that study of three languages:

(1) Mother tongue (regional language), (2) State language, Hindi and (3) One of the Indian or European languages. The Commission also recommended that the book of science and technology should be written in regional languages. In institutions of All India level, English should remain the medium of instruction, but by and by it should be replaced by Hindi. Hindi should be studied at all the stages, but it should not be thrust upon all the persons.

From the above discussion, it is evident that different Commissions have put-forth different views regarding the study of different languages, in our opinion mother tongue should be compulsory at primary and secondary stage of study. In addition to it, the State language should also find place in the curriculum. At higher stages of study too, Hindi should be compulsory. All out efforts should be made that the latest books of science and technology are written in Hindi Language and by and by English should be replaced by the State language Hindi. The development of regional languages is also very necessary. It is hoped that in a short span of time we should be in the position that all good books are available in State language Hindi and the regional languages.

8

Cultural Issues

Culture of every social order is unique. Culture has material and non-material aspects. Material aspects are the material object which we use in our day to day life. Non-material aspects are the value system, attitudes, opinions, beliefs etc. Education is an instrument that helps us to preserve and transmit the required aspects of culture. New aspects (both material as well as non-material ones) are also transmitted taking into consideration present and future needs if the society). Thus, there is a positive correlation between culture and education. Present Chapter deals certain aspects of culture and its relationship with education.

Cultural Concept

The word "culture" has been derived from a Latin word "culture" which means to "to cultivate." A few definitions are mentioned below:

1. *Cuber* : Culture, in terms of anthropology, is a continually changing pattern of learned behaviour and the products of the learned behaviour including attitudes, values, knowledge and material objects are shared by and transmitted among the members of society.

2. *Arnold Mathew :* The best that has been thought and known is culture. Culture includes the ways of life, the habits, the manners, the very tones of voices, the literature, the things which give pleasure to the community, the words, the thoughts, which make the furniture of their minds.
3. *Ottaway :* The culture of a society means the total way of life of a society.
4. *Taylor :* Culture is that complex whole, which includes knowledge, belief, art, morals, law, custom and any other capabilities and habits acquired by man as member of society.
5. *Brown :* Culture is the total behaviour pattern of the group conditioned in part by the physical environment, both natural and man made, but primarily by the ideas, attitudes, values and habits which have been developed by the group to meet the needs.
6. *Rugg :* Culture means the total life of the people that goes on with these groups; what the people in a given society do, think, feel, behave, desire, fear, etc.
7. *Maclver and Page :* Culture is the realm of styles, of values, of emotional attachments, of intellectual adventures. Culture, then is the antithesis of civilization. It is the expression of our nature in our modes of living and our thinking, intercourse, in our literature, in religion, in recreation and enjoyment.
8. *Ellwood :* Culture includes on the one hand the whole of man's material civilization, tools, weapons, system of industry, and on the other hand, all the non-material or spiritual civilization such as language, literature, art, religion, morality, law and government.
9. *Sutherland and Woodland :* Culture includes anything that can be communicated from one generation to another. The culture of the people is their social heritage, a complex whole, which includes knowledge, belief, art, morals, laws, techniques of food, fabrication and use, and modes of communication.

10. *K.M. Munshi :* Culture is the characteristic way of life inspired by fundamental values in which people live.
11. *Swami Dayanand :* Culture consists of the acceptance of truth and abandonment of untruth.
12. *Gandhi :* Culture is the foundation, the primary thing. It should show itself in the smallest detail of your conduct and personal behaviour.
13. *Nehru :* Culture is the widening of the mind and of the spirit.

Significant Features

1. Culture is a learned quality.
2. Culture is transmitted from person to person and generation to generation.
3. Culture is social but not the individual heritage.
4. Culture is idealistic. It stands for ideals and norms for human behaviour.
5. Culture meets and satisfies the social and ethical needs of man. Thus culture has the gratifying quality.
6. Each culture tries to adopt the qualities outside its own environment. The contact of two or more cultures takes place and the interaction of two cultures leads to adaptation. Thus culture has the adaptive quality.
7. Different aspects of culture have the integrative quality.
8. Culture is in a constant flux i.e., it is always in the process of change. Culture changes as the society changes. Thus culture is dynamic in quality.
9. Culture is the manifestation of man's mind in varying moods of nature and environment and in the changing course of history.

Various Dimensions

Material Dimension of Culture : Material dimension of culture includes material aspects e.g.:

1. Materials that contribute to better standard of living.
2. Materials that contribute to development of natural resources, human capital and technological resources.
3. Materials that contribute to control population problem.
4. Materials that contribute to control environmental problem.

Non-material Dimension of Culture : Aspects of non-material dimension of culture are human. Ideas, interests, appreciations, opinions, attitudes and values. The change in ideas and values is affected by a series of factors.

Specific examples:

1. Positive attitude for national and economic development of India.
2. Positive attitude for vocational and technical education.
3. Positive attitudes for savings.
4. Positive attitudes for small family norms.
5. Positive attitudes for improving standard of living.
6. Positive attitude for intercultural activities.
7. Values related to nationalism.
8. Values related to internationalism.
9. Values related to democracy.
10. Values related to socialism.
11. Values related to secularism (respect for every religion).
12. Values related to egalitarian society.
13. Values of cooperation and interdependence.
14. Social and cultural values related to industrialisation, modernisation and technological advancement.
15. Positive attitudes and values for maintaining healthy environment.
16. Scientific attitudes, scientific temper and rationality.
17. Respect for innovation, cultural diffusion and integration of new ideas.
18. Positive attitudes and values for conservation of natural resources.

19. Respect and tolerance for various ideologies or view points.
20. Appreciation for social-cultural problems and appropriate a participation towards their effective solution.
21. Tolerance for diversified socio-cultural values.
22. Respect for Indian Constitution.
23. Respect for law and order.
24. To feel proud of to be an Indian and buy Indian materials of consumption.
25. Respect for the process of Sanskritisation and Westernisation.

Educational and Cultural Relationship : There are two ways to discuss relationship between culture and education. The relationship can be discussed under the following two sub-headings.:

1. Functions of education towards culture.
2. Functions of culture towards education.

Education for Culture

Education influences culture in the following ways:

1. Preservation of cultural heritage.
2. Transmission of culture.
3. Development/promotion of culture.
4. New cultural patterns.
5. Maintaining continuity of culture.
6. Removing cultural lag.

Conservation and Preservation of Cultural Heritage : Education helps in the conservation and preservation of cultural heritage. The conservative function of education has been emphasized by many authorities e.g. Percy Nunn, Dr. Radhakrishnan, Pandit Nehru, etc. According to Percy Nunn, special functions of education are to: (a) consolidate nation's spiritual strength; b) maintain nation's historic continuity; (c) secure nation's past achievements; and to (d) guarantee nation's future.

According to Pandit Nehru, education must help in preserving the vital elements of our heritage. The core of India's cultural heritage is love of beauty and truth, spirit of tolerance, capacity to absorb other cultures and work out new synthesis.

Transmission of Culture : Education helps in the transmission of cultural patterns, traditions, experience, values and norms. There is no growth and development of man without transmission of culture, the chaos in the society may be there in case the transmission of culture is not done properly. Traditions may be destroyed which may cause the breaking of the society into pieces. This situation may lead to loss of values, truth, justice, ideals and that may lead to socially undesirable behaviours of individuals. This situation is harmful to the society. Education saves us from his situation. According to Ottaway, "one of the tasks of education is to hand-over the cultural values and behaviour patterns of the society to its young and potential members".

Development of Culture : Education causes the development of culture. A better and more developed society is formed through education. According to D.J.O. Connon, "If each generation had to learn for itself, what has been learned by its predecessors, no sort of intellectual or social development would be possible and the present state of society would be little different from the society of the old stone age." Education provides experiences that reorganize and restructure human experiences and as a result of this human culture and civilization develops.

Development of New Cultural Patterns and Adjustment with these Cultural Patterns : New cultural patterns are developed with the help of education as an instrument of social change. New knowledge, values, skills are generated through education which modify the behaviour of individuals. Education helps individuals in making adjustment with new cultural patterns.

Maintaining Continuity of Culture : Culture is the life blood of a society. Without culture, a society is bound to decay and die sooner or later Education upholds the continuity of culture through its diverse activities and programmes. The continuity of cultural condition is an essential condition for the survival of a nation.

Removing Cultural Lag : Due to certain type of crisis, lack of adjustment and constraints, the progress of culture comes to halt or there is a cultural crisis. This results into cultural lag. Similarly, when material culture develops at a fast pace due to scientific and technological developments, non-material culture consisting of ideals, values and norms lag behind.

There is no harmony between the two components (material and non-material) of culture. There is a clash of values as well as of ideologies. Education is the only means to bridge this cultural lag by its activities and programmes of development.

Cultural Effects

Cultural components, material and non-material influence the education which is considered as a social process or activity in a society. Educational aspects which are influenced by culture are briefly described below:

1. Aims of Education: Aims of education are determined taking into consideration the culture of the society.
2. Curriculum Development: Aims provide the guidelines for the development of instructional material to be followed in the educational institutions for the purpose of achieving desirable social aims.
3. Methods of Teaching: Culture helps in choice of appropriate methods of teaching to achieve aims.
4. Development of Social Discipline. Culture determines the nature of social discipline to be developed in an individual with the help of educational system.
5. Teacher and Teacher Education Programmes. Culture is the base for taking decisions regarding the roles of pre-service and in-service teachers in educational institutions.
6. Educational Environment in Educational Institutions: Cultural patterns, values, beliefs determine social environments in educational institutions.

Values

Meaning of Values : A few definitions of values are listed below:

1. *Kluckhohn :* Value is a conception, explicit or implicit, distinctive of an individual or characteristic of a group, of the desirable which influences the selection from available means and ends of action.
2. *R.K. Mukherjee :* Values are socially approved drives and goals that are internalised through the process of conditioning, learning or socialization, and that becomes subjective preferences, standards and aspirations.
3. *Parker :* Values belong wholly to the inner world of mind. The satisfaction of desire is the real value, the thing that serves is only an instrument. A value is always an experience, never a thing or an object.
4. *R.B. Perry :* Any objective whatever it be, acquires values when any interest, whatever it be, is taken in it, just as anything whatsoever becomes a target when anyone whosoever aims at it.
5. *E. Brightman :* In the most elementary sense, value means whatever is actually liked, prized, esteemed, desired, approved, or enjoyed at any time. It is the actual experience of enjoying a desired object or activity.
6. *John Dewey :* The term "value" has two quite different meanings. On the one hand, it denotes the attitude of prizing thing, finding it worthwhile, for its own sake or intrinsically. So, value in this sense is to appreciate but to value also means a distinctly intellectual act, an operation of comparing and judging to evaluate.
7. *Prem Kripal :* Values may be defined as:
   (a) What we believe (professed values);
   (b) What we practice (operational values); and
   (c) What we learn from experience.

In order to adopt and renew traditions received from the past traditional values, he further remarks, "Values should be operational and also relevant and dynamic. Values should not be crystallized and frozen to the point of rigidity, stopping further growth and renewal."

Importance

Values and Growth and Development of an Individual and Society : Different types of values (biological, economic, affecting, social, intellectual, aesthetic, moral, religious, etc.) affect the growth and development of an individual and the society. In the absence of moral, social, cultural, economic values, man stands zeroed and is considered insignificant. Society whose individuals have lost values is called poor and backward society.

Erosion of values is seen at all levels leading to spread of greed, injustice, insensitivity, and what not. Dr. Sampooran Singh writes on the erosion of social values in India, "Thoughts, ideologies, codes of conduct and sets of values, psychological pattern of behaviour have failed in transforming man. Man with the help of thought organisation has created a marvellous scientific and technological world, but human being, as an individual is unhappy and frustrated, not at peace with himself, not at harmony with different layers of his being."

Values and Sub-systems of the Society : Subsystems of the society (political, economic, educational, social, industrial, religious systems) depend upon values, e.g.

1. Political values affect everyone. We, in India and the world over, observe a decline in value system at political level. There is a need to check the erosion of values at this level and it is affecting at other levels also.
2. Economy also depends upon values of individuals.
3. Growth and development of industry depends upon values.
4. Religious values affect people's opinion and behaviour.

Values and Educational Institutions : The environment in different educational institutions depends upon value systems being followed. Decline in value systems leads to decline in educational standards. We see the effects of declining values in our schools, colleges and university. We have to follow values that may contribute to proper functioning of our educational institutions.

Values and Family : Family, peaceful environment and its development depend upon value system followed in a particular family. We generally find that disputes are there among family members. This is due to erosion of values. Respect for each other in the family is generally lacking. Cooperation, sympathy etc. are generally declining.

Values and Neighbourhood/Locality : Behaviour of individuals at a particular locality depends upon their values. We generally observe that people are least concerned with each other in the neighbour in big cities (in towns and villages, the feelings and values are different).

Traditions

Meaning

1. Traditions are unwritten body of beliefs, facts, etc. handed down importance to generation.
2. Traditions are the custom, or practice of long standing.

Importance

Conservation of Relevant Traditions : There are certain traditions which are still relevant and are needed at present for the present highly technological society. Good traditions should be conserved by different social groups i.e. family, school, organisations, social institutions.

Tradition is one of the Sources of Values : Traditions are one of the sources of values. Various sources of values are religion, philosophy, literature, traditions, science etc.

Religion

Meaning of Religion : Religion is the system of belief in worship of supernatural power of God.

Importance of Religion

Religion is one of the Sources of Values : Religion is one of the sources of values. Traditions, philosophy, literature, science etc. are other sources of values.

Different religions propagate different values. Hindu religion advocates self-realisation or Moksha. Everyone ultimately tries to merge his own self with universal God. Christianity, Islam, Sikhism emphasize a particular way of life based on the doctrines and principles of respective religions. All religions of the world recommend the following common values of life:

1. Simplicity
2. Pursuit of truth
3. Dignity of labour
4. Tolerance
5. Broadmindedness
6. Welfare of mankind
7. Attainment of bliss/Moksha
8. Holy life
9. Purity and simple living.

Religion and Values of Secularism : Religion can inculcate values concerning secularism. Different religious views can be presented through formal, non-formal and informal means of education.

The use of religious stories, biographies, legends, myths, morning prayers, celebration of religious festivals etc. may contribute to inculcation of common values which are within the framework of secularism.

Kothari Commission (1964-66) and Religion : Kothari Commission (1964-66) mentioned: "All religions stress certain fundamental qualities of character, such as honesty and truthfulness, consideration for others, reverence for old age, kindness to animals, compassion for the needy and the suffering."

Psychologists' View

According to Wilson (1978) artifacts have been found indicating that Neanderthals engaged in religious practices 60,000 years ago and since that time humans have produced about 100,000 religions. A few views about religion are given below:

1. *Allport's Views on Religion :* Religious orientation often characterizes the healthy adult personality. According to Allport there are two forms of religions:

(a) Extrinsic Religion (Unhealthy Religion) is the superficial religion that is participated in for entirely selfish and pragmatic reasons. Such a religion is also called unhealthy religion.

(b) *Intrinsic Religion (Healthy Religion) :* Religion that seeks a higher meaning and purpose in life and provides possible answers to the many mysteries that characterize human existence. Such a religion is also called as healthy religion.

Erikson's views on Religion : Religion is something that many people truly need. For centuries, humans have used religion to make the events of their lives more understandable and, therefore, less threatening. Without it, according to Erikson, the lives of millions of persons would be filled with uncertainty.

According to Erikson, a key function of religion is to provide a "shared world image. For only a reasonably coherent world provides the faith which is transmitted by the mothers to the infants in a way conducive to the vital strength of hope." In other words, for adults to instil hope in their children, they must have faith in their world. Erikson does not believe, however, that religion is the only thing that can provide a world image conducive to trust, hope and faith. Many people, he says, derive faith from such secular areas as science and social action.

Rollo Reese May's Views on Religion : According to May, true, healthy religion is defined as follows:

"Call it confidence in the universe, trust in God, belief in one's fellowmen or what not, the essence of religion is the belief that something matters presupposition that life has meaning."

According to May, a religious person is one who has found meaning in life, and an atheist is one who cannot, or has not, found it.

May considered religions that required blind acceptance of dogma to be unsound and unhealthy.

Healthy religion allows for creative living that May defines as follows:

"Creative living is that attitude..... which welcomes each day with calm enthusiasm instead of melancholy boredom. It is that state of soul by which one can work with success and satisfaction and occasionally a little joy, can love and move through love into a happy marriage and then enjoy the simple pleasures of a family. The creative person can affirm life in three dimensions - affirm himself, affirm his fellowmen and affirm his destiny. To him life has meaning. He is warmed by the friendship of his fellow and cheered by the confidence that he is of worth to them. Love can be supreme pleasure to him precisely because it is more than pleasure. His work can be satisfying precisely because it is part of a creative purpose larger than any particular work. All of which means that life's fundamental question receives a positive answer: the person has confidence in meaning in his destiny."

Wilson's Views on Religion : According to Wilson and other socio-biologists, "religion is culturally universal, uniquely human, and part of human nature."

Wilson says, "The predisposition to religious belief is the most complex and powerful force in the human mind and in all probability or ineradicable part of human nature."

According to Wilson, religion plays a vital role in allowing humans to live in groups such as tribes or nations. Wilson (1978) says, "Religion is above all the process by which individuals are persuaded to subordinate their immediate self-interest to the interests of the group." Religion does this in several ways but one way is to generate a feeling of kinship among persons who share common beliefs. By holding similar beliefs people, at least symbolically, become related and feeling related, they are more likely to engage in reciprocal altruism. Furthermore, religions almost always sanctify the principles by which believers should conduct themselves. Society depends on reciprocal altruism and religion encourages its practice and creates fear or guilt in those who are inclined to cheat.

Another important function of religion is to simplify life, and religion does this in several ways. In addition to providing believers with a feeling of kinship, religion also encourages the human tendency to divide humans into two categories such as believers and non-believers, members of the in-group and members of the out-group, and friends and enemies.

Social living requires rules and regulations and historically, it has been religion, in one form or another, that has furnished and enforced them. Although it appears necessary that these rules and regulations encourage altruism, give a sense of kinship to members of the community and discourage any practice that is not conducive to survival and reproduction.

Religion typically functions to strengthen and maintain the ethical code by which a society functions, therefore, it is not surprising to find that all of the major religions make strong statements about reciprocal altruism.

Thus religion facilitates societal living in several ways. On the negative side, however, is the fact that religions are seldom tolerant of each other. Wilson (1978) says, "The one form of altruism that religions seldom display to tolerance of other religions. This is as true for ancient traditions as it is for more modern religions. Each religion is made up of rules, regulations, myths, and ceremonies and rituals.

Each religion sanctifies a particular way of social life, provides answer to the great mysteries of life, and makes its adherents believe that they are special in some way, for example, that they are God's favourite people."

Freud's Views on Religion : According to Freud, religion is an illusion and it derives its strength from its readiness to fit in with our instinctual wishful impulses.

According to Freud, our ancestors created a God with the same characteristics as real fathers. When our ancestors were children they turned to their fathers for protection and guidance. Fathers tended to be revered, feared, and relied on. According to Freud, perhaps the uneducated masses will always need the illusions of religion to cause them to restraint their passions but educated, intelligent persons should live their lives according to scientific facts, not illusions.

It is time, said Freud, to admit that our ancestors were wrong about religion; miracles never existed; natural disasters kill both believers and non-believers; no life after death occurs; and the course of human history is explained by evolutionary principles rather than the unfolding of a divine plan. Furthermore, although civilization does requires rules, regulations, and inhibitions, these should be justified on rational grounds rather than claiming that they are the will of a deity. In other words, humans should be shown how various sanctions ultimately work to their own self interests and for that reason, should strive to preserve them.

The Correlationship

Value Oriented Education : There is a need of value-oriented education because of the erosion of social, moral, economic, political and cultural values in the present highly technological society. People have become materialistic. A few popular views are stated below:

Indian Education Commission (1964-66) : Indian Education Commission writes "The weakening of social and moral values in the younger generation is creating many social and ethical conflicts in Western societies and there is already a desire among some greater Western thinkers to balance the knowledge and skills which science and technology bring with the values and insights associated with ethics and religion at its best.

Challenge of Education : A Policy Perspective mentions the following:

"One of the major crises facing education in India is that of value-orientation. It has been usually argued that the main focus during the last three decades has been on quantitative expansion and consequently adequate attention could not be paid to maintaining standards and quality of education. The output of the educational system is not only of poor quality but degradation of the moral values has also been noticed."

National Policy on Education (1986) : "The growing concern over erosion of essential values and an increasing cynicism in society has brought to focus the need for readjustments in the curriculum for the cultivation of social moral values."

"In our culturally plural society, education should foster universal and eternal values, oriented towards the unity and integration of our people.

Such value education should help eliminate obscurantism, religious fanaticism, violence, superstition and fatalism."

"Value education as a profound positive content is based on our heritage, national goals, and universal perceptions. It should lay primary emphasis on this aspect."

Inculcation of Values

There are different approaches for inculcating values in others, which are briefly explained below:

Direct and Indirect Approach : Direct approach means teaching values directly to others. Here efforts are made cautiously to teach different values to others. The approach may work for some time but many a time it has its disadvantages. There may be reaction of the learners and sometimes they may give opposite opinions. That will prove rather more dangerous.

Indirect approach of teaching the different values is more convenient and effective. Here teaching is done incautiously. The learner reads books and is able to catch up values of life here and there. In day to day life situations, he learns values incidentally.

Formal and Informal Approach : When the learners are taught about difficult values by using formal ways, it may not have greater effect. Here materials from books are taught with the motive of teaching certain values. Television is shown by using formal situations in order to inculcate different values. On the other hand, the learner or the receiver of values is unaware of everything. He reads some material from the books and is able to pick up value of life incidentally. This type of learning is of greater value and lasts longer.

Curricular and Co-curricular Approach : According to curricular approach, separate syllabus is framed which aims at teaching different values to the learners. The syllabus is prescribed and teaching is done to finish the syllabus. In the textbooks, the different values may be integrated in different chapters. Thus the students have curricular programme which helps them to learn different values.

According to co-curricular programme, different activities such as singing, poem recitation, drama, debate, declamation contest, essay writing, competitions are organised with the main motive of inculcating different values of life in the youth. There can also be social service activities physical exercises, games and sports. Different activities will help in the inculcation of values.

Imparting Education along with Values : The authorities in educational institutions can organise various activities and functions for the purpose of inculcation of values in the youth. The head of the institution and the teaching staff can plan and organise a number of programmes for this purpose. A few such programmes are briefly explained below:

1. The textbooks prescribed for the students should contain stories with certain moral lessons. Teachers interested in writing textbooks for the children can help in making the textbooks of this type. Even supplementary readers or books for the children may be written by some teachers in collaboration with others and help in the achievement of the fixed targets.
2. Prizes may be given to the deserving persons for showing honesty, bravery, gallantry, truth, etc. The award of prizes be given to the students in social gathering.
3. Declamation contests may be organized in the institution on themes related to values of life. The contests may be

infra-school and then these may be inter-school. Participation in the contests by way of speakers and also by way of audience will have a good deal of impact.

4. National Service Scheme (N.S.S.) need be popularised and its programme of activities be organised vigorously. The students interested in social service at the railway station, at the general bus stand, in the social festivals, in the hospitals, in the villages, in the slum areas be able to do a lot. That way they will pick up those values of life permanently.

5. A few projects for value education may be started in the educational institutions under the guidance of some teachers. The students may start their own canteen with no-profit, no-loss basis. Different groups may control it turn by turn and make its functioning successful. Some students may start a cooperative store where books and stationery on wholesale rate may be purchased and sold to all the students studying in that school. The basis of the cooperative store should be no-profit, no-loss. It makes the students hardworkers and they will also understand this business and the margin of profit and loss etc.

   In the same way, students cooperative bank, students cooperative post office etc. may be set up in the institution under the guidance of some teacher. All this will inculcate good values of life among the students. Those students will come out as successful social beings.

   Educational institutions should shoulder the responsibility and strive in every possible way for the inculcation of values in the youth. The beginning years in the school are more conducive for it. The teacher will be able to achieve the aims by devoting less time and by paying far less attention as compared to the situation which would be otherwise.

6. Extension lectures based on morality or value-oriented education may be arranged in the institution. Eminent persons specialized in this field may be invited. Listening

to the lectures, discussions etc. will help a good deal in this direction.

7. The head of the institution and the teaching personnel should be living examples of values. The institution in itself should be made a centre for moral instructions. It should propagate all types of higher values of life.

8. Book exhibitions on literature related to values be organised in the institution by extending invitations to noted publishers/booksellers of this area of knowledge. The exhibitions should be thrown open to the students and the community. It will have its effects on one and all.

9. Educational TV can work wonders in this field. Some good teachers can bring out materials related to values in the form of TV serials. Showing such films to the students and the community be made a regular feature of the school.

10. Art and painting exhibitions on themes like moral, social, cultural values etc. be organised in the institutions. Paintings of distinguished artists depicting values be displayed. Such exhibitions will have their effects on the growing personalities of children. Some children might develop their interest in this area of knowledge. On the spot, Art and Painting competitions may be organised on themes related to different types of values. Students of different age groups may be invited from institutions of the region or the state as may be considered proper. Prizes may be given for excellent performances in different age groups. It will highlight the themes of values among the children and through them to the families and the community.

11. Some journal on the theme of values in life may be brought out by an institution. It can be done by some voluntary organisation also. Suitable articles can be invited for publication. The journal may be monthly or quarterly as is possible and its circulation should be popularised. It should be suitably priced so that it is within the reach of majority.

12. Skit, drama competition may be organised in the institution. Assistance may be sought from the District Public Relations Officers. The themes should be values in life- social, moral, cultural, political, educational etc. The different institutions should be encouraged to participate in the competition enthusiastically.
13. Value-oriented education should be made compulsory in all the schools. One teacher may be entrusted the duty of assessing the whole teaching of the school in terms of value education. Strenuous efforts should be made to achieve the desired aims with the cooperation of the staff and students.
14. Morning Assembly should be made compulsory in all the educational institutions. It can be of half an hour duration. Apart from morning prayer, good thoughts may be read out by some students and staff members. Religious and national songs may be sung or such poems may be recited.
15. House examinations may be arranged in value education. All students may be asked to qualify it at junior levels say in V standard, VIII standard and also at XII standard. It should be at degree level which may be organised by the university or by the college itself. No student should be considered to have passed the examination without having passed the value education or moral education or the so called religious education.

Correlationship of Education with Tradition and Religion : Traditions and various religions are the two important sources of values. Traditions and religions can be used for inculcation of values through value-oriented education. Following points point out the ways through which traditions and religions can be linked effectively with education in India.:

1. Fundamental principles of ethics are common to all the religions. Gandhiji suggested Wardha Scheme for teaching religious values through education.
2. School assemblies, including morning assembly can foster valuable moral truths.

3. Actual teaching of religious scripture can also be done.
4. Personal influence of teachers can be effective in inculcating religious values and values linked with traditions.
5. Celebration of religious festivals can help in inculcation of desirable religious values.
6. Simple and interesting religious stores and myths can develop desirable values. The religious stories and myths can be included in text books related to languages. Teacher can illustrate the values linked with these stories and myths.
7. Teaching of different religions can be a part of syllabus for social studies or history.
8. Extension lectures on traditional values and religious values can be organised under extracurricular activities.
9. Joint celebrations of religious functions in educational institutions can develop the feelings of respect for all religions.
10. Social service is emphasized in all religions. Social service activities can be organised by institutions on the guidelines of various religions and traditions.
11. Religious studies can be included in the timetable at various levels of education. Comparative studies on religions, history of religions can be taught.

Role of Government

National Policy on Education (1986) identified promotion of Indian Culture and Values in education as one of the goals of education. Centrally sponsored scheme of Assistance for strengthening culture and values in Education.

Bodies Eligible for Financial Assistance : Centre sponsors a scheme to assist the programmes that are in line with strengthening of Indian culture and values in education. The assistance is given to the following:-

(a) Government Agencies

(b) Educational Institutions

(c) Panchayati Raj Institutions.

(d) Registered Societies

(e) Public Trusts

(f) Non-profit making Companies.

Various Components

These are two components of the scheme;

1. Strengthening cultural and value education inputs in the school and non-formal education system.
2. The in-service training of art, craft, music, and dance teachers.

Finance : Budget provisions for this assistance programme are made by the Centre annually e.g. Five Crore for 1999-2000.

Centres for Promotion of Indian Culture

1. Centre for Cultural Resources and Training (CCRT)

Establishment

* It is an autonomous organisation established in May, 1979.
* It is under the administrative control of Department of Culture, Ministry of Tourism and Culture with Headquarter at New Delhi and two regional centres (Udaipur and Hyderabad).

Revitalisation of Education System : The central goal of CCRT is to revitalise education system by creating understanding and awareness among students about the plurality of the regional cultures of India and integrating this knowledge with education.

Programmes for In-service Teachers : Organisation of training programmes orientation programmes for in-service teachers from all parts of the country to achieve the following aims:

Development of awareness among students and teachers about problems e.g. environmental problems; conservation and preservation of Indian culture.

Programmes for Foreign Teachers : Programmes are also organised for foreign students and teachers.

Organisation of Workshops, Seminars and Training Programmes for Students and Teachers : Various types of workshops, seminars and training programmes are organised e.g. emphasis is given to Indian culture through drama, art, & other ways. A list of the programmes is given below:

Educational tours to monuments, museums, art galleries, craft centres, zoological parks and gardens:

* Camps on conservation of natural and cultural heritage.
* Extension lectures and demonstrations by artists, experts related to arts from schools & colleges.

Collection of Multi-Media : Efforts are being made to collect a variety of mass media on Indian culture and civilisation for use under various programmes of the centre throughout the country.

Scholarships : Scholarships are being awarded to students of age group 10-14 years under cultural talent search scholarship scheme. Students who are studying in schools, are eligible for these scholarships. These scholarship are also considered for those children who belong to such families who are practicing arts and are significant as Indian heritage. Scholarships continue upto 20 years of age or first year of a university degree. 322 students have got scholarships upto 1999-2000.

Teachers Awards : Awards are also given to teachers every year. Each award carries a citation, a plaque, an angavastram and an amount of Rs. 10.000/-.

Zonal Cultural Centres : Aims of Cultural Centres are as follows:

* To project cultural kinships transcending territorial bonds.
* To develop awareness about local cultures.
* To highlight cultural integration irrespective of geographical boundaries.
* To develop national integration through integration of culture & development of awareness.

Seven Cultural Centres : There are seven cultural centres:

1. North Zone Cultural Centre, Patiala.

2. East Zone Cultural Centre, Calcutta.
3. South Zone Cultural Centre, Thanzavur
4. West Zone Cultural Centre, Udaipur
5. North-central Zone Cultural Centre, Allahabad.
6. North-east Zone Cultural Centre, Dimapur.
7. South Central Zone Cultural Centre, Nagpur.

Assignment

1. Define the term "culture". Discuss briefly its material and non-material components.
2. Write varies characteristics of culture. Comment upon the following:

   (a) Views of Indian thinkers on culture.

   (b) Views of Western thinkers on culture.

   (c) Indian culture and its material and non-material components.
3. Discuss the relationship between culture and education. Justify the impact of culture on education. Justify the impact of education on culture.
4. Describe briefly the meaning and importance of values.
5. Explain briefly the meaning and importance of traditions.
6. Discuss the meaning and importance of Religion.
7. Comment upon the types of religion according to Allport.
8. Briefly discuss the views of psychologists on the meaning and importance of religion.
9. Comment upon the views of Freud on religion.
10. Comment upon the views of Wilson, a socio-biologist and psychologist on religion.
11. "Education and values". Comment.
12. Comment upon need of value-oriented education in India.
13. Discuss briefly the value-oriented education in India.
14. Comment upon traditions, religion and education.
15. Discuss briefly the relationship of values, traditions and religion with education.

9

Professional Issues

Growth Pattern

The Rigveda indicates that, since the very emergence of Indian culture and civilisation, the people of that ancient period had learnt to make dams for irrigational and other purposes. The ruins of Mohanjodaro and Harappa are concrete proofs of the fact that India had always been the leader in the technical and vocational spheres. Even Alexander the Great took many objects made of iron from India, a fact that proves the excellence of this industry. Not merely this, concrete products of the Indian industry and profession are to be found in every part of the world. However, with the passage of time, India fell behind in the race for progress, and, as a result, the countries which used to be considered backward in cultural terms, are today giving advice to India in the technical and vocational fields.

The modern period in the history of technical education has its beginnings in the administration of the East India Company. It began when the company felt the need for some workers and technicians. A few schools were set up to train skilled workers for; certain specific tasks. Although the Christian missionaries repeatedly emphasised upon the company administration the need for setting up technical education institutes in India, the company failed to pay much attention to it.

The history of technical education in pre-independence India can be divided into three periods.

From 1800 to 1857 : It was proposed that in the educational field, the organisation should be such as to offer practical benefits to the people of India. The administration did not attach much importance to this statement, but the Roorkee Engineering College did come into existence in 1847. Later on, in 1857-58, two engineering colleges were established at Madras and Calcutta. A mechanical school came into existence in Poona in 1854, but considering the situation of the country during this period, this progress can be termed negligible.

1857 to 1902 : Although Mr. Wood was deeply influenced by the- arts and sciences departments in England in the preparation of his famous despatch, he did lay very deep emphasis upon vocational education. He proposed the introduction of technical education in his Despatch, but the British government, adopting the policy of laissez faire, unburdened itself of this responsibility. Only such institutions were set up as could be of use to the administration. In consonance with this policy, the Poona Engineering College (1886) and the Victoria Jubilee Technical Institute (1887). Bombay, were established. Most of the work was done by the Christian missionaries because it was necessary to provide employment to the new converts to Christianity. In their schools, the apprentices were trained in woodwork and smithy (iron-mongering). By 1902, the total number of students studying in technical schools was 4105.

On the 18th of June, 1888, the government published a proposal, pointing out the need for and importance of technical and vocational education, along with literary or liberal education. Besides, it made clear the fact that such education should be specialised according to industries, for instance, the cotton textile industry etc. It was stressed that this kind of education should be organised with the help of the local administration, and according to local needs. Besides, some thought was given to providing technical education in colleges and universities.

From 1902 to 1947 : During this period, the Indian National Congress took birth, and it soon pressed the government to make prompt arrangements for technical education for the development of the country. In addition, it suggested that students should be given scholarships for studies in America and the Commonwealth countries. It was with this object in view that in 1904, the Association for the Advancement of Scientific and Industrial Education was established. By 1905,103 scholarships were granted to Indian students for studying abroad. These scholarships were meant for training in such industries as consumer goods manufacture, mines, pottery, tanning, match-making, glasswork, pencil, paper, etc. At the same time, an Institute of Mines was set up at Dhanbad, and an Institute of Textile Industries at Kanpur, and an Engineering College at Bombay were also established.

This progress, of course, touched only one aspect of the advance in technical education, and hence it never became available to the masses in general, despite the fact that the College of Engineering and Technology, Jadavpur, the Tata Institute, Jamshedpur, and the Banaras University had already come into existence to provide technical education.

Out of many other, two factors in particular have influenced technical education- (1) the unemployment resulting from the spread of education, and (2) the need for skilled workers after the World War I, and in preparation for the World War II.

Both these factors were responsible for bringing technical education to India. After the World War I, the British government had come to realise that it could not fight another: war successfully by confining itself and its resources to Britain alone. Consequently, it set up Ordinance factories at a number of places. In 1941, a polytechnic school was set up at Delhi, and, in 1945, a committee was constituted to' study the possibilities of technical education in India, based on the working of the Massachusetts Institute of Technology, England. This committee was referred to as the 'Government Committee'. On the basis of its suggestions, institutions were set up in all parts of India, though these institutions were set up primarily to meet the requirements of war.

On 30th November, 1945, the government set up the All India Council for Technical Education, while in March 1947, the Scientific Manpower Committee was constituted, and entrusted with the task of estimating the need for scientifically trained manpower in various spheres in the coming years. This committee projected that 54,000 engineers and 20,000 technicians would be required by the end of 1947.

Present Situation

In 1947, after independence, India possessed 38 technological institutions providing education to 2,940 students annually. There were 53 polytechnic schools educating 30,670 students every year and giving them diplomas. These educational institutions were made capable of playing a constructive role in the country's five year plans. In the First-Five Year Plan, many new courses were introduced at the degree level, particularly the courses which the country was in dire need of. The following was the nature of technical education in free India:-

Administration : Technical education has generally been directed jointly by the central and state governments. The All India Council for Technical Education, set up by the central government, has done much to encourage it. The centre's purpose is to provide for the technical development of the whole country, to make arrangements for higher technical education, to provide finance for these institutions, to give grants to universities and states, and supervise the functioning of all these various institutions. All these functions come within the jurisdiction of the ministry of education.

The aforementioned council created four regional councils, and entrusted them with the tasks of constituting boards of studies,- introducing national diploma courses, part-time courses and postgraduate courses. At the state level, too, technical education is supervised by the relevant departments within the departments of education. This department provides for technical education through a council consisting of 17 members and the education minister as its chairman.

Institutions : Institutions providing technical education can be divided into three main categories-

A. These are institutions which provide education through degree and postgraduate courses as well as research. The subjects covered by them include Mining, Metallurgy-cum-Engineering, Highway (Roads) Engineering, Irrigation, Soil Mechanics, Foundation Engineering. Production Technology, Chemical Engineering, Electrical Communications, Advanced Electronics, Geophysics, Petroleum Technology, Textiles, Architecture, Leather technology, Aeronautical Engineering, etc.

B. Institutions of this category include those which conduct diploma courses, and they provide training extending from 1 to 3 years in a variety of courses. They are called polytechnic institutions. Some of them have been established primarily for girls.

C. Institutions of the third kind provide vocational and industrial training. They conduct two kinds of courses-

   (a) The first include courses connected with art and handicrafts, such as - domestic industries, weaving, dyeing, printing, metalwork, leather dyeing, leather working, metalwork, iron-mongery, jewellery making, carpentry, pottery, utensil making, weaving of cane furniture, etc.

   (b) The second kind of courses are intended to produce partially skilled and semiskilled workers, and for admission to them students require knowledge only of reading and writing. In 1947, the country had 53 schools and 38 colleges of this nature, providing diplomas to 3670 students, and degrees to 2940 students. By 1962, these numbers had swelled to 221 schools and 114 colleges in which 38,826 students received diplomas and 17,074 degrees. For the third five plan, it was proposed that the engineering profession should be expanded. Consequently, Regional Engineering Colleges were established at Warangal, Bangalore, Nagpur, Bhopal, Durgapur, Jamshedpur, Allahabad, Delhi and Srinagar.

New Schemes : Among the new schemes was the provision of postgraduate education and research at the Indian Institute of Science at Bangalore, while the institute at Kharagpur was converted into a research institution, conducted on the lines of Massachusetts. Besides, Indian Institutes of Technology were established at Bombay, Madras, Delhi and Kanpur, in which education in a variety of courses is provided, with the purpose of developing technical education in the country. In the technical field, new courses in publishing, printing, town and rural planning, printing technology, and diplomas in management were introduced. The Council has also made arrangements for providing scholarships ranging from Rs. 50,75,150 and 250 for students studying under various courses.

Temple of Science : By 1964, the ministry of education, with the cooperation of the ministry of community development had set up 'temples of science' in various parts of the country. In these, students residing and studying in rural areas were kept in touch with the latest scientific information. However, for a variety of reasons, the government has now closed down these institutions.

Research : The Council has given even more encouragement to the existing institutions to encourage research in the technical sphere. These researches have proved fruitful for technical education in such matters as progress, improvement guidance and maintaining liaison. The Council has also sought to ensure that the knowledge produced by these researches should find actual use in workshops. For this, there are provisions for attractive scholarships.

In the light of the progress of other nations, we, find that our country is quite backward. Even today, our country stands in great need of vast developments in technical education, and the need will be met only when the government decides to spend at least 7 per cent of the national income upon education.

Difficulties Ahead

While the British government failed to take adequate interest in the spread of technical education in India because of its own vested interests, the government of free India has come to feel need for it. The existing government wishes to put India on the path to progress through five year plans, proof of which lies in the various technical schools polytechnics and engineering colleges, etc., established in various parts of the country. The skilled individuals produced by these institutions have played some role in the country's development, but, the sphere of technical education is riddled with certain problems which are preventing the desired progress. The main problems of technical education are outlined below:-

Need for Technical Manpower : India has generally suffered from the lack of mobility of manpower. The rising needs have necessitated an increase in the demand for both quality and quantity in technical education. But, because of hampered mobility, our trained manpower has not developed as rapidly as in other countries. Wood's view was that it was India's great misfortune that, despite receiving technical education, an Indian does not get the opportunity to apply it in practice, and consequently, he lags behind individuals of other countries. The people of India begin the chapter of their development at which the people of other countries complete the process of their growth.

The conflicts with China and Pakistan, too, have further highlighted the dearth of technicians. Today, apart from the other spheres of activity, the work of security and defence also requires skilled technicians, but their shortage can be overcome only when condensed courses are introduced.

Demand for New Institutions : Another reason for the shortage of trained individuals is that we could not establish a sufficient number of such training institutions. At present, the country has 120 such colleges. The setting up of one college means that Rs. 4.15 lakhs are needed for buildings, Rs. 0.08 lakh, for recurring expenses, and Rs. 3 lakhs for materials, but unfortunately our country cannot afford to spend so much in this one sphere alone. Hence, the

Technical Education Council set up 9 Regional Colleges and 27 Polytechnic Colleges, which provided a variety of courses. Even today, continuous efforts are being made to procure more and more trained individuals.

Dearth of Technicians at the Lower and Middle Levels : In technical education, it is possible to obtain individuals at the middle and higher levels in adequate numbers, and, unfortunately, most of them get into the habit of getting the work done by mechanics. The outcome is that, when there is a dearth of mechanics, these individuals just sit idle. Hence, it has become necessary to provide training for semiskilled technicians also. Such individuals can develop skills for working in various spheres, such as starting an engine, fitting machines, carrying out electrical repairs, etc.

Efficiency of the Administration : In India, it is being increasingly felt that if an administrative department takes interest in its work, it usually shows satisfactory progress. Administrative departments face two major obstacles- (i) in some spheres, individuals have an excessive workload, which prevents them from increasing their efficiency; (ii) in some cases, more than enough staff is provided for a single piece of work, with the result that they pass the responsibility to the next man, thus ensuring that nothing actually gets done.

Hence, the Planning Commission has suggested that, in the entire sphere of technical education, the workload and the responsibility should be collectively and individually put upon the workers. Statistics show that, in the administrative sphere, the real need is for workers actively working in the field rather than in the office. Hence, the administrative departments should be revamped in such a manner that the emphasis shifts to the creative work in the field. There should be more creative and active workers in every department.

Narrow or Limited Curricula : So far, people have generally assumed that the purpose of technical education is to produce an educated manual worker or labourer, while in reality, technical education induces profound respect for labour, and awareness of the dignity of labour. Hence, it is necessary that, technical education everywhere should be accompanied by general education so that the curriculum of technical education should not remain rigidly stuck to training in a particular field of technology. The Council too has been making efforts to overcome this narrow approach, and also to achieve an increase in the number of skilled and semiskilled technicians.

Medium of Education : Pandit Nehru had recommended that English should be the medium of technical education, since he felt that almost all the literature in this sphere was available only in English. But, the question, is, how many Indians know English? Not very many. The result has been that the common man has been kept away from technical education. It is possible to evolve a technical terminology in the various Indian languages, and it can be argued that rapid progress can be achieved in the sphere if technical education is available in Indian languages, just as education in law is available in them.

Lack of Teachers : There has usually been an acute shortage of teachers in technical and engineering education, because of the fact that the demand for engineers and technicians is very high in the country. Teaching does not offer very attractive scales of pay, and besides, it offers very little scope for working with one's own hands. Besides, the teacher does not enjoy a very high social status. For instance, even at the national level, the engineer is given more importance than a teacher, although the former is the product of the teacher. The dearth of teachers can be overcome if teachers are given better scales of pay, more attractive facilities, more importance than engineers, and importance at the social, economic, cultural and national levels.

Proper Arrangements for Practice in Workshops : The absence of well equipped workshops in engineering and technical colleges has, for long, been a sore point. This problem manifests itself in two ways -(i) lack of good workshops, (ii) presence of excessive trainees in the workshops. Thus, even if the workshop is itself satisfactory, the number of trainees is so large that the workshop cannot achieve its real objective. If workshops are organised on the following bases, technical education can progress more rapidly

(a) workshops should not depend upon imported machines. (b) New workshops should be established and equipped with Indian materials and machines. (c) Industrialists should be induced to cooperate in this collectively. (d) As in the case of the USA, cooperative programmes should be taken up, and students learn to produce the maximum quantum of goods through the most modern technology.

Post-school Education **:** After emerging from the engineering school or college, the student finds himself backward when confronted with the real work situation. His knowledge once again takes a backward path. In order to confront this problem, it is necessary to introduce morning and evening classes to provide the latest information. The benefit will be that the students will keep in touch with the latest progress in their field, and also make the best use of their time. In-service training courses should also be organised at regular intervals.

Research **:** India spends only 0.2% of its national production upon research, whereas Russia and America spend as much as 2.8%. And, in fact, it is India which has the greatest need for research into such spheres as improvement in the quality of goods, production of new goods, recycling of waste products, reduction of costs, reduction of the risks in productive processes, overcoming difficulties, and determination of basic standards, etc. For this purpose, through engineering design, structure, method of working, etc., research can be made capable of developing techniques which will help the country to create international markets for its goods.

Absence of Cooperation between State Industries and Technical Education **:** Occasionally, our newspapers report that thousands of overseers are unemployed in a particular region. In planning for the spread of technical education, the state must keep in mind its manpower needs, since it is being observed that engineers and overseers are being produced without any planning. It would be far better if the state first conducted a survey of its manpower needs and then made arrangements for the training of a sufficient number of engineers and technicians.

Technical Education Commission

After reflecting upon the problem of unemployment, the Kothari Commission has expressed its view on technical and vocational education in the following terms:

1. By 1986, 20% of the lower secondary students and 50% of the higher secondary students should receive vocational education.
2. Vocational courses should be introduced at the school level. Brilliant and talented students must get adequate opportunities in this sphere.
3. Arrangements should be made for training skilled and semiskilled workers. For this, the following kinds of institutions should be established:-
   (a) I.T.I.
   (b) Junior Technical School
   (c) Technical High School.
4. In the courses for skilled workers, the courses below class 10 should be included in the polytechnic.
5. The rigidity of the present curriculum should be abandoned.

Technician Training : According to the Kothari Commission, in our educational system, the second level of skill which exists at the secondary level produces a middle level specialist whose functions are understood very little in our country. Hence, the following suggestions have been offered:

1. Technician training should be restructured in the light of modern knowledge, and training should be based upon professional differentiation and specialisation.
2. Diploma training will be particularly useful for institutions.
3. Polytechnics should be established in industrial areas.
4. Teachers in polytechnics should be recruited from the industries, and there should be flexibility in evaluating their academic or educational qualifications.

5. There should be different kinds of courses for girls, including diploma as well as certificate courses.
6. In polytechnic schools, wastage and stagnation should be prevented, in view of the labour and power involved in training students.
7. Some selected polytechnics should provide post diploma courses also.
8. Keeping in mind the mobility of labour in the country, polytechnic schools should have courses based on local needs and available resources, but special emphasis should be given to the teaching of science and mathematics.

Other Vocational Education : Today, an almost unaccounted variety of vocational courses have emerged. For their best development, it is necessary to be cognizant of the following facts: (i) Commercial, clerical, and scientific education should be imparted in classes 11 and 12. The interests and aptitude of girls should be kept in view. (ii) Students emerging from polytechnics, etc., should be encouraged to set up their own enterprises.

Engineering Education : In the opinion of the Kothari Commission; the progress of industrialisation depends upon the proper understanding of science, and, it also necessitates the best possible training for engineers. It is suggested, therefore that- (i) in some subjects of engineering, students with B.Sc. degree, for instance, in electronics, should be granted admission. (ii) The differences in the pay scales of teachers in various institutions should be eliminated. (iii) Practical training should be given for one full year, after the third year of education. (iv) Mixed courses should also be introduced. (v) More productive work should be done in the workshops. (vi) There should be variety in the courses so that they may meet the changing needs of changing times. (vii) The curriculum should be edited and reviewed from time to time, and the various subjects should be given a progressively more scientific shape.

Teachers : The attractions in the engineering professions are so powerful that hardly any engineer is attracted towards teaching. Private firms offer better scales of pay as well as better working conditions and facilities. To overcome this difficulty, the following steps should be taken- (i) Teachers should be allowed to take up consultancy work for industries. (ii) Summer courses institutions should be introduced. (iii) The scale of pay should be made more attractive. (iv) Teacher training courses should be introduced to overcome the present shortage of teachers. (v) The policy of transferring teachers should be suitably modified.

Resources : The best possible education in engineering depends upon the availability of necessary resources. For this, the following suggestions have been offered- (a) Facility of utilising foreign exchange should be given. (b) Machines of the best quality should be installed so that they may be utilised for longer periods. (c) Postgraduate courses should be introduced. (d) The training and education should be practical (e) There should be close cooperation with industries.

Medium of Education : At the secondary, polytechnic and other levels, the medium of instruction should be the regional language. It is suggested that (a) vocational education should be given via the regional language, and hence the literature needed for the course should be prepared in the regional language. (b) Postal coaching or teaching should also be introduced so as to spread vocational education rapidly.

Administration : Good administration is needed for the proper running of engineering institutions. For this, it is suggested that- (i) There should be an organisation similar to the UGC for technical education. (ii) IIT etc. should be granted the status of universities. (iii) Technical education boards should be set up at the state level. (iv) Principals of institutions should have complete powers regarding administration.

The Kothari Commission has thought extensively and deeply about engineering and technical education, and as a result, it is hoped that our country may soon be free of the spectre of unemployment. This Commission has made complete provisions for manpower planning for vocational education. It has also stressed specialised studies. However, what we have before us is only a plan. This alone will tell us how much success it has attained.

Growth under Five-Year Plans

First Five-Year Plan : Rs. 23 crores were spent upon the development of technical education. In this plan, the Indian Institute of Science, Bangalore, was enlarged and arrangements were made for imparting training in crafts, Polytechnic, technical, high schools and industrial training schools were increased and enlarged, while more scholarships were also provided.

Second Plan : The allocation for technical education in the second plan rose to Rs. 48 crores. During this period, the number of institutions offering degree and diploma courses was doubled. New institutions were set up and more scholarships provided.

Third Plan : In this plan, Rs.142 crores were provided for technical education. The new institutions were set up, while the curricula of 12 institutions were reconstructed and enlarged.

Fourth Plan : A sum of Rs. 253 crores was allocated for technical education in the fourth plan, and arrangements were made for the appointment of teachers; creation of hostels, establishment of new institutions, and introduction of correspondence courses.

Today, our engineers are faced with unemployment. This is obviously a very grave problem, and it is reflected in the fact that the enrolment in technical institutions fell to 64%. In the fourth plan, emphasis was laid upon the consolidation of the existing institutions. Besides, the curricula of technical education was remodelled in the light of the requirements of our industries.

Differences in the Rate of Progress : The pace of progress of technical education has continued to vary. The work in technological institutions was started after delays, besides which, the state governments, too, showed little interest in the consolidating and strengthening the existing institutions. The outcome was that even the allocated sums were not fully expended.

Difference in Certificates : Many states committed the folly of issuing different kinds of certificates. Sandwich courses were initiated. The polytechnic method was revaluated, and efforts were made to see how these courses could be made more practicable.

Educational Plan : The need for an educational plan for postgraduate education and research was soon felt. At the same time, management studies were also introduced. The consequence of this progress has been that technical institutions are now capable of offering enrolment to 74,000 students, while this figure was only 2000 a few years ago.

In view of the existing facts, an effort should be made to formulate a plan for the next 15 years, with the object of creating a technical society. For this, the objectives should be clearly defined, so that the necessary flexibility in the method of education may be maintained. In the fifth plan, the following aspects were considered, in the light of the need for rapid development in this sphere - (i) Technical education should be directly linked to economic development. (ii) The curriculum should be restructured so that primacy is given to the generation of skills in addition to imparting of knowledge. It is also necessary to develop practicability and enterprise. (iii) Technical extension services should be introduced, because these services will bring about coordination between the masses, the institutions and industries. (iv) For the growth of technical education, state, regional and institutional plans will be prepared. (v) Provisions will be made for the Continuing Education so that, even after the completion of training, the trainee should maintain his contact with knowledge and new skills. (vi) Provisions will be made for every kind of technical education in the light of the need for technically skilled manpower. In this context, thought is being devoted to (a) joint centre state responsibility, (b) blueprint of a plan, (c) an enrolment policy, and (d) Multiple Entry Points.

In the fifth plan, the following provisions were made for technical education, keeping in view, the points elucidated above:-

Programme : Thought has been devoted to various programmes with a view to achieving long-term goals and objectives. Every technical institution was consolidated in terms of its needs for buildings, resources, aid, etc. A detailed plan was prepared for the reorganisation of polytechnic education.

Qualitative Development : Efforts were made to bring about a qualitative improvement in technical education through the development of faculties, curricula and preparation of teaching materials. It was opined that the workshops and laboratories should be equipped with the latest machines and tools. Besides, such varied courses as practical art, commercial conduct pharmacy, etc., were also developed.

Training of Teachers : The training necessary for teaching technical courses is in itself a serious problem, and hence much thought was given to the training of teachers. According to the recommendations of the All India Council for Technical Education, it is necessary to provide at least short term training to teachers.

Postgraduate Education and Research : For the fifth plan, arrangements have been made to ensure that, in the various institutions, advance study centres should be set up and activated in a planned manner. In the Regional Engineering Colleges, practice workshops and industrial orientation courses have been introduced, with the cooperation of local industries. It was also proposed that in certain selected institutions, there should be arrangements for higher studies and research.

Management Education : It was proposed in the fifth plan, that management education, instead of being limited to merely four management institutes, should be made available through university departments also. Besides, there should be provisions at many centres for training of foremen and supervisors.

Establishment of Specialist Institutions : Institutions related to specific industries should be established, along the lines of such existing institutes as the National Institute of Foundry and Forge Technology, the National Institute for Training in Industrial Engineering, the Central Institute for Industrial Design, etc. The Regional Training Institutes should introduce courses for the training of teachers of training institutions through such courses as pedagogies, creative programmes and industrial experience.' Teachers of polytechnic institutions must also be trained.

Scholarships : The number of scholarships based on ability and resources was increased in the fifth plan. It was suggested that the Apprentice Act should be amended and individuals holding certificates should be taken within the purview of this Act. Archives would be set up in selected institutions while textbooks of a superior standard would be produced, and thus science will be brought close to technology.

Administration : It has been felt that there is need for a good administration for effective planning and organisation at the state and national levels. It was suggested that boards of technical education should be set up in state by legislative acts, and in addition, the ministry of education should set up a department for manpower planning, monitoring and evaluation.

The Economic Aspect : Rs. 300 crores were allocated for all these programmes. 2200 crores were provided for all educational programmes, but it was not possible to accommodate technical education within the general education budget. The Working group suggested reconsideration of the plan, pointing out that the expenditure on construction could be reduced. Thus, it suggested the allocation of Rs.190 crores.

The Sixth Plan : In the sixth plan (1978-83), the emphasis was mainly upon a continuation of the programmes of the fifth plan. It was felt that the existing system of technical education was adequate for the forthcoming decade. At present, 25,000 students gain admission to degree courses and 50,000 students to diploma courses. The sixth plan provides that technical education may be revaluated in case of need. Five centres for advanced studies into energy, materials, oceans, etc., will be set up. The plan provides Rs.150 crores for this purpose.

Some of the proposed programmes are - (i) Setting up institutes of management at Lucknow and Bangalore, to be run by such institutions as the NCERT and UGC (ii) Establishment of a national council of science education, similar to the NCERT and UGC (iii) Introducing R & D projects. (iv) Providing for Apprenticeship. (v) Modernizing the new programmes such as Archives and Laboratories.

10

Democratic Issues

In the hands of man, Education is a useful weapon. It can work wonders if used rightly. The need of the hour is to make it society oriented. Only a good society which has definite principles and ideologies pledged to the nation can take humanity to do yeoman service in these times of crisis. Let us, therefore, revolutionize our system of education to reach the right goals without any type of wastages.

India became a democratic country with the dawn of independence. The leaders of the free country accepted democracy for the people of the country. Ever since then, efforts have been to make it a successful democratic republic. Undoubtedly, a good deal of work has been done in this direction but much more needs to be done. Then and then only we shall say that ours is a successful democratic republic.

Education is the basis with the help of which the edifice of strong democracy can be built firmly. The country has been in the grip of problems like poverty and illiteracy. And then the problem of population explosion became a big hurdle in its way of progress. Education has been used as a weapon for bringing about all round progress of the country. Due to knowledge explosion all over the globe, education is also expected to be abreast of the latest advancements in the field of science and technology. Only the use of right type of education can help really in the fast changing political and social set-up of life whose foundations are laid on democratic philosophy. So the need of the hour is to keep education upto the mark and upto date in every respect.

Democracy : Meaning and Definition

Let us understand the word 'democracy' in its true perspective. The word 'democracy' is derived from two Greek words 'demos' and 'kratos' which mean 'people' and 'power', respectively. So it means the rule of the people. Democracy means, "A form of government in which the supreme power is vested in the people collectively." Abraham Lincoln said, "Democracy is government by the people, of the people and for the people." According to Seeley, "Democracy is a government in which every one has to share."

Lord Bryce said, "Democracy is the form of government in which the ruling power of the state is legally vested, not in any particular individual or class but in the members of the community as a whole." According to Radhakrishnan University Education Commission Report. "Democracy is the way of life and not a mere political arrangement. It is based on the principle of equal freedom and equal rights for all its members, regardless of race, religion, sex, occupation or economic status."

Mazzine says, "True democracy refers to the progress of all under the leadership of the wisest and the best."

Thus democracy is a way of life where we have sympathy, cooperation and the spirit of understanding. Everyone has the freedom to grow and develop as per his own potentialities. There is equality of rights and opportunities. There is liberty of thought, belief, faith and worship. It is political democracy.

Fundamentals of Democracy

True democracy is based on the following basic principles:

Respect for Everyone : Everyone in the society has his worth and importance. In a democratic set-up of life, the dignity of an individual is held in high esteems. "Each individual is a sacred legacy of society." Democracy believes the dignity of every individual.

Freedom : 'Freedom is the soul of democracy.' Democratic set-up of life believes in the freedom of all. Every individual enjoys freedom of thought, expression, belief, faith, worship, movement and so on. Here freedom does not mean that a person may do any illegal work or do something which is anti-national. It is freedom within definite limits.

Equality of Opportunity : Every individual lives on the basis of equality. There are equal opportunities given to every one irrespective of caste, colour and creed. That way nobody has any type of grudges against anyone else.

Fellow-feelings : Everybody in the democratic society has fellow-feelings. They understand their own duties and share their feelings of oneness with the other fellows of the society. Everybody believes in mutual cooperation and the policy of give and take relationship. Democracy believes in fraternity and group living.

Toleration : The quality of toleration exists in everyone. Everybody tolerates well the leader and the other fellow-beings who are together followers of the same leader. There are healthy relationships among them all with proper toleration.

Good Citizenship : In a true democracy, every human-being happens to be a good citizen. They understand their duties and responsibilities as true citizens.

Faith in Change : Life is dynamic and so are the ways of life. Many things in life go on changing with the passage of time. A true democrat does not resist any change because he/she knows that change is natural and it may be for betterment. They always believe in cooperative living and combined efforts. Moreover, they are staunch believers of peaceful methods.

Thus democracy is a popular way of life. It is the basic philosophy of life on the basis of which our nation exists and is to make progress. Education has to be in tune with the life and philosophy of the people. Then only it is worthwhile. In the absence of a suitable type of education, the democratic society cannot exist well.

Education is the weapon of democracy and without good education for all, democracy will not be successful. Democracy without education is a contradiction in terms. The purpose of education is to ensure that human behaviour conforms to the values and ideals of democracy. Education must build the democratic convictions in the people. Democracy is a practical creed. The principles of democracy influence the theory and practice of education. They are both interdependent.

It may, however, be borne in mind that this concept of Democracy means only political democracy. In this sense, democracy is a formal structure of government through the elected representatives of people in general. This view of democracy is just a misconception. To make the real concept of democracy workable and truly effective, democratic principles and values should pervade all fields of human activity, be it political, social, economic and so on. Democracy is, in fact, a way of life, a method of approach in the settlement of problem an instrument of the development of social and economic aspects of society.

Economic and social democracies are also equally important. Economic democracy means that only a few capitalists of the nation will not have the economic power in their hands. All individuals or people as a whole have that power. In other words, the production and distribution of wealth will be by the people, for the people and of the people. There is economic equality and no economic exploitation.

Social democracy abolishes all distinctions of colour, caste, creed and sex. It ensures equality of opportunities to all. Social democracy does not believe in distinction of birth, class or money. It allows maximum freedom to grow and develop to one and all. In short, justice, fair play, freedom, equality and fraternity are the watchwords of social democracy.

Thus it is clear that democracy is not a mere political deal. But it not came in gap is a way of life where community has unity in its political, economic and social aspects. Bode rightly says, "Democracy is a way of life and a way of life means a determining influence in every area of life."

Characteristics of Democratic Education

Democratic type of education is needed in our country. Only then we can have successful democratic social set-up. The main features of democratic education are:

Universal and Compulsory Education : In a democratic country, education is made available to one and all. It is of universal nature and is compulsory for everybody. Such an education makes people conscious of their duties, rights and other obligations.

Free Education : Education is given free upto a certain standard. In fact, education is regarded as the birth right of every individual. Some people who are unable to receive education due to physical deformity or mental retardness are also provided with special type of education. Thus free education is provided to the blind, deaf and dumb children.

Broad-based Education : Democratic education is broad based. It has wider visions. It caters to the needs of requirements of variety of people. Thus it is found to satisfy one and all in the democratic set-up of life.

Child-centered : Democratic education is child-centered. Every child receives full attention and gets all types of facilities for his proper growth and development. Here education is provided according to the abilities and aptitudes of the child.

Community-centered : Community is the centre 'round which the whole process of education takes place. Needs and requirements of the community are well taken care of. It is related to the social environment of the community.

Provision of Adult Education : Democratic education makes provision for the education of the adults. In the society, some people fail to receive their fundamental education due to one reason or the other. It may be due to dropouts. Democratic education provides non-formal education for such adults.

Good Citizenship : Democratic education helps in producing good citizens. It enables the Individuals to understand their duties, responsibilities and obligations towards the society and above all the nation.

Decentralized : For giving democratic education, the environment is made fully democratic. The functioning of the institution is all decentralised. There is student's self government. The institution gives training for leadership and democratic living.

For National Unity : Democratic education keeps all the nations fully united. There may be people with different languages, different religions, different cultures but democratic type of education unites them together under the banner of democratic republic.

For International Understanding : Democratic type of education has now become the heartfelt requirement of one and all in this universe. One brotherhood, one universe, one humanity- are now fully understood by the whole humanity. Democratic education provides International understanding by developing democratic values of life.

The National Education Association of America has given 'hallmarks' of democratic education as given below:

1. Welfare of all.
2. Equal educational opportunity for all.
3. Respects the basic civil liberties.
4. Promotes economic, political and social conditions.
5. Right to determine the purposes and policies of education.
6. Favours democratic methods.
7. Efficient use of various personnels.
8. Teaches through experiences.
9. Liberates and uses intelligence of all.

10. Gives knowledge of democratic efficiency.
11. Respects humanity, tolerance, occupational efficiency and civil responsibility.
12. Promotes loyalty to democracy.

Education in Democracy

Democracy and education are inter-linked and interdependent. Democracy affects education and education affects democracy in a number of ways. Democratic principles and values have recently entered the field of education. The credit for this goes to John Dewy - the well known American educationist. According to him, "A democracy is more than a form of government, it is primarily a mode of associated living, a conjoint communicated experience." His ideas of democracy have greatly affected education. Now education has become a weapon with the help of which meaningful democracy is possible. K.G. Saiyitiain rightly said, "Education must be so oriented that it may develop basic qualities for the functioning of the democratic." Let us now study about it in details.

Aims and Objectives : Democracy desires the attainment of the following aims :

(1) To make the individuals good citizens.

(2) To help everyone to become cooperative.

(3) To give training of leadership.

(4) To help in character building.

(5) To make the individuals vocationally efficient.

(6) To help everyone have good health and thus have a sound mind.

Secondary Education Commission (1952-63) has suggested the following aims of education for a democratic country.

Development of Democratic Citizenship : The success of democracy largely develops in them the qualities of (a) clear thinking (b) receptivity to new ideas (c) clearance in speech and writing, (d) the art of living in a community, (e) passion for social justice, (f) tolerance, (g) true patriotism and (h) internationalism.

Improvement of Vocational Efficiency : It includes (a) healthy attitude to work and dignity of labour, (b) technical skills and efficiency, (c) self-reliance.

Development of Personality : Democratic education is to develop the individuality of a child into a balanced and harmonious personality. Development of personality includes (a) releasing the sources of creative energy in the student, (b) cultivating rich interests (c) giving due place in the curriculum to subjects like art, craft, music, dancing, etc.

Development of the Qualities of Leadership : This is important for successful functioning of democracy. Education must train our students to shoulder the responsibility in social, political, industrial and cultural fields. Education should instil in children the readership qualities from the very beginning. Children are the future citizens and they have to assume leadership in different fields.

Development of National and International Feelings : This is very essential for the success of democracy.

The first need is development of the sense of oneness and the unity of the nation. National integration requires international understanding. No nation can exist in isolation. There is interdependence which is so essential for world peace.

The Curriculum : In a democratic country, curriculum is constructed with the purpose of realizing democratic values. Only those subjects, activities and programmes are included in the curriculum with the help in the realization of democratic values.

Democratic curriculum is organised on the basis of the following principles:

Broad-based Curriculum : Curriculum should include totality of experiences that a child receives In the classroom as well as outside the classroom. It is not just subject-centered curriculum.

Flexibility : Democratic education envisages a curriculum which is varied and flexible and satisfies the individual needs and interests. It also caters to the demands of society. Such a curriculum is not rigid. It allows necessary changes whenever situation demands or need arises thereto.

Diversified : Democratic curriculum is diversified to suit the needs of all children with different tastes, aptitude and. Intellectual background.

Related to Life, Needs and Aspirations of the Pupils : The democratic approach to curriculum is based on practicalism. It is a curriculum which is directly related to the realities of life, needs and aspirations of the people. It also attends to the local needs and available resources.

Provision for Vocational Needs : It must include general 6s well as vocational aspects of eduation.....an Inter-blending of course. Democratic curriculum very well meets the needs of vocations, professional and economic requirements.

Integrated Curriculum : Democratic curriculum is constructed on the principles of integration. It is a balanced curriculum and includes different subjects, experiences and activities.

It is life-centered, activity-centered and child-centered curriculum.

Teaching Methods : Democracy ideals and values exert a powerful influence upon the methods of teaching also. It has given birth to a number of progressive methods of teaching which are based on individual differences, learning by doing, activity method, Dalton Plan, Heuristic Method, Experimental Method and Socialised classroom techniques.

The traditional methods are discarded. Democratic methods of teaching foster and develop the intelligence of children. Their critical reasoning has the freedom to exercise initiative and originality. Teaching and learning become a joyous experience and a shared activity.

The Discipline

Self-discipline : Democratic discipline is self-imposed. It does-not believe in repression or compulsion. It is discipline from within.

Democratic Discipline is Free Discipline : It is based on love, sympathy, cooperation, responsibility and human relationship.

Social Discipline : It develops in the pupils social attitude, habits and ideals of conduct, through the joint activities of the school which function as a community centre. Students learn self-control through social service, student's councils and social consciousness.

Role of Teacher : In a democratic set-up, the teacher is a friend, philosopher and guide. He holds a key position in the educative process. Every teacher is well-versed in the knowledge of his subject and he is professionally efficient.

The teacher is wholeheartedly devoted to his job and the ideals of democracy. He constitutes the environment making it congenial for the optimum development of children in terms of their talents and capacities.

The teacher in a democratic set-up has to work in close cooperation with different social groups, parents and members of the community. The purpose is to develop children as good citizens, socially oriented and dynamic members of the society.

He himself becomes a model for his students and exercises positive influence on them.

Administration of School : In democracy, school administration is based upon democratic principles and values. It is decentralised administration. It is a means to realise the goals of education i.e. to produce dynamic and productive citizens. It also works in the direction of training children in democratic living and leadership.

School administration is based on democratic spirit. It provides necessary conditions for the proper development of children's personalities. It is based on team spirit, sharing of responsibility and associated living.

It provides adequate rights and freedom to teachers in framing the school policy and programme. Teachers have their say in determining the school curriculum and methods of teaching. The school becomes a community and functions as a social organisation with democratic environment. The organisational climate is quite congenial, free and democratic in spirit.

Ways and Means : Ever since Independence, India accepted democracy and now it has not only to maintain but has also to flourish it. Plans and programmes are prepared from time to time for keeping the flame of democratic life burning successfully. Here below are suggested some ways and means which can help in a number of ways:

1. The controlling authorities of school education, the heads of the institution and the teaching personnels should plan together and then work in close collaboration with one another. That way goals will be achieved rightly without any type of wastage of energy and time and also without overlapping of efforts.
2. The curriculum for the schools should be made broad based and it should be based on the sound principles of democracy. There should be provision of diversified courses so as to give importance to individual differences and variations of attitudes and aptitudes.
3. The textbooks prescribed in the school should propagate democratic values. A few chapters in the textbook may be based directly on democracy and in a few other lessons, there should be indirect preaching of democracy. This type of subject matter contained in the books will have a very good impact on the growing and developing personalities of school children.
4. The curriculum should have sufficient scope for work experience. A number of crafts may be introduced as per the requirement of the community and the locality. Thus towns having industry may introduce industry-oriented practical work. In the case of rural school, provisions of crafts concerning agriculture may be introduced.
5. Efforts should be made to give workable knowledge of different things to the students. A few projects of work experience are repairs of watches and clocks, cycles, scooters, cars, radio, T.V., electrical appliances, wood works, mason work etc.

6. The administration of the institution may be fully decentralised. The Head, the teachers and the students should realize that they are equally involved in the functioning of the institution.
7. Training for human relationship need be provided in the educational institutions. The students must acquire the spirit of cooperative living. The school authorities should try to set up residential schools as far as possible. It will develop fellow-feelings and cooperative living among the students. The Head of the institution and the teachers may plan together the whole teaching programme of the school. Methods such as learning the whole teaching programme of the school. Methods such as learning by doing, group discussions, individualized instructions etc. should be used to the maximum in classroom teaching programme. It will develop in the students confidence and self-reliance.
8. Critical thinking should be developed in the students. This is possible if teaching is carried on by using mother tongue. It is very important at the early stages of growth and development. It is bound to help the students have creative thinking. Every type of creativity on the part of the students should be encouraged.
9. A few projects such as students cooperative store, student's cooperative bank, student's post office, student's canteen may be introduced in the schools with the sole purpose of imparting education to the children. It will help them to learn how they can work as a team and learn many things for their future careers.
10. Training in leadership need be given in the educational institutions. Every child has the potentialities which may be hidden but they can be recognized by the teachers. They can be given very good training of readership. The more the leaders, the more successful will be the democracy of the country. Thus we find that educational institutions can work wonders in making the country truly democratic.

Education revives democracy, maintains democracy, refines democracy and glorifies democracy. In return thereto, democracy makes education fully democratic. Both are interlinked and interdependent. Each One helps the other to become better for the next moment. These two together make human life worth living. Surely education is very good weapon with the help of which democracy may be made all successful.

Works Ahead

1. Discuss in details the relationship that exists between democracy and education. Why is education for true democracy very essential for our country today ?
2. If we accept the attainment of democracy as our ultimate goal, what policies and practices must be followed in our schools ?
3. Liberty and equality are two great principles of democracy. How can we promote them through education ?
4. There is a functional relationship between democracy and education. Bring out the relationship between the two and discuss the important ways and means of achieving this relationship.
5. "If democracy is to be stable form of government of a country, education for democracy must be introduced and maintained at all costs." Discuss the statement briefly.
6. How can education for democracy be imparted successfully in the present day situations prevailing in the schools?
7. What do you understand by democratic conception of education ? Discuss briefly the views about curriculum, methods, teacher and discipline of the democratic education.
8. Discuss the importance of 'Education for Democracy' keeping in view the democratic set-up of our country.

Education requires democracy, pragmatic democracy, welfare democracy and [illegible] in [illegible]. In a democracy, proper education only democratic. Both are interrelated and interdependent. Each helps the other to become better or more [illegible]. These two together make happen the [illegible] [illegible] education, a very good system, with the help of which democracy may be said as [illegible].

[illegible]

11

Social Issues

In culture, the material and non-material aspects depend upon the needs of the society. The change occurs in these material and non-material aspects with the passage of time. New challenges are there before every society. New technologies develop for the benefit of mankind. The structure and functions of different social orders change as a result of a number of interrelated and interdependent factors. The present chapter deals with the concept of social change and the factors that influence these social changes in our social orders.

The Concept

1. Talcott Parsons and others believe in the structural and functional sub-systems of social system. The change in structural and functional sub-systems of social system is the social change.
2. *Dawson and Gatis* : Cultural change is the social change. Cultural change can be grouped into two categories: material and non-material. Material aspect of culture deals with material of utility while non-material part constitutes habits, ideals, beliefs, attitudes and values.

State of social development is called as civilization. In the light of above facts, social change means change in material and non-material aspects of society.

3. *Johnson :* According to Johnson social change may be defined as modification in the ways of doing and thinking of people.
4. *Maclver :* According to Maclver, change in social structure is called social change
5. *Kuppuswamy :* According to Kuppuswamy, social change is the change in social behaviour and social structure, norms, roles, cultural values and personality of individuals.
6. *V.R. Taneja :* According to V.R. Taneja, change in manners, customs, habits, attitudes and purposes is called social change. He is also of the view that open mind and interaction of varied factors (historical, environmental, technological, scientific and so on) brings in social change. There are innovations.

   An innovation is a new way of looking at things in the light of felt experiences and knowledge, a departure from the old to the new in order to make it relevant to the times. Innovations must be examined, tried and adapted and if found good for society, they must be integrated for the development of society. Regarding types of social change, it is of two types: exogenous and endogenous depending upon the exogenous and endogenous factors bringing about social change. Social change can also be classified as planned change and unplanned change.
7. *Gupta :* Socio-cultural change can be characterised by three stages (Gupta, 1995): innovation; diffusion; and interpretation. Innovative stage deals with new discovery either in the shape of a machine or an idea. The diffusion stage requires social interactions in which choices or decisions are made by individuals or groups of individuals. The interpretation stage involves the actual adaptation of existing system in order to implement the innovation.

Influencing Factors

There are many factors (causes) that are responsible for social change. Economic, social, psychological and political factors of social change are briefly described below:

Economic Factors : Economic factors are important for social change. For example, low per capita income of a citizen of a country affects consumption pattern (a social factor), savings (economic factor), investment (economic factor), production (economic factor).

Low per capita income affects other economic factors (low savings, low investment and low production) and social factors (low consumption).

Social Factors : Social factors affect the social change. For example, education, health, housing, social services, food and nutrition, employment are the social factors related to standard of living in a society. These factors affect human resources (non-material component of culture), natural resources (material component of culture), technological resources (material component of culture).

Human resource development depends upon various factors of standard of living e.g. education develops human resource. Better health provisions contribute to his health maintenance. Social services meet the individual's needs. Employment provides economic security. Sufficient per capita income helps an individual in improving consumption pattern, saving and investments.

Human resource development as a result of factors of standard of living also contributes to improve human capital and technological resources. The improvement in resources (human resource, human capital and technological resources) improve economic conditions of the country and the individuals.

Psychological Factors : Psychological factors e.g. personality, intelligence, problem-solving skills, reasoning, creativity, motives, adjustments, needs, physical, social, emotional and moral development of individual, group behaviour etc. affect social change. Fully developed personality of a citizen contributes to social, economic, political, cultural development of a country. Intelligent persons, with well developed reasoning abilities, creativity, contribute to social development. Well adjusted individuals do their best for social development.

Political Factors : Political factors like political system in a country foreign policy, etc. affect social change. For example, democratic political system in India is causing social change in line with parliamentary system of democracy. In America, social change is in progress in Line with Presidential system of democracy. In China, communism is bringing change in Chinese society according to philosophy of communism.

Political philosophies and actions also affect foreign relations, foreign aid which have their own implications on social, economic, and psychological factors.

Political decisions in different countries are different on environmental issues, population regulation, drug abuse, literacy, education, economic decisions, industry etc. Hence social change in a society depends much upon political factors.

Miscellaneous Factors : Geographical factors, environmental factors, population, developmental priorities etc. are other major factors of social change.

Educational Significance

Education is a dominant factor which affects the social and cultural behaviours of individuals directly and indirectly. Let's have a brief discussion on the direct and indirect effects of education on socio-cultural changes in context of Indian population. The description on this aspect can be done on the following major headings:

1. Education, standard of living and social change.
2. Education, resources and social change.
3. Education, population situation and social change.
4. Education, environmental problems and social change.
5. Education, existing socio-cultural patterns and social change.

I Standard of Living

Resources.

Population Situation.

Environmental Problems.

Existing Socio-cultural Pattern.

Education, Standard of Living and Social Change : Factors related to standard of life are education, health, social services, food and nutrition, employment, per capita income and national income, employment, etc. Education is a dominant factor in bringing about change in socio-cultural behaviours of people. Educated members of a society are today developing interest, appreciation, attitudes and values related to factors like health services, employment, per capita income, social services, etc. They are constructively engaging themselves in bringing improvements in these factors and thus trying to improve their standard of living. Education is a single factor which is developing awareness about he contributions of these factors in improving their quality of life.

Thus, we can conclude that education is bringing change in the social behaviours of people through the development of awareness of factors of improving the standard of life. Secondly, education is encouraging them to participate in activities related to these factors besides simple awareness. Thus the awareness component as well as developmental component are the functions of education with specific reference to social change in the area of standard of living.

Education, Resources and Social Change : Education affects the development of resources which bring a significant change in the material and non-material aspects of culture of any society.

A few examples are described below:

Education, Human Resource Development and Human Capital Formation : Education contributes to human resource development and human capital formation. Human capital is the sum total of knowledge, skills, initiative, resourcefulness, capacity for sustained work, right interests, attitudes, values, aptitude, and all other human qualities conducive to higher output and accelerated economic growth. The human resource development and human capital constitute components which are the non-material components of culture. Thus education is instrumental in bringing about changes in knowledge, skills, interests, attitudes, values, etc. which are the non-material components of culture.

Education, Technological Resources and Social Change : Technological resources are developing due to new researches and technical education. These resources are being appreciated and utilized by members of the society. People have developed positive attitude for vocational and technical education. Modern values related to industries based upon current technologies are being internalized by business community. Scientific and technological attitudes and rationality are being given preference today. Thus, education is contributing towards the development of a highly technological society where material and non-material aspects of Indian culture are changing rapidly.

Education, Natural Resources and Social Change : Natural resources like water, forests, petroleum, minerals, etc. are available in plenty in India but we lack adequate knowledge and right attitudes to manage these resources for maximum economic output. Education is providing technical knowledge, and managerial skills. Education is also emphasizing for development of desirable attitudes and values in this regard. For example, through education, desirable attitudes regarding conservation of natural resources. It is only through the development of right attitudes regarding conservation, we will be able to utilize our natural resources for a longer period.

Education, Population Situation and Social Change : Population explosion is a major problem in the national development of under-developed and developing countries The economic resources are utilized mostly in meeting the basic needs of people and investment in productive activities is less. Investments in developmental plans are to be increased. There is a need to change the opinions and value system of people with specific reference to population problem. Education can be instrumental in the internalisation of right value systems to control this problem.

Education, Environmental Problems and Social Change: Technical advancement and industrialisation are good for us in terms of economic development, but industrial growth and other factors are causing environmental problems which have become a serious threat to the very existence of human race. Educational measures can be adopted to develop awareness among people. Attitudes for healthy environment can be inculcated through education. Thus education is being used today as an instrument to inculcate desirable values related to environmental problems.

Education, Existing Socio-cultural Patterns and Social Change : The existing political systems, cultural systems, social systems and consumption patterns can be analysed and desirable changes can be brought about using education as an instrument. The values of democracy, socialism, secularism, egalitarian, social order, nationalism, modernisation, internationalism, Sanskritisation, Westernisation, etc. can be inculcated through education strategies.

1. Discuss varied views on the concept of social change.
2. Comment upon the importance of social change with specific reference to India.
3. Discuss various factors or causes that contribute to social change. Support your answer with suitable examples.
4. Discuss the relationship between education and social change.
5. Comment upon the following:
   (a) Education, standard of living and social change.
   (b) Education, human resources and social change.
   (c) Education, technological resources and social change.
6. "Education is an instrument of social change." Comment.

12

Role of Secularism

Role of Education

Ever since India got freedom in 1947, the word 'secular' has been used very often by the national leaders. Every one says, "India is a secular-country." In every political and educational corner, secularism is being propagated. Let us now acquaint ourselves with the word 'secular'. The word 'secular' has been derived from the Latin word "Seculum" which means 'age' or 'generation'.

The term 'secularism' was first used by George Jacob Holydake in the nineteenth century. He used this word in the context of social and ethical values. According to Holydake, the concept of socialism may be defined as a system, "which seeks the development of physical, moral and intellectual nature of man to the highest possible point as the immediate duty of life which inculcates the practical sufficiency of natural morality apart from Atheism, Theism or Bible which selects as its methods of procedure of promotion of human improvement by material means."

As per Oxford Dictionary, the word secular means sceptical of religious truth, opposed to religious education. It does not mean irreligion or anti-religion or irreligiousness. In fact, the word secularism shows our broad mindedness.

Bradlaugh, a successor of Holydake says, "Secularism is hostile to religion."

According to Chambers Dictionary "secularism is, the belief that the state morals, education etc. should be independent of religion."

Webster's Dictionary states that secularism is, "the belief that religion and ecclesiastical affairs should not enter into the functions of the state." Webster further says, "A system of doctrines and practices that rejects any form of religious faith and worship."

The pluralistic view is that secularism is an attitude of accepting all religions rather than rejecting any or all religions. This view was put forth by Mahatma Gandhi and Dr. S. Radhakrishnan.

Mahatma Gandhi put forth his view, "The soul of religion is one but it is encashed in a multitude of forms. Wise men will ignore the outward crust and see the same soul living under a variety of crusts." Then in 1928 he said, "After long study and experience, I have come to the conclusion that

(1) All religions are true.

(2) All religions have some errors in them.

(3) All religions are almost as dear to me as my own Hinduism. My veneration for other faiths is the same as to my own faith."

In this context Dr. S. Radhakrishnan says, "Secularism does not mean anything irreligious or atheism or even stress on material comforts. Rather it lays stress on the universality of spiritual values which may be attained by a variety of ways."

There is establishment of a secular polity. Every religion is important and so every religion should be respected. All religions basically have the same beliefs and ultimately advocate to reach the same goals. There is need of imbibing qualities like tolerance, cooperation and understanding. There should be no place for religious prejudices. According to Mahatma Gandhi, "My veneration for other faiths is the same as for my own faith." "We believe in Sarva-Dharma-Samantar having equal regard for all faiths and creeds."

Regarding the secular state, Donald E. Smith says, "A state which guarantees individual and cooperative freedom of religion, deals with the individual as a citizen irrespective of his religions, is not constitutionally connected to a particular religion nor does it seek either to promote or interfere with religion."

Dr. B.R. Ambedkar explained the concept of secular state, "All that a secular state means is that this parliament shall not be competent to impose any particular religion upon the rest of the people."

Indian Scenario

India is a multi religious and culturally varied society. People have different religions and they have different beliefs. A large number of people is uneducated. That is why, people have narrow mindedness. Value crises have also deteriorated the social set up of life. Fanaticism and communalism are on the increase. During the recent past, people started believing in regionalism. Ram Janam Bhumi and Babri Masjid became the issues of great struggle between the different communities. In this type of prevailing situations, there is great need of educating the people on the right lines. That way only selfishness and narrow mindedness of the people can be ended. And they can be made to realize the importance of national unity and emotional integrity.

There is need of making the people open minded. Only a broad minded person is able to make adjustment in any and every type of situation. Equality, liberty, fraternity, national outlook and international understanding need be propagated. Moral values have to be imbibed. Scientific attitude in order to have rationality and objectivity need be developed in the fast growing and developing generations.

In the present set up of life where there is erosion of values, narrow mindedness and selfishness spreading, trifles over petty religious matters are caused. Corruption and disbelief are rampant. How can all this be improved? Who can be entrusted with the job of shouldering the whole responsibility? The only suitable weapon for this is Education. In the words of D.E. Smith, "Secularism's best hope for future in India lies in its classrooms."

Secondary Education Commission says, "The educational system must make its contribution to the development of habit, attitude and qualities of character which will enable its citizens to counteract all those fissiparous tendencies which hinder the emergence of a broad, national and secular outlook."

The National Policy on Education (1986) says, "In our culturally plural society, education should foster universal and eternal values, oriented towards the unity and integration of our people. Such value education should help eliminate obscurantism, religious fanaticism, violence, superstition and fatalism."

Concerns of Commissions

Major recommendations of different commissions are as under :

University Education Commission (1948)

1. That all educational institutions start work with a few minutes for silent meditation.
2. That in the first year of degree course, lives of great religious leaders like Gautam, the Buddha, Confucious, Zoroaster, Socrates, Jesus, Sankara, Ramanujan, Mohammad, Kabir, Nanak, Gandhi be taught.
3. That in the second year some selections of a universal character from the scriptures of the world be studied.
4. That in the third year, the central problem of the philosophy of religion be considered.

Secondary Education Commission (1953)

The Commission is of the view that "Healthy trends in regard to religious or moral behaviour spring from three sources:

1. The influence of the home which is the dominant factor.

2. The influence of the school through the conduct and behaviour of the teachers themselves and life in the school community as a whole.
3. Influence exercised by the public of the locality and the extent to which public opinion prevails in all matters pertaining to religious instruction or moral instruction, the Commission has recommended.

"One of the methods adopted in some schools is to hold assembly at the commencement of the day's session with teachers and pupils present, when a general non-donominational prayer is offered. Moral instruction in the sense of inspiring talks given by suitable persons selected by the headmaster and dwelling on the lives of great personages of all times and of all climes will help to drive home the lesson of morality. In view of the provision of the constitution of the secular state, religious instructions cannot be given in schools except on voluntary basis and outside the regular school hours; such instructions should be given to the children of the particular faith and with the consent of the parents and the management concerned.

Sri Prakasa Committee (1959) : Sri Prakasa Committee, 1959, constituted for this purpose, gave the following suggestions:

Educational Programmes

Elementary Stage

1. The School Assembly should be held for a few minutes in the morning for group singing.
2. Simple and interesting stories about the lives and teachings of prophets, saints and religious leaders should be included in the syllabus for language teaching.
3. Audio-visual material connected with the main living religions of the world should be included especially in the teaching of Geography.
4. In the school programme, two periods a week should be set aside for moral instruction. Dogmas and rituals should be excluded from moral instruction. Kothari Education Commission has also made similar recommendations.

5. Physical education and all forms of play in the school should contribute to the building of character and the inculcation of the spirit of true sportsmanship.

Secondary Stage

1. The Morning Assembly should observe two minutes's silence followed by readings from the scriptures and classics. Community singing should also be encouraged.
2. The essential teachings of the great world religions should be studied as part of the curriculum pertaining to Social Studies and History. Simple texts and stories concerning different religions may be included in the syllabus.
3. One hour a week should be assigned to moral instruction. Suitable speakers may be invited.
4. Organised social service during holidays and outside class hours should be an essential part of school programme. This is very helpful in teaching the dignity of manual labour, love of humanity, patriotism and self-discipline. Participation in games and sports should be compulsory and physical education including sex education, should form a normal part of school programme.
5. Qualities of character and behaviour of students should form an essential part of the overall assessment of a student's performance at school.

University Stage

(a) Silent meditation should be encouraged.

(b) General study of different religions should be an essential part of the general education course in degree classes. In this connection, the recommendations made by the University Education Commission should also be incorporated.

(c) A Course in Comparative Religions may be introduced. In other words, there should be University Department in the comparative study of religion.

(d) A fairly long period of social service should be introduced by all universities.

National Education Policy

Change in Curriculum : The growing concern over the erosion of essential values and an increasing cynicism in society has brought to focus the need for readjustments in the curriculum in order to make education a forceful tool for the cultivation of social and moral values.

Universal and Eternal Values : In our culturally plural society, education should foster universal and eternal values, oriented towards the unity and integration of our people. Such value education should help eliminate obscurantism, religious fanaticism, violence, superstition and fatalism.

Positive Content : A part from this combative role, value education has a profound positive content, based on our heritage, national goals and universal perceptions. It should lay primary emphasis on this aspect.

Action Programme

The "Programme of Action" which is the follow up measure to National Policy of Education, has laid down some concrete steps to achieve the desired goals as stated below:

"A special place has been assigned to imparting of value oriented education in the Education Policy document. A beginning would be made by instituting a special study value-oriented education. Based on its analysis, it would in collaboration with NCERT and State institutions, help in suggesting broad parameters of values of integrity, truth, devotion, loyalty etc. with particular reference to their embodiment in Indian heritage so as to blend naturally with the overall educational process."

Naturally then the authorities concerned with education will have to work vigorously to achieve the desired ends. Now let us see what can be possible at the hands of different authorities concerned with education.

Authorities of Administration

The controlling authorities of education can play a vital role as suggested below:

1. Universal compulsory and free education for all upto 14 years of age has been the slogan of the government ever since India got freedom. Good many efforts have been made for this but the overall achievement is much below the desired targets. The obvious reason being poverty stricken ever growing population.

   There is need of making provision of part time education facilities. Special type of education need be provided to the children of this category which should help them to earn sufficiently along side their learning. There is need of introducing practical oriented education, work based education which would enable the learner to become proficient in some vocation or job. When the children will learn by working with their hands, they will become an asset to their families as well as to the community and the nation they belong to.

2. Suitable type of curriculum should be prescribed in the schools. The different activities and the textbooks should propagate the chief characteristics of secularism. Different lessons in the books should reflect love and respect for all religions.

3. The authorities can introduce moral education as a compulsory paper for all the students. It will change the outlook of the students. They will have good qualities like honesty, sincerity, hardwork, fellow-feeling, coexistent, non-violence etc.

4. Efforts can be made to introduce a subject like 'Comparative Religions Study'. Efforts should be made to popularize this subject in the senior classes. Of course for juniors there may be elementary type of study of different religions. For example in the lower classes, the textbook on this subject

may consist of biographies of founders of some popular religions.

5. Newspapers and journals can play a leading part in propagating the characteristics of secularism. Some journals may be selected which can educate the masses. The newspapers may also have, one page per week, totally based on secular education. The intellectuals may be asked to write their articles for the newspapers and also for the journals.
6. Radio and T.V can also be used to educate the public fully about secularism. The Public Relation Officers (PROs) at district headquarters can use T.V. and Radio for the achievement of goals.

Teacher's and Headmaster's Role

In the schools, the teachers and the headmasters can play significant roles. No doubt, the higher authorities can prescribe certain things but it is the teachers community that can actually put those things in practical shape. Without their whole hearted cooperation nothing in this regard can be achieved. Now let us see how the schools can help in imparting secular based education:

1. *Moral Education, Religious Education, Comparative Religious Studies :* All these subjects should be entrusted to the matured teachers. In the hands of such teachers, there will be no misunderstanding and no basic misrepresentation of facts and figures. The personalities of such teachers in themselves will be good examples for the students to follow.
2. *Every School should Celebrate Religious Festivals Pertaining to Different Religions.* At least one function of each religion must be celebrated in the institution. Efforts should be made that festivals of all religions should be celebrated with equal pomp and show. In the celebration of each such function, students belonging to different religions should be associated. The school authorities should ensure that all religious festivals are given equal importance.

3. The school authorities should organise declamation contests on topics related to all religions. While doing so, it must be ascertained that nothing happens which injures the feelings of one religious group or the other. There should be some internal checking of the material being presented by the students in the gathering. The teachers incharge of declamation contest should make all efforts to maintain that the central string of all religions is one.
4. Extension lectures on topics of comparative religious study may be organised in the schools. Eminent scholars of different religions may be invited for giving lectures to the students. Only those persons should be invited who have made comparative study of different religions.
5. In the institutions, tours and trips may be organised. The students may be taken to different centres of religions. Thus the students may be taken to see 'Guru Gobind Singh Bhawan' in the Punjabi University, Patiala. The very sight of the building, showing the studies of different religions and all ultimately uniting and showing oneness will have deep impact on the personalities of the children. Just possible some students may take up comparative religious studies for their postgraduate degree.
6. In different religions, many things are common such as social service at the time of celebrations, service to humanity etc. may be highlighted in the schools. The students may be encouraged to take up such activities. Once the dignity of social service is realized by the students, it has then everlasting impact on their personalities.
7. The institutions should lay greater emphasis upon teaching religious studies through informal type of instructions. The students can be encouraged to think of points common in different religions. Those thoughts/ideas may be highlighted in the morning assembly or at some other occasion when there is a gathering.

No doubt, our country is secular and we are expected to believe in secularism. For this we shall have to make efforts in different ways. Only then people will become fully conscious of it and the goals behind would be achieved. Both formal and informal ways need be applied for it. Education can certainly deliver the goods if it is planned with those motives in mind.

1. What is secularism? Discuss the need and importance of secular based education.
2. What are the characteristics of a secular state? How is our educational system trying to create a social climate in the country in which secular values are sought to be promoted?
3. Write short notes on:
   (a) Secular based Education.
   (b) Secularism and Education.

13

Directionless Education

The development of education gives birth to several types of problems. With the development of Indian education, problems of Indian Education also increased. Some of the problems are as old as the modern education system itself. We will briefly discuss the chief problems of Indian Education.

Education without Aim

The aim of education which was in the pre-independence period cannot continue to be accepted in the independent India. It is a matter of great regret that there is no definite aim before the Indian students. Innumerable young men and women are receiving education in schools and colleges without having any definite aim before them. They have no goal or aim in their life. Most of the young students consider the getting of jobs as the ultimate aim of their education.

It has to be admitted that we have not been able to change aims of our education in accordance with the changing situation and circumstances of the country. Kothari Commission has remarked in very clear words that the most important reform in the education is to change it or to make endeavour so that it may be related to the life of the people, their needs and aspirations and, thus, we will have to develop education as a powerful weapon for bringing about social, economic and cultural changes, which are necessary for the achievement of national objectives. According to this aim, the development of education be made in such a way so that it may lead to social and national unity, tendencies of modernisation may be made mobile and social, and moral values may be established.

In short, we may say that modern education should aim at fulfilment of the needs of the citizens and develop the feeling of universal brotherhood among them. Thus, under the present political, economic and social changes the aim of education should not remain bound to the old route of the period of British regime. Structural changes are needed in the present system of education.

Uncompatible Curriculum

Another chief problem of Indian education is defective and unbalanced curriculum. The curriculum which is prescribed for the study of the students emphasises only bookish knowledge. The relation of curriculum has not been established with life and consequently many young persons who have received higher education are facing the problem of unemployment.

The Secondary Education Commission has pointed out the following defects of the curriculum:

(a) The present curriculum is very narrow.

(b) It is bookish and theoretical.

(c) It includes more subjects than are required and many of them are useless and unnecessary.

(d) Emphasis is not given on teaching the boys practical subjects and other types of activities, which may help development of the versatile personality of the child.

(e) The curriculum does not fulfil the different needs and interests of the students.

(f) The curriculum lacks technical and professional subjects.

The Kothari Commission has also dealt with in detail the defects of the curriculum. The Commission has pointed out that in the background of the important efforts that are being made in the foreign countries in the development of curriculum, it appears that the basis of the curriculum in India is very narrow and out of date. The Curriculum emphasises bookish knowledge and cramming. There is insufficient provision for practical activities and experience and there is prominence of external and internal examinations. Besides since adequate importance is not given to the development of skills, proper aptitude, tendencies and values, the curriculum is not complete to keep pace with the lives of the people. Keeping in view these things, the Commission has recommended that there is urgent necessity of improving the curriculum, raising its standard and for reforming it.

Outdated Teaching Methods

Another serious problem of our education is that teaching methods have not been changed in accordance with the change of tune and circumstances. Even today the education is not child-centered in India whereas in other countries, endeavour has been made to make it as much child-centered as possible. While other countries of the world have been adopting new methods of teaching, even today we are adopting the conventional and out-of-date teaching methods. The conventional and out-of-date methods are very much detrimental for the education of our country and hence new teaching methods, keeping in view the needs and circumstances of the present times, should be adopted with immediate effect

Defective System of Examination

The problem of examination system in India is as serious as the problem of curriculum and the methods of teaching. The aim of our education has become only to pass examination.

Mostly, only one examination is held in a year, with the result, that the student are not able to acquire proper and real knowledge. The number of the examiners is so large that no harmony can be established in their decisions. It depends upon the mood, individual ability, knowledge of the subject and environment to award marks to the examinees. Mostly, essay type of examinations are organised, which are completely unpsychological.

The different Committees and Commissions, which have been appointed to suggest ways and means to reform education, have pointed out the seriousness of the problem of defective examination system. The University Education Commission has remarked that although the seriousness and complication of this problem has been increasing with great speed, constructive steps have not been taken to reform it. The Mudaliar and Kothari Commissions also have pointed out the seriousness of this problem. It is, therefore, necessary that all-out efforts should be made to solve this problem as expeditiously as possible.

Stagnation and Wastage Problem

India is an underdeveloped and poor country and the percentage of literacy is very low. Keeping this situation in view, it is very unfortunate that the problem of wastage and stagnation has been existing in the field of education for a very long time. Because of the defective administration, defective environment, defective curriculum and defective examination system, lakhs of students fail every year. Kothari Commission has expressed the view that the rate of wastage is from 1/3 to 1/2 in class 1. The problem of wastage and stagnation exists at all stages of education. There are some students, who leave education in the middle and there is a large number of students, who fail every year in the examinations.

Control and Management Problem

The problem of control and management of education is also one of the chief problems in India. Mostly, the education up to primary and junior high school is organised by the local district board and municipalities. Some schools are directly under the control of the State Government, whereas some institutions are under the control of private managements. Some institutions are also under the control of religious institutions. Likewise, secondary schools are also under the control of local boards, private and religious institutions. There are also Government schools. Most of the schools are non-government and they are managed by the management committees of the schools concerned. Generally, the members of the managing committees are such as make the institutions serve their personal interests.

It is a matter of great regret that some members of the management committees are so influential that even the higher officials of the State Education Department hesitate to take any action against them. The Education Board of the State are not able to function properly because of groupism and party politics. It is a matter of great regret that groupism, favouritism, corruption etc. are rampant in primary as well as secondary schools. Teachers of secondary schools are also the victims of anger of the members of the management committees. Most of the managers of non-Government schools are not competent and fit to shoulder the grave responsibility of education. Caste feeling, individual rivalry, jealousy, groupism and corruption are rampant in the management committees of the non-Government schools. The poor teachers of these schools become the victims of these difficulties.

Most of the universities in India are under the control of State Governments. Only 5 Universities are under the control of Central Government. In the universities also, the control and administration are very loose. The problem of control in the affiliated colleges of the universities has become so serious that its solution seems to be very difficult. Many colleges are run by private and religious institutions and they include all those defects which exist in the field of secondary education. There are very few institutions at present which are run with the feeling of public welfare. Most of the teaching institutions have become the means of earning money and their managers consider it their aim to realise utmost money from the Government and the people.

It is important to note here that the condition of the Government schools and colleges is far better than the non-Government institutions. Kothari Commission has made important suggestions in regard to the management, administration and control of education at different stages. If the suggestions of the Kothari Commission are properly implemented, the problem of control, management and administration of education at different stages can be solved.

Menace of Indiscipline

Indiscipline is increasing day by day among the Indian students. It is such a serious problem that it has attracted our attention and anxiety of all the scholars and educationists of the country. This problem is absent at the primary stage. By the time the students enter the secondary stage, they become adolescent. They tend to flout the established rules. Their indiscipline takes the collective form of Individuality, the student continues the old tradition of discipline, but when he is swept off by the mounting tides of collective tendency, he becomes a prey of indiscipline. There are many causes for the prevalence of indiscipline among the students. The prominent among such causes are (a) defective examination system; (b) defective economic system; (c) impracticable curriculum; and (d) wastage and stagnation. According to Kothari Commission, the modern, social and economic system are, to a great extent, responsible for the indiscipline among the students. The Commission has also pointed out that the chief cause of indiscipline among the students is the interference of the politicians in the schools, colleges and universities.

The Commission has seriously analysed the causes of unrest among students. Explaining its causes, the commission observes that "there is a variety of causes which have brought about these ugly expressions of uncivilised behaviour *e.g.*, the uncertain future facing educated youngmen leading to a sense of frustration which breeds irresponsibility, mechanical and unsatisfactory nature of many curricular programmes, the totally inadequate facilities for teaching and learning in the large bulk of institutions; the poor student-teacher contact, the inefficiency and lack of knowledge on the part of many teachers and their failure to interest themselves in student's problems; the absence of imagination and tact combined with firmness on the part of heads of institutions; the prevalence of what has come to be known as teacher's politics.......

The attempt by political parties to interfere in their work, and by no means the least, the impact of the conditions of public life in the country, the falling standards of discipline among the adults and a weakening of their civic consciousness and integrity."

In order to solve the problem of indiscipline, it is necessary to remove the above mentioned causes. It can be suggested that the number of students in classes should be reduced, the curriculum should be made useful and practical; examination system should be reformed, aimlessness of education should be ended, sports, games and cultural programmes should be organised, well-trained teachers should be appointed and they should be kept away from party politics. If we really wish to improve the education in the country; we shall have to uproot the causes of indiscipline.

The Education Commission has classified the remedies for student indiscipline into two categories viz. removal of education deficiencies that contribute it and setting up of a consultative and administrative machinery to prevent the occurrence of indiscipline.

The remedies of the first group are regarded as the core of the problem. In fact, "the incentives to positive discipline have to come from the opportunities that the institution presents and the intellectual and social demands it makes on the students". As regards second remedy, it has been suggested that polarisation between teachers, students and administration should be avoided. Joint councils of students and teachers should be appointed. All this should create a spirit of comradeship between the teachers and the students. If this "spirit could be created, many of the problems of discipline which are disastrous to our academic life at present will become easier to solve and, will be hoped, disappear in course of time."

Problem of Medium Selection

It is very difficult and complicated problem in India as to which language (national language Hindi, international language English or regional languages) should be the medium of education. Since the beginning of 19th century, the medium of instruction has remained a controversial issue. Different Scholars and Commissions have given different views in this regard. In 1956, the State Organisation Commission defined the frontiers of all states. This gave rise to the controversy of language issue. In 1957, the official language commission suggested that Hindi should be developed as the obvious linguistic medium of instruction and ruled out English as the language of India's mass medium. The Radhakrishnan Commission also recommended that the medium of instruction should be any Indian language except Sanskrit. In 1966, Kothari Commission recommended that the regional language should not only be made the medium of instructions at the primary and secondary stages but they should also be made the medium of education at the university stage. Hence, Hindi should be developed as a link language and the use of English should also be continued. The language policy of Kothari Commission was severely criticised and many scholars even remarked that it was only a conspiracy to continue the use of English in India.

At present in different states, education is imparted through the medium of regional languages at the primary and secondary stages. At the higher stages also, endeavours are being made to make the regional languages as the medium of education. But the influence of English has yet not declined at this stage and English language continues to be the medium of education in different universities. Thus, the problem of language still remains a problem and it is very essential that this problem should be solved in the earliest possible time and the language controversy should be at rest forever.

Education of Women

Another chief problem of education in India is the problem of education of women. The Constitution of India has enshrined in the principle of equality of men and women. However, we find that women of India still flag behind in many respects. In 1932, as compared to 100 boys, only 55 girls were receiving education at the primary stage. At the secondary stage, this number was only 26. Thereafter, the education of women has greatly expanded but still the percentage of women is very low. The main cause of this narrow viewpoint "is the failure to understand the importance of education. It is really a matter of great satisfaction that our Government is conscious of its responsibility towards the education of women and is taking every possible step to encourage the education of women." The Kothari Commission has also emphasized that for some time priority should be given to the education of women in our educational system and only then the problem of education of women can be solved.

Education of Adults

It was pointed out earlier that the number of illiterates is far greater in India than the number of literates. At present, the population of India has swelled near about 90 crores. About 70 per cent of the total population is illiterate. There has been no appreciable increase in the percentage of literacy.

The efforts that have been made by the Government in regard to education of adults have not met with much success. Proper curriculum and proper teaching method should be adopted for the education of the adult and able sufficient teachers should be appointed to make the scheme of adult education a success. The Kothari Commission has made some very important suggestions to achieve these goals. The prominent among such suggestions are the establishment of 'Adult Education Department in Universities', proper provision of libraries and the establishment of Social Welfare Councils. It may be admitted that we cannot achieve the goal determined by the Kothari Commission so soon. But we can certainly act according to the suggestions of the Commission so as to solve the problem of adult education in India, so that the problem of illiteracy may be solved in India in near future.

Worker and Disabled Person's Education : Industrialisation is progressing with great speed in India. Consequently, the number of weak persons is constantly increasing. The education of these workers also pose serious problems before as. Although Government has been emphasizing on the education of the workers is the programmes of the expansion of adult education yet sufficient success has not so far been achieved in this field.

Along with the problem of education of the workers, the problem of the education of the disabled persons is also very serious. There are mainly two types of disabled persons (a) mentally retarded persons, and (b) physically disabled persons. Mentally retarded children are those, whose I.Q. is below 35. At present about 33% of "school going children are mentally retarded to varying degrees. According to Kothari Commission the number of disabled children in India was 25 lacs out of which 14 to 18 lacs were said to be mentally retarded children.

With the expansion of civilisation, mental diseases are also increasing. Poverty, bad company, lack of opportunities to education, cruel and apathetic behaviour of the parents, family quarrels, *etc.* are the causes of mental diseases. There are also lacs of physically disabled children in India. The Government have made many efforts for the education of disabled persons, but so far sufficient arrangement has not been made for the education of all types of disabled persons.

Technical and Professional Education Problems : With the rapid development of industrialisation in India, the problem of technical and professional education is also becoming complicated. No special provision was made for the professional and technical education before independence.

Great efforts have been made in this direction after the achievement of independence. Despite tremendous increase in the number of schools and the students, there is still shortage of skilled craftsmen and trained persons in the field of different professions. It is true that many engineers and overseers are facing the problem of unemployment but in other professions there is still shortage of skilled and trained persons.

System of Education

Last but not the least problem that we have before us, is that our educational system is not in accordance with the political, social and economic conditions of the time. In the modern period, India has adopted a democratic set up and hence education should also be completely democratic. In the economic field, importance has been given to the socialist programme and hence, our education system should also aim to inculcate the feeling of socialism in the citizens. Because of the social changes, the feelings of caste distinction and untouchability have greatly reduced but still these evils exist in the society. Our educational system should be organised in such a way as may be able to root out completely these evils from our society. Education plays an important role in establishing harmony with the vast changing world and hence our education should be able to adopt itself in accordance with the rapid changes that are taking place in different fields in the world. If we are able to solve only this problem and make our educational system in accordance with the changing circumstances, the rest of the problems will automatically be solved.

Conclusion : It is obvious from the above discussion that in the modern period, there are many problems in the field of Indian education. These problems are so serious that they cannot be solved within a very short period. They require constant study and research and sincere efforts for their solution. However, it may be remarked that our progress depends upon the solution of these problems and the sooner we solve these problems the better it will be. If we are able to solve these problems within a short span of period, India will find her place among the progressive and developed nations of the world.

Monetary Hurdles

The problem of finance is probably the greatest obstacle in the expansion of Indian Education. Although different types of schemes are formulated for the expansion of education but it is not possible to implement them properly because the Government is not able to provide necessary finance for them.

Various Stages of Education and Educational Finance : In all the provinces in India, primary education has been made free and hence the complete responsibility of the primary education is on the local Government. The responsibility of secondary education is also on the State Government and it is the duty of the Government to make necessary provision of finance for it. The Central

Government is to a great extent, responsible for higher education. In order to give financial help to the universities, the Central Government has established an institution known as University Grants Commission.

It is true that most of the burden of the primary and secondary education is shouldered by the State Governments but the Central Government also gives financial aid to the State Governments in this field and local institutions such as Municipalities, Corporations, District Board, Gram Panchayats etc., also share some of the responsibility of primary education. Thus, we see that the Central Government not only gives utmost help in the field of university education but it also grants financial help to the State Governments in the field of primary and secondary education.

In view of the provision of free primary education, the whole responsibility of collecting money for the same has come on governments. The State Governments grant financial help for the pre-primary education also. At both these stages two types of institutions are working. Most of the schools are run by Municipalities, Corporations, District Boards, Panchayats, etc. There are also schools which are run by non-government institutions and local bodies. Provision of free primary education has been made in the Non-Government schools also. Besides these schools there are also such schools which receive no financial help from the Government and carry on their work only by the fee received from the Students.

At the secondary stage also, there are three types of schools. Some schools are run by the State Governments and the responsibility of their finance is wholly on State Governments. Some schools are run by local bodies, such as Municipalities, Corporations, etc. The responsibility of finance of these institutions is both on the local institutions and the State Governments. The Central Government also gives some financial assistance to the State Governments in this respect. The number of Non-Government schools is much at the secondary stage. These schools receive financial help in the form of grant-in-aid from the State Governments.

14

Reformation of the System

The existing structure of the Indian education is based on the suggestions of wood's Despatch, 1854. In this Despatch there were 4 steps for educational programmes:

(1) Primary, (2) Secondary, or Middle, (3) High School, and (4) University. There have been some changes in the structure proposed by Wood's Despatch, but still it is almost the same. Until the 20th century, the period of school education was 9 years. Later on, the period of 9 Years was extended to the period of 10 years. There was provision for the 4 year's Primary Education, 2 years lower middle education and 2 years High School Education.

The Secondary Education Commission or the Mudaliar Commission proposed this very structure. This Commission was of the opinion that the period of Primary Junior Basic Education should be of 4 or 5 years. The period of Middle or Junior Secondary or Senior Basic Education should be 3 Years while that of Secondary Education be 4 Years. There should be provisions for the 3 Year's Degree Course, and 2 Year's Postgraduate Course. In this way Mudaliar Commission suggested that the period of Secondary Education should be 7 years. Though Mudaliar Commission was entrusted with the job of making recommendations for the secondary Education but the Commission also gave certain valuable suggestions for Degree Education. The Commission was of the opinion that we have to face a lot of difficulties because in some provinces there was the degree course of 3 years while in other it was of 2 years. The Commission proposed that 'there should be uniformity in all the provinces. It was the reason that the Commission proposed that total period of primary and secondary education should be of 11 years. While there should be 3 years Degree Course and a period of 2 years should be allotted for the Post-Graduate Education.

Kothari Commission and the Reorganisation of Education : In 1964, Commission under the Presidentship of Sri D.S Kothari was appointed to give its suggestions regarding the Education System and the changes to be made. The Commission submitted its report in 1966. Kothari Commission was of the opinion that the entire structure of Indian Education should be reorganised. The Commission recommended that educational system should consist of:

A preschool stage consisting of one to three years:

- a primary stage of seven or eight years divided into substages, a lower primary stage of four or five years and a higher primary stage of three years:
- a lower secondary or high school stage of three or two years in general education or one to three years in vocational education;
- a higher secondary stage of two years of general education or one to three years of vocational education;
- a university stage having a course of three years or more for the first degree and followed by courses for the second or research degree of varying durations.

Kothari Commission also gave valuable suggestions for the 10 years education. The Commission also recommended for the modification of higher secondary pattern course corresponding to Higher Secondary stage. About the transfer to pre-university course, it also recommended for the lengthening of duration of Higher

Secondary Course and Reorganisation of education at the University stage.

Here we are giving a number of accounts of its recommendations:

First Decade Improvement

The Commission visualises:

(i) The first ten years of schooling, covering a primary stage of seven or eight years and lower secondary stage of three or two years, will provide a course of general education without any specialisation.

(ii) The primary stage will be preceded, wherever possible by pre-primary education period of one or three years.

(iii) The age of admission to Class Ist should ordinarily be made not less than six years.

(iv) At the end of primary stage, about 20 percent students will step off the school system and enter working life, about 20 percent will step off the stream of general education into different courses whose duration may range from one to three years and the remaining 60 percent may continue their general education.

(v) One external examination will be held after ten years of school education.

(vi) At the end of ten years of school education, about 40 percent students will get into working life, others about 30 percent will go to vocational courses and the remainder will continue further in the stream of general education.

Improvement and Modification

The Commission attaches great significance to the changes that have to be made in the existing higher secondary pattern in the light of the above proposals and recommends as follows:

(i) The system of general education which now begins in Class IX, should be given up and no attempt of specification should be made till after class X. This will need a considerable reorganisation of the existing curricula of the higher secondary schools.

(ii) The idea of raising every secondary school to the higher secondary status should be abandoned. It is unwise in rural country to try to raise every high school to the higher secondary status. The Commission has, therefore, visualised as a permanent feature of educational system, secondary schools of two types, first, high schools of ten years course and the higher secondary schools of twelve years course of education. An essential requirement for raising the standard should be that the institutions need be large, centrally located and equitably distributed between rural and urban areas. It would also be necessary to review the status of the existing higher secondary schools and those which are uneconomic or are substandard may be reconverted into high schools.

(iii) There should be an integrated course of studies beginning from class IX if we want to provide specialised studies in different subjects at the higher secondary stage.

(iv) There should be an external examination at the end of Class X to mark the termination of the first ten years of general education. A student studying in a ten year high school will thus have to appear for two external examinations at the end of Classes X and XI at the interval of one year. This handicap can be removed by extending higher secondary course to two years.

(v) Existing higher secondary schools with a well organised integrated courses in Classes IX, X and XI may be permitted to carry on if they so desire, with such course until they add Class XII. It will not be obligatory for the students of such schools to appear for an examination at the end of Class X. They may take one final examination at the end of Class XI or take in two parts at the end of Class X and XI.

Vocational courses at the end of primary stages will need that the schools should provide adequate facilities for suitable form of education either part-time or on a full time basis.

Corresponding Courses of Higher Secondary Stage : The name, duration, location and control of courses corresponding to higher secondary stage vary from State to State. In all the States, where the higher secondary pattern is adopted but all high schools have not been raised to the higher secondary status; the stage is provided as Class XI in the secondary schools and pre-university courses in the colleges.

The main reforms are needed for reorganisation of educational structure at this stage:

(a) The transfer of pre-university course from the universities and the colleges to the schools; and

(b) The lengthening of duration of the courses of general education uniformly to two years.

The programmes may be implemented in successive stages.

Expanding the Duration

The duration of the higher secondary courses should be lengthened to two years and the whole programme be spread over to 20 years divided into two stages. The first stage of five years should be devoted to secure a better utilisation of existing facilities and to make required preparation for a successful implementation of this important reform. Even during this period selected higher secondary schools should be allowed to add the twelfth year and even some high schools of good quality and possessing the necessary facilities may be allowed to introduce two year higher secondary course as pilot projects. The stage will cover a span of 15 years which will be completed by the end of seventh.

The next popular demand is related to lengthening the total duration of higher education. The duration for the professional degree is not less than sixteen years practically in all the advanced countries. Hence, the demand only refers to the first degree in Art and Science, which is four years after matriculation or equivalent examination. It is generally contended that this duration should be lengthened by a year. This view accords with the thinking of several bodies on the subject. The Calcutta University Commission, the University Education Commission and the Committee on Emotional Integration also support the view. The State Education Ministers' Conference in 1964 proposed twelve year course of schooling before admission to degree course. The Commission agrees with the recommendations in full.

Educational Structure Reorganisation

Besides lengthening of the duration of school education, it is recommended that the reorganisation should be carried out through a phased programme spread over at least twenty years, keeping in view the variety of educational patterns, limited resources and the vastness of the country. The pre cent higher secondary pattern in which specialisation begins from class IX, need be abandoned. Along with this measure, a systematic attempt should be made to transfer the pre-university course to secordary schools. The next step would be to increase the total duration by adding a year to the higher secondary course.

University Level Reorganisation

The Commission observes that the principal criticism of higher education is directed, not so much against the pattern of organisation as against comparatively low standards of the degree awarded by the Indian universities in arts, commerce and science. Several factors are responsible in respect of the structural reorganisation of the university stage:

(1) The duration of the first degree should not be less than three years and second degree may be two or three years.

(2) Some universities should start graduate schools with a three year Master's Degree course in the subject which they purpose themselves.

(3) Three year special courses for the first degree need be started in selected and in selected institutions.

(4) Suitable bridges need to be built between the present courses and the new courses of longer duration.

(5) Those who offer the longer course should be given incentives in the form of scholarships.

(6) In Uttar Pradesh, the degree should be lengthened with the establishment of three years graduate schools in selected subjects and in selected universities. The first degree colleges should be raised to three years; to other colleges, fifteen or twenty years.

Efforts made by the NATO : A Council or Educational Research and Training for the Reorganisation of Education. The suggestions of Kothari Commission for the reorganisation of Indian Education were very valuable. On the basis of these suggestion National Council of Educational Research and Training proposed a new scheme of Education which is popularly known as 10 + 2 + 3 scheme. Following were the chief suggestions made by the Council.

15 Year's Degree Course : National Council of Educational Research and Training proposed out the Degree Course should be of 15 years instead of 14 years, in India, period of Secondary Education was in various forms from State to State. In Some States, it is of 12 years while in some other States, it is of 11 years. In some States the Degree Course after the Secondary Education is of 2 Years, while in some it is of 3 years.

National Council of Educational Research and Training proposed that there should be general education for 10 years. After that, there should be 2 year's academic and vocational education and the Degree Course should be of 3 years.

10 Year's General Education : According to the Plans of National Council for Educational Research and Training, period of general education was kept as 10 years. The proposals were that the diversification of the curriculum should not be there within the 10 years of education. The Curriculum for Class 1 and 2 should be as follows:

(1) Mother Tongue, (2) Mathematics, (3) Environmental studies, (4) Practical experience, and (5) Health Education.

The curriculum for classes 3 to 5 should be as follows:

(1) First Language, (2) Mathematics, (3) Environmental Studies, which should include Social Studies as well as General Sciences, (4) Practical Experience, and (5) Health Education and Games.

Syllabus of Class 6 to 8 should be- (1) First language (Mother Tongue), (2) Second Language (where the mother tongue is not Hindi, the second Language should be Hindi), (3) Mathematics, (4) Science, (5) Social Studies (History, Geography, Civics and Economics), (6) Practical experience, and (7) Health Education and Games.

Courses for class 9th and 10th were following :

(l) First Language (mother tongue), (2) Second language, (3) Third language, (4) Mathematics, (5) Scientific subjects (Physics, Chemistry and Biology etc.), (6) Social studies (History, Geography, Civics and Economics), (7) Different Fine Arts, (8) Practical experiences, and (9) Health education.

Abolition of Public Examination System : Under the scheme of National Council of Educational Research and Training, there was no scheme of public examination system. A proposal was, that the existing examination system shall not be useful under the new scheme and so it should be abolished.

No Question of Failures : Under the scheme of National Council of Educational Research and Training, there was no question of any failures. Under these plans there was the system of grades A, B, C, D etc.

Diversification of Curriculum after 10 Years general Education : National Council of Educational Research and Training proposed that there should be diversification of curriculum only after 10 years of general education. Those who have received 10 years general education, 50 per cent should go for the vocational education while the 50 percent should opt for academic education. Those who do not have much interest in the academic education, should opt the vocational and technical education. Those who receive higher grades, should be allowed to proceed for the academic education while those who get inferior grades should be diverted towards the vocational and technical education.

3 Year's Degree Course : Under the Plan of National Council of Educational Research and Training there was provision of 3 Year's Degree Course. In this plan 2 year's Degree Course was totally abolished.

Scheme of 8+4 and Reorganisation of Education : In 1977 there was fall of Congress Government at the Centre and under the Janta Government Dr. P.C. Chunder was entrusted with the job of Education Ministry. At this time, in some States the scheme of 10+2+3 was implemented while it was not implemented in others. Janta Government was of the opinion that the scheme of 10+2+3 was roll of difficulties. It was not practical. Dr. Chunder himself was against 10+2+3 system. He was of the opinion that in this scheme Degree Course shall be of 15 Years. This Period should only be of 4 years. He also criticized the heavy curriculum at the secondary stage under the 10+2+3 years scheme. In July, 1978 there was a conference of Education Ministers of all the States of the country. This Conference proposed for the abolition of 10+2+3 scheme.

The period of secondary education was divided into 3 parts- Primary, Secondary and Higher Secondary. The period of Primary and Secondary Education would be 8 +2 or 7+3. It was for the different states to opt for 8+2 or 7+3 according to their needs and resources. Conference also proposed that the period of Higher Secondary Education should be kept as 2 years. The Conference proposed that the Degree Course shall be of 2 years. However, the Honours Course shall be of 3 years. The Conference of Education Ministers held in 1978 gave certain valuable suggestions but they were not properly implemented.

Re-implementation of 10 + 2 + 3 Scheme : After the fall of the Janta government, it was again felt that the 8 + 2 or 7 + 3 scheme was not useful for all-round development of the country and it should be properly implemented. The present situation is that the structure of education is almost the same as it was proposed by the Wood's Despatch. After the implementation of 10 + 2 + 3 scheme in all the states, it is expected that revolutionary changes shall take place in the sphere of education.

15

Organisational Management

Organisational Body

The organisation of education in India can ordinarily be divided into the following parts:

(i) Pre-primary education.

(ii) Primary education.

(iii) Secondary education.

(iv) Higher or university education.

Pre-primary Education : Pre-primary education is organised for the children of the age 1 to 2 years to 6 years. There are following types of pre-primary schools in India:

(a) Nursery schools.

(b) Kindergarten schools.

(c) Montessorie schools.

(d) Pre-basic schools.

(e) Schools for the poor,

(f) Schools of unitary education and

(g) Child Centres.

The number of Nursery Schools is very less in India, most of the Kindergarten schools are run by Missionary Institutions and mostly, the children of rich people receive education there. Common people are not able to send their children to such schools. The provision of Montessorie schools has been made by Government and many private agencies. For several years the number of Montessorie Schools is increasing day by day. The number of pre-basic schools is also very less. Some schools have also been opened for the education of poor children. There are very few schools of unitary education and the number of such schools is decreasing day by day, although even today many schools of this type are found in villages. Child centres are also making useful contributions in the field of primary education.

Primary Education : According to Article 35 of the Constitution of India. "The State shall endeavour to provide within a period of 10 Years, from the commencing of this Constitution for the free and compulsory education for all children until they complete the age of 14 years, "According to this Article, this work should have been completed by the State by the year 1960. But this objective could not be achieved until now because of economic and administrative Obstacles. However, an endeavour has been made to expand primary education by opening different types of schools. From the point of view of organisation there are following types of primary schools:

(1) Schools organised by District Boards,

(2) Schools organised by Municipal Boards,

(3) Schools organised by Notified and Town Areas,

(4) Schools organised by Cantonment Boards,

(5) Schools organised by Religious Institutions,

(6) Schools organised by Gaon Sabhas,

(7) Schools organised by Private Individuals,

(8) Schools organised by Collective Organisations,

(9) Schools organised by the Government.

Missionary Institutions have also contributed much in the expansion of primary education. District Boards have also performed praiseworthy work for the expansion of primary education. The Government gives grant-in aid to different types of schools to give impetus to the expansion of primary education.

Secondary Education : According to Mudaliar Commission Secondary Education should be for the boys and girls from 11 years to 17 years of age. The Mudaliar Commission has divided the whole system of secondary education into two parts- (1) 3 years of Junior Secondary Education; and (ii) 4 years of higher Secondary Education. It has also been recommended by the Commission that Intermediate classes should be abolished and 11th class should be joined with the high school and the 12th class should be made a pan of the degree course of the university.

Kothari Commission has also divided the secondary education into two parts (i) Secondary, and Higher Secondly. According to the Commission, the period of secondary Education should be 3 years and the period of higher Secondary education should be for 2 Years.

We will now discuss the organisation of the secondary education under the following headings:

Two Forms of Secondary Eduction : At present two forms of secondary education are found in India. In some provinces classes from 6th to 12th have been included under the secondary education, but in most of the provinces classes from 6 to 11 have been included under the Secondary Education. In the provinces where 12th class has not been included under the secondary education and it has been joined with the degree course, the term of which has been extended to 3 years.

Lower Secondary Education : The lower secondary education starts after the completion of the primary education. In Utter Pradesh its term has been fixed for 3 years. This type of education is imparted in Junior High Schools or Senior Basic Schools. The lower secondary education includes classes from 6th to 8th. The boys and girls of nearly 11 or 12 years receive this type of education which is also called the education of Junior Higher Schools. There are 3 types of schools for imparting lower secondary education. The first type of schools are such which impart primary and lower secondary education. The second type of schools are those which impart only lower secondary education. In other words, such schools made provision of education from classes 6th to 8th. They are called Junior High Schools. The third category of schools are such where secondary education is also imparted along with the lower secondary education.

Secondary Schools are of three types:

(1) Government Schools.

(2) Government Aided Schools.

(3) Schools run by Local Bodies.

Higher Education : In India, autonomy has been given to the universities. The government do not interfere in their activities and works.

There are following 3 types of universities:

(i) Affiliated Universities.

(ii) Unitary or Residential Universities:

(iii) Federal Universities.

Affiliated Universities : The jurisdiction of these universities is very vast and the colleges affiliated to it are spread far and wide. The are affiliated to it. The universities inspect and supervise the colleges affiliated to it. The affiliated colleges have to follow and observe the rule of the universities and their curriculum is also determined by the universities. The universities possess the power to affiliate or recognise any college within its jurisdiction. The universities of Agra, Meerut, Kanpur, Calcutta, Bihar, Andhra Gorakhpur, Guwahati, Gujarat, Madras, Nagpur, Osmania, Punjab, Rajasthan Poona and Saugor, etc., are affiliated universities.

Residential Universities : The jurisdiction of the Unitary University is limited to only one centre. They are called Residential Universities. This type of universities themselves organize the whole teaching work. They themselves organise teaching, administration, and management. The universities of Lucknow, Patna, Allahabad, Aligarh, Baroda, Jadavpur, Vishwabharti, etc. are the Unitary or Residential Universities of the country.

Federal Universities : The Federal Universities are those Universities whose jurisdiction is limited to one centre or place but some colleges are also affiliated to them. Each college takes part in the administration of the university and has to surrender some of its freedom and autonomy to the university. All the colleges mutually cooperate with each other under the direction and supervision of the university. Bombay and Jabalpur, etc. are such type of universities. From the point of view of administration, there are two types of universities. Some universities are central universities and the rest of them are autonomous universities having no control of the Central Government. Aligarh, Banaras, etc., are the universities which are under the control of Central Government

Forms of Affiliated Colleges : The colleges which are affiliated to the universities are of two types: Government and non-Government. The Government colleges are directly administered by the Government; whereas there are Managing Committees for the administration of the Non-Government Colleges. The Government exercise some control over these Managing Committees.

Keeping in view the rapid growth in number of the students in the modern period, some colleges have been affiliated with the unitary or residential universities also. For example many colleges such as Lucknow Christian College, Shia College, Kanyakubja College and Manila Degree College, etc. have been affiliated to the Lucknow University. But the university exercises full control over these affiliated colleges. These affiliated colleges have no freedom in respect of examination, etc. and they have to carry on their whole works in accordance with the direction and instructions of the university. The affiliated colleges are also two types. In some affiliated colleges, teaching is imparted only for graduation course whereas some universities have certain affiliated colleges which impart teaching of postgraduate courses also.

The Management

The whole educational administration of India can be studied under the following three headings:

(i) Central Government, (ii) State Government, (iii) Local Bodies.

Central Governments Educational Administration : The following three units are available for the educational administration at the central or National level:

(A) Ministry for Human-Resources and Development.

(B) University Grants Commission.

(C) Central Educational Council for Research and Training.

Ministry for Human Resources and Development : Now, the education is under the concurrent list Minister for Human Resources and Development is the highest authority at the Centre in the field of education. His main task is to plan the educational policies of the country and put them before the Cabinet. There is an Education Department in the Central Secretariat to help him. There is a Deputy Education Minister and separate advisors for Lok Sabha and Rajya Sabha. Under his Ministry, there is deputy secretary, superintendent and other personnels to assist him. There are many departments for education at the central level.

Under the Minister, there is 'Central Advisory Board', 'Central Education' and a 'Foreign Education Bureau'.

University Grants Commissions : University Grants Commission has a President and other members. Amongst them there are three vice-chancellors of universities, four educationalists and two representatives of the Central Government. University Grants Commission has to perform the following chief functions:

1. To advise for the improvement and raising of standard of higher education.
2. To examine the economic needs of the universities and make policies for giving grants to the universities from its own funds.
3. To collect datas regarding the examinations, curricula and research-works of the universities.
4. To have discussion with the educationists, traders,

industrialists and representatives of different private agencies on educational matters.

5. To hold discussions with the vice-chancellors of different universities.

The University Grants Commission is doing a commendable job in the field of education.

Central Educational Council for Research and Training : 'Central Educational Institute' performs the functions of this council. Under it, there are eleven departments and four Regional Colleges. The council works on the problems and the research in the field of education. Kothari Commission suggested that it shall be the apex body for improvement of higher education and shall work in coordination with the education departments of different states. There is provision for a full time Director and an Assistant Director in the Council. The four Regional Colleges attached to the Council give emphasis to multi-propose education and its different departments are in New Delhi.

State Level Educational Administration : Education was included under the State List in the Constitution of India but now it is in the Concurrent List. The structure of the administration of education at the state level is almost same in all the provinces. Only a time difference is found in some States. We will here discuss the administration of education at the State Level as is found in Uttar Pradesh:

Education Minister and other Officers : The Education Department of the State is under a Minister, who is called the Minister of Education. He is appointed by the Governor on the advice of the Chief Minister. There are also Minister of State and Deputy Minister. There are also the following officers to work under the Education Minister at the Secretariat level:

(a) Education Secretary,

(b) Special Secretary,

(c) Joint Secretaries,

(d) Deputy Secretaries, and

(e) Under Secretaries.

With the assistance of different officials, Education Minister puts-up the budget for Education in the legislature. There is also a 'Permanent' Council of the members of the legislature to advice the Education Minister.

Directorate of Education : In Uttar Pradesh, there are three Directors viz.. Director of Higher Education, Director of Secondary Education, and Director of Basic Education. All the Directors are responsible for the administration of their Directorates. In the Directorate there are Additional Directors, Joint Directors, and Deputy Directors to help the Director of Education in the administration of the Department In U.P. there are eight Deputy Directors at the Directorate level:

1. Deputy Director, Finance, 2. Deputy Director, Training, 3. Deputy Director, Urdu, 4. Deputy Director, Women, 5. Deputy Director, Sanskrit, 6. Deputy Director, Camp, 7. Deputy Director, Basic, and 8. Deputy Director, Secondary. There are also Assistant Deputy Directors to perform different functions.

For the convenience of administration, the entire state has been divided in thirteen educational zones viz. Paudi, Faizabad, Meerut, Agra, Bareilly, Muradabad, Varanasi, Gorakhpur, Lucknow, Jhansi, Allahabad, Kanpur and Nainital. There are separate Deputy Directors for each zone, having some districts under their educational purview.

District Inspector of State and other Officials : Each province has been divided into many districts and in each district a District Inspector of Schools is appointed to look after the Educational administration of the district. The District Inspector of Schools are the highest officials of the Education Department of the District Under them, there are Assistant District Inspectors of Schools at some places.

Educational System of Autonomous Bodies : For the educational systems of the cities and villages there are some local institutions. City Corporations are established in big cities. In these city Corporations, there is a separate officer for Education Department and all the primary schools of the city work under his control. This education officer works under the control and supervision of the Executive Officer and Chairman of the Municipality. In rural areas, the organisation of the primary education is made by the District Boards. The District Boards have been conferred wide power in the field of educational administration. The President of the District Board and his Education Committee make provision of appointment of the teachers and the maintenance of the Schools.

In this connection, the Board has to work in accordance with the advise of the District Inspector of Schools. The main responsibility of the District Board is in the field of primary education. As far as the secondary and higher education are concerned they are under the control and supervision of the State Government.

16

College Education

The Backdrop

The system of higher education, which we see today in our country, started after the advent of British in India. The development of this education can be conveniently studied under following four heads:

(a) Periods of Colleges (from beginning of the British rule to 1857),

(b) Period of the first University (from 1857 to 1917)

(c) Establishment of new Universities (from 1917 to 1947)

(d) Higher Education in Independent India

Colleges in Colonial Rule

The higher education was in a very disorganised condition at the time when the Britishers established their authority in India. The British rulers established many Government and private colleges till 1857. The more prominent of such colleges were Banaras Sanskrit College, Hindu College, Calcutta Christian College, Madras and Agra College. There were 23 colleges of general education - Medical Colleges, 1 Civil Engineering School in the year 1857.

First Indian University

Accepting the recommendations of Wood's Despatch of 1855 the Universities of Calcutta, Bombay and Madras were established in 1857 on the model of London University. All universities performed the functions of only conducting examinations. Emulating the examples of these universities, Punjab and Allahabad Universities were established in 1882 respectively. The college education received a great impetus during 1901-02. The number of colleges which were 68 in 1881-82 increased to 179 in 1901-02. University education made a great progress during the reign of Lord Curzon, Viceroy of India. In order to give a fillip to the university education, be appointed the Indian University Commission in 1902 in order to enquire into the conditions and working of the Indian Universities and make necessary suggestions. Two years later, Indian Universities Act was passed. This act brought about many important changes in the organisation. Jurisdiction, powers and administration, etc. of the Universities. Consequently, the expansion of the university education was checked for some time. However, it must be admitted that this act went a long way to improve and reform the conditions and standards of the contemporary universities and colleges.

Establishment of New Universities

After the establishment of Allahabad University in 1887, no new university was established for a period of 30 years. However, the number of colleges, increased to 185 during this period. In view of the increase in the number of colleges, it was felt that 5 universities at Calcutta, Madras, Bombay, Punjab and Allahabad were incapable to cope with the increased work. Hence, it was thought necessary to increase the number of universities. The Government Resolution of 1913 emphasised the establishment of new universities. The Calcutta University Commission, 1917 also advised the establishment of new universities. Consequently, following universities were established by the year 1947. Mysore

University (1916), Patna University (1917), Banaras Hindu University (1917), Osmania University (1918), Aligarh Muslim University (1920), Dacca University (1920), Lucknow University (1920), Delhi University (1922), Nagpur University (1923), Andhra University (1926), Agra University (1927), Annamalai University (1929), Travancore University (1937), Utkal University (1943), Saugoi University (1947) and Rajputana University (1947).

Post-independence University and Higher Education

At present higher and university education is imparted through arts, science and commerce and professional colleges, research institutions and institutions deemed to be universities under the Universities Grants Commission Act, 1956.

In addition to Central universities, State Universities and their affiliated colleges, Indira Gandhi Open University and other open universities are doing a commendable job in the field of higher education.

It is clear from the above discussion that the expansion of higher education has received a great impetus after independence. However, it may be mentioned here that the expansion of higher education has not taken place in accordance with the new needs and interests of the country. Generally, the policy of the government has been to increase the number of institutions of higher education rather than to aim at the qualitative progress of higher education. Besides this, there are multilateral problems of higher education, which have not attracted the proper attention of the Government and hence special efforts have not been made so far to remove the defects of higher education. It is good that after the declaration of the Education Policy of 1986, more emphasis is being given to the specialization in higher education.

Difficulties and Remedial Measures

The problems of higher and University education in India is nothing but the problems of Indian society in general. If we wish to establish a society based on the principles of democratic socialism, we will have to reorient the entire educational structure.

But unfortunately there is still a lag between our ideal and reality. Our universities have not been able to shake off the heavy load of bookish learning. The Kothari Commission has very aptly quoted Sir Eerie Ash by on the real condition of Indian universities:

> "Looking at Indian universities a century after, their foundation, one cannot but help feel that they have failed to adopt themselves sufficiently to the vast and unique opportunities which surround them; they seem to have lost enthusiasm and initiative under the crashing problems which have beset them. Despite three major commissions they have not been able to extricate themselves from their own brief history. With a few notable exceptions they remain examining bodies. As universities multiply in number, their academic standards, relative to those elsewhere, do not improve... the universities remain alien implantations, not integrated into the new India...

This is one reason why, to the observer from outside, the Indian intellectually displaced person nostalgically treasuring his threads of communication with England... Universities have responded to reply to the challenge of Asiatic culture." The main problems of higher and university education in India are as follows:

Far from Goal

One of the chief problems that confronts the higher education in India is its aimlessness. Most of the students are receiving higher education in India without having any definite aim.

Change in Aims : It is most essential that the students receiving higher education must have some definite aims before starting higher education. The aims of higher education should be changed. While describing the aims of University education in 1952, Newmen remarked, "if a practical end must be assigned to a university course, then I say it is training of good members of society." The University Education Commission visited many universities and made the following remark in this connection: "We are everywhere struck by a deep general awareness of the importance of higher education for national welfare and uneasy sense of the inadequacy of the present pattern. The universities as the marks of the future, cannot persist in the old pattern. With the increasing complexity of society and its shifting pattern universities have to change their objectives and methods, if they are to function effectively in our national life."

The University Education Commission has determined many aims of higher education. We have discussed it earlier while dealing with the recommendations and suggestions of the University Education Commission. The aims are no doubt praiseworthy but most of them are based on idealism. It may also be pointed out that these aims have neither been achieved since 1949 to this date nor are they expected to be ever achieved. The aims determined by the University Education Commission are very good but it is not easy to provide facilities, so that the said aims may be achieved.

Curriculum with Flaws

The curricula of the institutions of our higher education are full of many defects. The subjects of study in most of colleges are old and out of date. The curriculum fails to fulfil the interests of different types of students and consequently their intellectual development is checked. Radhakrishnan Commission has remarked, "A Curriculum which had validity in the Vedic period or the renaissance cannot continue unaltered in the 20th century."

Some Suggestions : As pointed out earlier the curricula of our universities are not in accordance with the interest of different types of students. In order to remove this defect, it is necessary that there should be diversification of courses in curriculum of the universities in the same way as determined by the Mudaliar Commission for the curriculum of the secondary schools. The curriculum of the universities should be flexible so that it may be made in accordance with the changing conditions and need of the changing society. In this connection, the University Education Commission had rightly remarked, "Educational systems are built for the time and not for all time. There are no changeless ways of educating human nature. A curriculum which, vitally in the

Vedic period or the renaissance cannot continue unaltered in the 20th century."

Educational Specialisation

In university education, emphasis is given on the specialisation in different subjects. Consequently, when the students complete the university education they acquire special knowledge and skill in some particular subjects but their viewpoint remains unbalanced and narrow but they do not become completely educated in real sense. Explaining its reason, K.G. Saiydain remarks, "there is certain narrow, unimaginative type of specialization which results in the science being complacency ignorant of arts and poetry and social and political problems, and arts students having no appreciation of how science and scientific technique have transformed the world in which they are living."

Suggestions : It is necessary that different branches and experiences of knowledge should be interlinked and harmonious relations established among them. The balanced development of the mind of the students will not be possible unless and until they experience the integration of knowledge and experience. It may, therefore, be suggested that along with the education of art and science in secondary schools, colleges and universities, provision should also be made for imparting general education so that the students of arts and literature may acquire the knowledge of the subjects of science and the students of science and commerce may acquire the knowledge of the subjects of art and literature. Thus, the defect of narrow specialisation can be removed by establishing harmony between general education and specialisation. This will also help the development of personality of the students and they will become able and dutiful citizen.

The subjects and curriculum of the general education should be selected in accordance with students of particular fields. It is heartening to note that University Education Commission has suggested the inclusion of general education in the curriculum of the universities. This suggestion has been accepted by some universities, namely Aligarh, Andhra, Banaras, Baroda, Jadavpur,

Karnataka, Kerala, Mysore, Poona, Rajasthan, Saugor, S.N.D.T., Bombay, Sri Vainkateshwara, Utkal and Vishwabharti.

Need of Counselling and Guidance

In the institutions of our higher education, there is no provision for giving proper guidance and counselling to the students. In the absence of such a provision, the students select their courses either according to their own choice or with the advice of some inexperienced persons. Consequently, many students select subjects which are either against their interest and tendencies or they are not capable of studying those subjects.

The Provisions

It is necessary that in the educational institutions of higher education, there should be a provision of experienced and trained persons to provide guidance and counselling to the students from beginning to the end. The suggestions given by Mudaliar Commission and Kothari Commission in this connection hold good for the educational institutions for the higher education also.

Low Teaching Standards

The standard of teaching in our colleges and universities is very low. In this connection in his book, 'A new deal for our Universities', K.R.S. Iyenger has rightly remarked, "Our standards, whether in scholarship or teaching, were never very high or exacting, are now fast racing to the bottom." It is very difficult to raise this standard as pointed out by Dr. S.N. Mukerjee, "Academic standards once lowered are not retrievable and Gresham's law is applicable to them."

Suggestions : Many suggestions can be given for raising the standard of teaching. The more prominent of such suggestions are increase in the salaries of teachers; not more than 18 hours of teaching work in a week; improvement in the condition of the services of teachers; provision of tutorial classes; well-organised libraries and laboratories and encouragement to debates and discussions. The Kothari Commission has made some praiseworthy recommendations in this connection such as giving professional training to junior lecturers, organisation of Reorientation Courses for new lecturers etc.

Medium of Instruction: English

More than 50 years have passed since the attainment of independence but as yet English continues to be the medium of instruction in the institutions of higher education. Our subservience to the British for a long time has created so much reverence and love for English that we still find ourselves unable to replace English as a medium of instruction with some other Indian language or national language. It is a matter of great regret that due consideration has not been given to the loss which English as a medium of instruction is causing to our youth.

Federal Language as Medium of Instructions : It has become expedient that English should be replaced as a medium of instructions as soon as possible. The University Education Commission has suggested the regional language or federal language. Most of the universities of the country have been endeavouring to give practical shape to the suggestion of making federal language as medium of instructions so that it would be convenient for the persons of different States of the country to establish contacts among themselves. It would be proper and convenient to conduct the examination of Indian Services in the Federal language.

However, we should not totally ignore English. We should remember the words of Dr. Radha Krishnan, "We might have banished Englishmen, but not their language, and English is not the monopoly of Englishmen."

Defective Examination System

The present examination system of our universities has been subjected to severe criticism by Indian and foreign educationists. All the Committees and Commissions that have been appointed so far have thrown special light on the defects in the prevalent examination system. Indian University Commission in 1902 pointed out in its report, "The greater evil from which university education in India suffers is, that teaching is subordinated to examination, and not examination to teaching." The University Education Commission of 1949 also pointed out, "If we are to suggest one single reform in university education, it should be that of examination."

***Suggestions* :** The present examination system can be reformed by including scientific methods. In our examination system, examination of students by progressive tests and determination of 70, 55 and 40 per cent marks for awarding first, second and third division to the students is necessary. Besides this, it has also been suggested that abolition of external examination, start of internal assessment or evaluation system and training of teachers with the new system of assessment or evaluation etc. may go a long way to remove many of the defects to the present examination system.

Breaking Rules and Regulations

The problem of indiscipline among the students has assumed so much seriousness and complications that it is eating the very vitals of our educational system. Prof. N.K. Siddhant, former Vice Chancellor of Calcutta University has mentioned the following types of activities coming within the indiscipline- (1) Financial irregularity, (2) Minor misconduct, (3) Disorderly misconduct, (4) Theft and burglary, (5) Sex misconduct, (6) Misuse of privilege, and (7) Cheating in examination. As pointed out rightly by Prof. N.K. Siddhant in his book 'Indian University Administration', "The problem of maintaining discipline in the seats of higher education is assuming greater importance every day."

***Suggestions* :** According to Prof. Siddhant the best way of solving the problem of indiscipline is to divert the activities of the young students into healthy channels including sports, games, cooperative living in hostels, self-management of masses debates and symposia. However, the lead in all these matters should be given by the teachers themselves.

Prof. Siddhant had also made the following suggestions for solving the problem of indiscipline among the students:

1. The statistics of different types of indiscipline in each centre of higher education should be maintained.
2. The family and social life of the students and records where the student has studied earlier should be studied.
3. The cause of each crime committed by the students should be discovered.

Interview of indisciplined students should be arranged with an expert who should be acquainted with the seriousness of the crime and should try to explain them that acts of indiscipline and crime which the students were committing were not proper. It has rightly been suggested by the Education Commission that not only the teachers but the students, their guardians and parents, society, Government and the political parties will have to work in order to solve the problem of indiscipline among the students. Besides this, the defects of educational system should also be solved at the earliest possible time. Vice Chancellor's Conference of 1969 suggested, "It is desirable that student is exposed to and acquainted with national development programmes, secularism, national integration, the constitution, and citizenship." Radhakrishnan Commission was of the view, "great literature sets fire to the highest emotion and promotes the highest ideal and aspiration. A study of great books that fills us with hope is essential in university course." Kothari Commission, while giving the various suggestions for removing the indiscipline remarked, "It is necessary to remember that the responsibility for the situation is not unilateral it is not merely that of the students or parents or teachers or state governments, or the political parties, but multilateral. All of them share it."

Societies of Students

The student-societies in educational institutions of higher education also pose serious problems before us. The harms which these student-societies cause to the students are well known. The workers of these societies interfere in each and every work of the college. If the teacher, principal or managers of the college do any work which is against their wish but they want that the appointment of the teachers, their teaching work and all the policies connected with the college should be done with their advice. Thus, these student- societies prove to be scourge for colleges.

Registration of Student's Society : The Indian Educationists are not against the student societies. On the contrary, they want that these societies should be organised because they provide opportunities of exhibition of intellectual powers of the students, develop their qualities of leadership and develop their homely relation. But mostly these societies start working in the wrong direction. In this connection V.K.R.V. Rao has pointed out "Unfortunately, we have in our universities certain very undesirable elements, many of whom are in contact with embassies, planning trips abroad and obtaining money from outside sources. All these have a demoralising effect on the student-community and should be stopped. Again, I should like to suggest that legislation be introduced for the registration of university or college societies to ensure that they observe certain rules in elections, method of keeping accounts and similar other things."

Almost all the above problems have attracted the attention of the University Education Commission, which has made many suggestions to solve these problems. Most of these suggestions have been accepted by the Government and many of them have already been implemented. It may, therefore, be hoped that after being free from the present problems, the higher education will make the complete development of the personality of the youths and by developing their intellectual and physical powers will make them able citizens of the country.

It is a matter of great regret that in the present scientific period, when the standard of higher education should be very high, the standard of higher education in India is declining day by day. K.R.Y. Iyengar is of the opinion, "our standards whether in scholarship or teaching never were very high or exacting are now fast racing to the bottom." There are many reasons for this decline in the standards of our education. Following are some of the main causes which are responsible for the decline of standards of higher education in India.

Number of Students Increasing

The development of education in India is taking place rapidly. The number of students receiving higher education is constantly increasing and it is likely to increase more in the near future. Although the number of students is rapidly increasing, yet it has not been possible to provide them with necessary facilities. The number of able teachers is also not increasing with the same proportion. University Grants Commission is of the opinion, "If increasing number of students continue to be admitted in our universities without corresponding expansion of facilities, there is great risk of the academic standards being impaired further."

Suggestion : In order to solve the above-mentioned problem, Kothari Commission has recommended that selective system of admissions should be adopted in the universities. The number of students in the educational institutions should be determined keeping in view the facilities available in the institutions concerned and the number of teachers.

The university should prescribe necessary qualification for admission and the best students should be selected from among them desiring to seek admission in the universities. The new and modern methods should be adopted while selecting the students. Until these methods are fully developed, the percentage of marks secured by the students in pre-university examinations should be made the basis of their admissions. Each university should establish a Board of University Admission which should solve all the problems concerning admission. In order to help the students to select different subjects of higher education, the University Grants Commission should establish Central Testing Organisation.

Lack of Basic Facilities

Yet another reason for the low standard of education in universities is that in universities the students do not have the same faculties which are provided to the students of the universities in other countries of the world. The students have to face the shortage of books. The libraries of the universities are not properly equipped and are not able to make available all the necessary books to the students. The environment and the condition in which our universities are imparting education is likely to lower the standard of education. In many degree colleges, there is not even proper seating arrangements for the students. There are thousands of such degree colleges, which do not possess even playgrounds. In such conditions, the lowering of the standard of the education is quite natural.

Suggestions : To solve this problem, a high level committee should be appointed for providing necessary facilities to the students. The Government of India and the State Governments have been making every possible endeavour to provide grants in order to remove the difficulties of the students and to equip properly the libraries, etc. But it may be made clear that only Government's efforts alone will not solve this problem. The non-government institutions should also come forward and make as much contributions possible in this field. It is the sacred duty of the rich class of the society to spend as much as possible money to raise the standard of higher education. In progressive countries like America, non-government institutions contribute a lot in the field of higher education. The rich class and non-government institutions of India should also emulate the example of America. If the big capitalists and industrialist come forward to make their contribution in this field considering it as their sacred duty, this problem can be solved to a great extent

Teacher's Poor Condition

The poor condition of the teachers is yet another reason which is responsible for the low standard of higher education. The teachers of degree colleges and universities get so less salaries that they adopt other means in order to meet their expenses. Consequently, they are not able to devote themselves heart and soul into the teaching work. A teacher who is always busy in finding means to meet his expenditure cannot be expected to render much help to the students in research work.

Suggestions : It is necessary and expedient to improve the financial conditions of the teachers for raising the standard of teaching. The Kothari Commission has made many important suggestions in this connection. The Commission had recommended the salaries of the teachers at different stages. The Mehrotra Commission has recommended new grades for university teachers.

Besides the increase in their salaries the teacher should also be provided with other types of financial facilities. The teachers doing extraordinary work at the University stage should be given promotions. The qualification and the salaries of the teachers of the affiliated colleges as well as the universities should be the same.

Terms and Conditions

Another reason for the low standard of education is that the teachers have been burdened with too much work. The condition of working of the teachers are such that they are not able to perform the teaching work properly. At the university stage where prominence is given to the research work, it is completely improper to burden them with too much work. Kothari Commission has remarked, "There is much serious concern that in many places there is too much teaching but relatively too little of good teaching."

Suggestions : In order to remove the above mentioned defects, it is necessary to reduce the hours of working of the teachers. Besides this, they should be encouraged to devote their utmost time in the research work. Each teacher should be given one year leave with salary within a period of five years of service for increasing his knowledge and for travelling to foreign countries. They should have complete freedom in performing the teaching functions. Only teaching work should be taken from them. It is very bad practice to burden the teachers with administrative and other works of educational institutions. The suggestion made by Kothari Commission in respect of the promotion of teachers, improvement in the conditions of their service and other works, etc. are very important and should be implemented in all institutions of higher studies.

Teacher-students Gap

Another reason for the decline in the standard of higher education is the fact that there is a wide gulf between the students and the teachers. The number of students in each class is so much that the teacher is not able to recognise each student with much less talk for establishing close contact. Consequently, there exists a wide gulf between the teachers and the students. While in western countries the students and the teachers work together like a family and perform some type of functions in their interests, in India it appeals that the interests of the students and teachers are separate from each other.

Suggestions : In order to establish close contact between the teachers and students, it is necessary to adopt tutorial system. Besides reducing the number of students in each class, at different hours 4 or 5 students should meet a teacher and hold discussions with him in respect of his subject. Debates and discussions should also be organised. These debates and discussions help to establish close relations between the teachers and the students, and the students are able to increase their knowledge with the help of the teachers.

Defective examination system is also one of the chief causes leading to the decline in the standard of university education. It was pointed out by Radha Krishnan Commission "If only one suggestion is made to reform university education, it should be in respect of present examination system. Too much importance is given to the essay type of examinations. Consequently, the students think that they will achieve success by studying some selective questions and so they do not devote themselves heart and soul into the studies throughout the year. Most of the students study only selected questions and thence the standard of education is constantly declining. Besides this, the number of pass mark is so low that they secure it very easily."

Suggestions : To reform the present examination system, it is necessary to give less prominence to the essay type examination and shift emphasis on internal assessment or evaluation. In place of essay type examination, tests would be more useful. So far students securing 60 per cent, 45 or 48 per cent and 33 per cent marks are awarded first, second and third divisions respectively. The above mentioned percentage of marks should be increased to 70, 55 and 40 respectively.

Party-politics and Groupism

The prevalence of group party-politics is yet another cause which is responsible for the decline in the standard of education in Indian universities. Different political parties endeavour to make their influence in the University. In every province, there are some particular persons who are ever eager to establish their control over universities. Consequently, because of party- politics such teachers are appointed who are not properly suitable for teaching work. The groupism of the teachers also lowers the standard of teaching work. The teachers remain busy in group party-politics and they do not get sufficient time to throw themselves heart and soul into the teaching work.

Suggestions : The need for keeping the colleges and universities away from party-politics need not be over-emphasised. All the political parties and scholars consider this problem seriously. We should think that the future of our country depends upon the progress of higher education. If the standard of higher education goes on constantly declining, we cannot make progress in any field. The conferences should be organised for keeping the universities away from party politics. There should be a free discussion in these conferences over this problem. Thereafter, a date should be fixed on which the suggestions should be submitted in this connection.

Government should implement the suggestions of the said conferences. As far as possible, the politicians should not be appointed in the universities. The debates and discussions should also be organised. These debates and discussions help to establish close relations between the teachers and the students, and the students are able to increase their knowledge with the help of the teachers.

Last but not the least, the growing indiscipline among the

students is also one of the chief causes responsible for the decline in standard of higher education. This indiscipline among these causes are the social and economic difficulties; growing unemployment; non availability of educational facilities, group party-politics; lack of interesting subjects in the curriculum etc.

Suggestions : To resolve this problem, Kothari Commission has suggested that not only the teachers but the students, parents and guardian, society, Government and political parties should work together to solve this problem. Such type of programmes should be organised in colleges and universities that may keep the students busy in constructive work and keep them away from party politics. Every possible endeavour should be made to solve the problem of unemployment.

Unless and until the problem of indiscipline is satisfactorily solved in the colleges and universities, it would be wishful thinking to hope for an improvement in the standard of our higher education. Kothari Commission is of the opinion, "whatever else education may or may not aim at doing, it should at least strive to enable youngmen and women to learn and practice civilized norms of behaviour."

It is explicit from the above discussion, there are many reasons which are responsible for the decline in the standard of higher education. It is not only necessary but also expedient to check the decline in the standard of education and every possible effort should be made to improve the existing standard of higher education. If we intend to come at par with other advanced countries of the world then it should be our sacred task to work sincerely to raise the standard of higher education.

similar [illegible] of the city [illegible] to [illegible] these [illegible] social and economic [illegible] availability of educational facilities [illegible] in the [illegible]

[illegible] problem [illegible] Kerala [illegible] has suggested that not only [illegible] and [illegible] social [illegible] and political [illegible] [illegible]

[illegible] said the problem of [illegible] would [illegible] [illegible] to [illegible] education [illegible]

[illegible] which [illegible] in the standard of higher education [illegible] and every [illegible] should [illegible] the existing standard of higher education [illegible] with [illegible] of the world [illegible] should [illegible] to raise the standard of higher education.

17

School Education

Importance of Education

Secondary Education has a vital role to play in any programme of education for the community. It provides teachers for both elementary and adult education. It also prepares pupils for the universities and other institutions of higher education. Besides, it is the stage which in all countries marks the completion of education for the vast majority. Even the minority which goes for higher education can not take full advantage of the under opportunities offered by the universities unless they have received their grounding in a system of sound secondary education.

Set-up of Secondary Schools

Secondary school is the gift of modern education. This type of schools were not prevalent in ancient and medieval India. This type of schools were started in India for the first time by the foreign missionaries and thereafter, by the Indian education-lovers. These efforts were started in the end of 18th century and in the 19th century. The chief purpose of the establishment of secondary schools in India was to teach English to Indians.

From 1835 to 1854 : The report of Lord Macaulay which was accepted by Lord William Bentick, the then Viceroy of India in 1835, paved the way for the expansion of secondary education.

From 1854 to 1904 : Wood's Despatch also contributed much in the development of secondary education in India. It was suggested in the said Despatch that Indians should be made acquainted with the books written by European writers. Wood's Despatch has also credit, of starting the grant-in-aid system, which further encouraged the establishment of secondary schools.

By this time, certain defects had crept in secondary education. In order to remove these defects, Hunter Commission suggested in 1882, that the education of High School should be devised into 2 parts (a) 'A' Course which should be for those students, who wish to take admission in universities to receive higher education and (b) 'B' Course, which should be made more practical and which should prepare young men for professional and non-literary works. Neither the Government nor the people paid any heed to the recommendation of Hunter Commission. Consequently, the secondary education continued to expand in its former way. This process of expansion continued from 1882 to 1902. There were 3,916 secondary schools in 1902. The number of secondary schools increased to 5,124 in 1902.

From 1904 to 1917 : Indian Universities Act of 1904 empowered the universities which desired to send their students for matriculation examination, thus, a restriction was imposed upon the secondary schools because they could not send their students for matriculation examination without obtaining recognition from the University. Consequently, many undesirable secondary schools had to be closed down and new schools were established after considering all the facts and circumstances thus created.

From 1917 to 1947 : The Calcutta University Commission which was appointed in 1917 made a study of the defects of the secondary education and arrived at a conclusion that unless and until the secondary education would not be reorganized after removing its defects, it would not be possible to make any sort of reform in the University education. The said Commission recommended the establishment of a Board of Secondary and Intermediate Education in each Province. This was a novel thing, which was made for the first time by this Commission.

In 1929, Hartog Committee accepted that as compared to the education of common people, secondary education had made more progress. However, the Committee added that because of large number of failures in matriculation examination, the rate of wastage in secondary education was very high. In 1936-37, Abbott and Wood suggested in their report that upto the stage of High School, Indian language should not be given in literary form. The Sargent Report of 1944 also made many important suggestions in regard to secondary education, such as high school course should be made of 6 years, no students below the age of 11 years should be admitted in high school.

In spite of the suggestions made by the above mentioned Committees and Commissions, no restrictions were imposed on secondary education and it continued to expand in an unrestricted manner. The number of secondary schools, which was 2,953 in 1916-17 increased to 4,883 in 1947-48.

Secondary Education in Independent India

Several Committees and Commissions have been appointed in the post independence era. The prominent among them are being described below:

Tara Chand Committee 1948 : One of the important suggestion of the Committee was that secondary school should be multilaterally but keeping in view the local conditions and circumstances unilateral schools should also be encouraged. This Committee also recommended that a Commission should be appointed in order to investigate the problems of secondary education.

University Education Commission, 1948-49 : The chief aim of this Commission was to investigate and make suggestion in regard to university education. But it also considered different aspects of the secondary education and made many important suggestions.

In the opinion of the University Education Commission, the secondary education was the weakest link in the whole structure of education. The Commission recommended that students should be admitted in the university only after completing 12 years of study in school or intermediate college.

Secondary Education Commission, 1952-53 : As a result of the suggestions of Tara Chand Committee and Central Education Advisory Board, Secondary Education Commission was appointed to study in detail the different aspects of secondary education and to make different suggestions to reform it. We have already discussed in detail in an earlier chapter the different suggestions made by this Commission to reform secondary education in India.

Secondary Education Development

The development of secondary education has received an impetus after the attainment of independence. At present, secondary education is free in Andhra Pradesh, Gujarat, Karnataka, Uttar Pradesh, Kerala, Tamil Nadu, Andaman & Nicobar Islands, Arunachal Pradesh and Lakshadweep and in Government institutions in Jammu and Kashmir, Nagaland, Dadra and Nagar Haveli and Pondicherry. It is free for girls in Madhya Pradesh, Manipur, Orissa, Rajasthan and Tripura.

Under the new educational policy of 1986 emphasis was laid on the new educational policy and for the formal education National Open Schools were established. In 1992 a new workshop scheme was introduced.

Open Schools are contributing a lot in the field of secondary education. By the end of 1992-93, 305 Navodya Vidyalaya came into existence. 17 more were to be established in 1993-94. It was proposed that by the end of 1996, there shall be atleast one Navodya Vidyalaya in every district.

Difficulties and Remedial Measures

Many defects have crept in the secondary education that if they are not solved within a short period of time, the progress of Indian education will receive a great set-back. We will now attempt to discuss the different problems of secondary education and their solution.

Aimlessness : One of the chief problems of secondary education is its aimlessness. It would not be improper to remark that the aim of education is independent. India is the same which was before independence. Education is acquired only with the aim so that the students may get employment or for getting admission in an institution of higher education, which is also sought with the aim of getting employment

Definite Aims : In order to make the secondary education successful and effective, it is necessary to determine its aim. So long as the aims of this education are not property determined, its utility will continue to be doubtful. Now, the question arises what should be the aim of secondary education? The first and foremost requirement for this is that the secondary education should be made an independent unit and not complimentary of higher education. Thereafter, the following aims of secondary education should be determined:

(i) To make students skilled in some work after completion of their education.

(ii) To increase their professional and productive powers.

The secondary Education Commission determined the following aims of Secondary Education:

(a) Development of democratic citizens

(b) Increase in professional skill

(c) Development of personality

(d) Development of leadership.

Unsuitable Curriculum : The curriculum of secondary schools is unsuitable because of being single track. All the students have to study one prefixed curriculum. The students do not get opportunity to select subjects according to their interests and desires. Besides this, their curriculum is not related to the environment and practical life. We observe that many political, economic and social changes are taking place in the country but our education in general and secondary education in particular has failed to keep pace with the changes. The curriculum does not appear to be related with the practical life. The pupils read the traditional curriculum, without interest, understanding or appreciation. Their chief aim is to get through the examinations.

Interesting and Diversified Curriculum : In order to remove the defects of the curriculum, it is necessary that it should be extended in different trades, professions and agricultural subjects should be included in it and the help of the experts should be taken in order to cater the interest and aptitude of the students. With these aims in view, the Secondary Education Commission recommended the diversification of courses and in this connection made the following suggestions:

(i) The curriculum should be such as may develop the different abilities and capabilities of the students.

(ii) The curriculum should be diversified and flexible so that it may be according to the needs and interests of the students.

(iii) The curriculum should be closely related to the social life of the students.

(iv) The curriculum should be such so that the students may not only be encouraged to work but also to make proper use of leisure.

(v) The curriculum should not include such subjects as are not related to each other. Although the subjects of the curriculum should be interlinked with each other.

Indiscipline : Indiscipline is yet another main problem of the modern secondary education. It is not proper to accuse only the students of being indisciplined. In fact, the present educational system, examination system, aimless education etc. are the factors which are responsible for the indiscipline among the students. It may be mentioned here that the indiscipline among the students is increasing so far that if something is not done to remedy this evil, it will not only be harmful for the students but would jeopardise the whole education system.

There are various factors involved in the causation of indiscipline. Chief among them are as follows: (1) Loss of higher spiritual values, (2) Political changes, (3) Defective mode of examination, (4) Wretched economic condition of teachers.

Besides this, the role of teachers is also of paramount importance. According to Prof. Humayun Kabir, "If education trains the future citizen, it also determines the shape of future society, the value of such education depends upon the character and competence of the teachers who impart it that is why the fate of society depends on the quality of its teachers. It is no exaggeration to say that incompetent and dissatisfied teachers undermine the very foundation of society.

Suggestions : As pointed out earlier, students alone cannot be held responsible for the growing indiscipline among them. Those who hold students alone responsible for this evil, have not cared to consider all the aspects of this problem. Political movements are, to a great extent if not wholly, responsible for the growing indiscipline among the students. Low social values have also influenced the students as the members of the society. Besides this, economically hard pressed teachers have left thinking as to which direction the students society is proceeding to. In addition to this, obscene films, film songs, racialism, favouritism, indifferent attitude of the persons, etc. have also led to the growing indiscipline among the students.

If we want to remove widespread indiscipline among the students, we will have to give proper attention to the above mentioned factors which are responsible for growing indiscipline among the students. This herculian task can be achieved only when the government, people and guardian jointly take active and constructive measures in this connection.

Undesirable Growth of Private Schools : After the attainment of independence, there has been an unprecedented increase in the number of secondary schools in the name of expansion of education. But this increase has not only proved to be undesirable but has proved to be scourge for the students, teachers and ultimately for the country. Most of these schools are the private properties of some particular caste, political party or capitalists and casteism, favouritism, etc., are rampant in these schools. We can easily have idea of the discipline of such schools, standard of teaching and the character of the students and the teachers.

Abolition of Private Schools : Private schools are a slur on the forehead of secondary education. It is necessary to remove this slur as soon as possible. Only the Government is capable of performing this work and nationalisation of education is the only way through which (his slur can be removed. But at present, nationalisation of the entire secondary education does not appear practicable. However government can regulate the management and administration of private institutions. In this connection the Raghukul Tilak committee had recommended that in order to improve the management of private institutions, the managing committees must include one representative of teachers and three other members nominated by the Education Department

Low Standard of Teaching : Low standard of teaching is also one of the chief problems of the secondary education. Government has mainly concentrated their attention towards the expansion of education and have not devoted their proper attention towards the qualitative progress of education. The teachers do not get sufficient salaries to meet their daily needs and requirements. Unless the teachers are given proper facilities and are given the place of respect in society, we cannot hope good performance. Besides this, there are many schools which do not have sufficient funds to make proper provision of building and other necessary things connected with education. These shortcomings have also adversely affected the standard of teaching.

Suggestion : To talk of raising the standard of teaching only by spending the money is to build a castle on the sand. The standard of teaching can be raised by taking into consideration many factors, which have been mentioned earlier. The Government should appoint such Inspectors, who would make their contributions in this connection and should make necessary suggestions. Besides this, the teachers should be sent to training colleges from time to time in order to acquaint them with latest teaching methods. It is also necessary that only enthusiastic persons and the persons who wish to dedicate themselves for the service of the society should be selected for the teaching work. They should also be encouraged from time to time by giving them rewards for their meritorious work in this connection.

Defective Examination System

The system of examination of our secondary education is full of defects. There is the domination of matriculation examination over the whole secondary education. A school, its teachers and its students are tested in accordance with their success in the examination. Examination is not the real test of knowledge of the student and the working capacity of the teacher. According to S.N. Mukherjee "Worse than India's Communality ridden, social and political system is her examination-ridden educational system. In fact, the matriculation Examination dominates the entire work of our secondary schools. The prestige of a school depends entirely upon matriculation results and very little on real education merits of the institution."

Required Change

The suggestions made by the Secondary Education Commission are really praiseworthy. The Commission made the following suggestions to reform the present examination system:

(i) Number of external examinations should be reduced.

(ii) The method of the questions asked in the examination should be changed in such a way so that they may not remain merely essay type.

(iii) While making the final evaluation of the work of the students along with the internal examinations, proper importance be given to the periodical tests, and school records.

(iv) The public examination of the students should be taken only after the completion of the whole curriculum of the secondary schools.

If the suggestions made by the Secondary Education Commission are properly implemented, the defects of the modern examination system can be removed.

Absence of Living in Community

There is absence of well-organised community life in the secondary schools of the modern period. The main reason for this is that the sports and games, excursions, physical exercises, social activities etc. which may establish "lose contacts among the students, are not organised in the schools. Besides this, there is total absence of religious and moral education in the schools. Thus, the schools of modern time have just become a factory whose aim is to make the students pass the matriculation examination.

Centralised Community

The schools should be the centres of community life. Mudaliar Commission has rightly remarked, "School is a small community within a large community and the attitude, values and modes of behaviour which have currency in national life are bound to be reflected in the school." In fact, school has an idealist epitome of community life. Hence, schools should be a place which should reflect the elements of all the useful activities of the community.

Lack of Communication

For many years, our secondary education is single track. Neither is there diversification in its curriculum, nor has it given any importance to vocationalisation. The form of curriculum which was fixed by the British Rulers keeping in view their own interest generally continues to be the same even today.

Provision for Communication

There is great need of vocationalisation of secondary education. The Secondary Education Commission has remarked, "Secondary Education should be vocationalised in a large measure and enrolment in vocational course rest to 20 per cent of total enrolment at the lower secondary stage and 50 per cent of total enrolment at the higher secondary stage by 1986." Kothari Commission also suggested, "The link between education and productivity can be forged through vocationalisation of education especially at the secondary school level." The following suggestions may go a long way to bring about the vocationalisation in secondary education.

(i) Money should be taken from all the rich persons of the country in the form of education cess.

(ii) 50 per cent of the money thus obtained should be contributed by the Central Government and the rest 50 per cent contributed by the State Government.

(iii) In order to impart education of vocational subjects, persons of different profession of the district and the country should be invited from time to time. In this way, problem of the salary of the teachers can be solved for some time.

(iv) The student should be given opportunities for acquiring practical knowledge in the professions which are carried on in the neighbourhood of the school. In this way, the expenditure to be incurred on establishment of different types of workshop in the schools can be saved for some time. If the Government is not prepared to take full responsibility for giving the implements to the students learning different vocations then at least it should make full endeavours to do so. This will attract the students towards professional courses.

Secondary Schools Management

At present three types of secondary schools are imparting education at the secondary stage:

(i) Government school

(ii) District Board and Municipal school

(iii) Schools run by private bodies.

The number of Government schools is comparatively far less than the number of schools run by private bodies. The main cause of this is that instead of taking the responsibility of education the Government has been encouraging the establishment of schools by giving some grant-in-aid to the schools run by private bodies. As compared to the Government schools, the condition of the District Board and Municipal schools is very miserable. So far as the question of schools run by private bodies is concerned, they are run on the principle of business and are the definite means of income of their managers. Since they are run on profit basis, they cannot be expected to render the real service for the cause of education.

Management by Government

The above mentioned problem can be solved if the Government takes over the management of all the non-Government schools by making necessary laws in this connection. If this is not done in the near future, this problem would go on multiplying and would cause irreparable loss to the cause of secondary education.

We have discussed in brief the chief problem of secondary education. It need not be over emphasized that these problems should be solved within the earliest possible time. Unless this is done in the near future, it is futile to hope reformation in higher secondary education and subsequently the progress of the country.

18

Basic Education

History of the Development of Primary Education- We can study the history of development of primary education in India in two parts : (a) Primary education before the commencement of the system of compulsory primary education, and (b) Compulsory primary education.

The Backdrop

From 1757 to 1813 : After the battle of Plassey (1757), the East India Company started its campaign of expanding its empire and from that time a new chapter started in the history of Indian education. Although by that time the condition of Indian education had become miserable because of the widespread discontent and anarchy, yet there was a network of educational institutions in the whole of India, which had become a part of social and cultural life of the people. There were about one lac educational institutions in Bengal only. But the Britishers crushed and completely shattered the Indian education in order to establish their trade monopoly and political ownership.

From 1813 to 1854 : The modern educational system was started in India by the Christian Missionaries. They built up primary, secondary and higher educational institutions. Indian education was disregarded and ignored under the rule of East India Company. The charter of 1813 provided that at least one lac rupees was to be spent every year on the revival of Indian literature and expansion of scientific studies. But even this amount, which was not at all sufficient for so vast a population, could not be properly used for a period of 10 years. From 1824, some amount was sanctioned for education but it could not fulfil the needs of the education of Indians.

From 1854 to 1857 : It was accepted in Wood's Despatch of 1854 that the education of the common people had been completely ignored and disregarded. Wood's Despatch, therefore, suggested that provision should be made to impart practical and useful education to the common people. The number of primary schools should be increased. Native schools should be encouraged through grant-in-aid system. But the officials of East India Company ignored the primary education and spent more money on secondary and higher education. Consequently, the primary education could not make any progress.

From 1857 to 1882 : Stanley's Despatch of 1850 recommended that the Government of India should take up the responsibility of primary education and advised that the Government should impose local taxes to bear the expenditure of education. Consequently, primary education made some progress during this period.

From 1882 to 1905 : According to recommendations of Indian Education Commission of 1882, the management of primary education was transferred to the local institutions. This new system undoubtedly led to some progress but it cannot be called satisfactory. The real position was that by transferring the responsibility of primary education to the local institutions, the Government wanted to get rid of this responsibility. Lord Curzon, the Governor General of India, admitted that primary education was so far ignored and disregarded by the Government. He wrote: "I am one of those who think that Government has not fulfilled its duty in this respect."

Lord Curzon did praiseworthy works in the field of increasing the number of primary schools and in raising their teaching standards. But the partition of Bengal led to widespread discontentment and dissatisfaction among the people and his services in the field of education could not be taken into consideration by the people. At its Calcutta Session of 1905, the Congress decided to launch the National Movement, this Movement created consciousness among the Indians in regard to their rights. The primary education takes a turn from this period and advances towards the stage of compulsory primary education.

Compulsory Education

Early Efforts. Although no solid efforts were made till the beginning of 20th century in regard to compulsory primary education, yet some Britishers, who were the lovers of education, were inspired to work in the field of intellectual and social development. Some important suggestions were made in regard to compulsory primary education. Baptist Missionary, William Adam, was the first of such liberal persons. Revenue Survey Commissioner of Bombay, Capt. Wingate and educational Inspector of Gujarat and T.C. Hope were the other prominent Britishers who suggested the provision of compulsory primary education but unfortunately, the British rulers did not pay any heed to their suggestions and their suggestions were completely ignored.

Politicians' Efforts

The National Movement, which was gaining momentum slowly and gradually was bringing about the consciousness among the Indians. The field of education was also influenced by this Movement. Educated Indians, prominent among them being Sir Chimnun Lal Sitalvad and Sir Ibrahim Rahmatullah, started the Movement to make the provision of compulsory education. Since then the movement was limited to Bombay province only, it influenced only the Government of Bombay and in order to investigate the utility of compulsory education in Bombay city, a Committee was appointed in 1906. But unfortunately, this Committee arrived at a conclusion that the provision of the compulsory primary education would not be proper because the people were not prepared for it.

Successful Experiment : The king of Baroda, Maharaj Sayaji Rao Gaekwad had the credit of making the first successful experiment of compulsory education in India. Liberal minded and education-lover king of Baroda declared in 1892 that there would be compulsory primary education in a Talluqa of Amraili City, consisting of 9 villages in his State. All the boys from 7 to 12 years of age and all the girls from 7 to 10 years of age were to receive education in primary schools. This provision was started from November 18, 1893 and met with such an astonishing success that it was extended to 52 villages of the said Talluqa. Thereafter, primary education was made compulsory for all the children of the State by the Act of 1906.

Gokhale's Efforts

Being inspired with the feeling of nationalism, Gopal Krishna Gokhale presented a Resolution in the Imperial Legislative Assembly in regard to primary education. The Resolution suggested to take steps for making primary education free and compulsory throughout India. On being assured by the Government to consider over the said Resolution, Gokhale withdrew his resolution but the Government did not even dream of giving practical form to its assurance. After seeing the attitude of the Government towards the primary education, Gopal Krishna Gokhale submitted a bill in 1911, in the Imperial Legislative Assembly in regard to primary education. The bill aimed to implement the principle of compulsory primary education through stages. According to this bill, compulsory primary education could be started by seeking prior consent of the Local Councils of their areas where a definite number of children from 6 to 10 years of age were receiving education. But the efforts of Gokhale could not succeed. His bill was strongly opposed in the Imperial Legislative Assembly, and was defeated by 38 to 13 votes on March 19,1892.

Compulsory Education Act : Being inspired by the efforts of Gokhale, another great leader, Vithal Bhai Patel presented a bill in the Provincial Legislative Assembly of Bombay. The aim of this bill was to introduce compulsory primary education in the municipal areas of the province. The said bill became an Act in 1918 and was called Bombay Primary Education Act. This was the fast act, which accepted the principle of compulsory primary education by the Government of a Province. This was the pioneer of the revolution in the field of education. Consequently, by the year 1930, almost all the provinces passed the Acts in regard to compulsory primary education.

According to these Acts, responsibility of primary education was entrusted to the local institutions. It was the responsibility of these institutions to implement the provisions of these Acts. These institutions were also empowered to impose education cess in order to meet the expenditure to be incurred on education. The Provincial Government also promised financial help to meet the expenditure on education. Only those boys and girls who were ordinarily between the age of 6 to 7 years could take benefit of the provision of compulsory education.

Expansionary Phase

As a result of Compulsory Education Acts and the feeling of nationalism, the expansion of compulsory education received an impetus. Under the guidance of the father of the nation, Mahatma Gandhi, women also demanded their rights. They organised All India Women Educational Conference in 1927 and demanded the right of receiving education equal to those of men. The efforts of Mahatma Gandhi and Dr. Ambedkar not only brought about consciousness among the Harijans but they also went a long way to expand the education. Because of the efforts of these great leaders, the people started taking interest in primary education. Fortunately for India, the organisation of the provincial education came into the hands of Indian Ministers and Government contributed much for the expansion of primary education.

This progress of compulsory primary education continued till 1930 but thereafter from 1931 to 1937 the development of compulsory education received a set-back. There were two main reasons for this. The first cause of this set-back was the worldwide economic depression, which also influenced India. Hence, it was quite natural that the expensive schemes of compulsory education were postponed. Secondly, the Hartog Committee which was appointed in 1927, emphasised that instead of aiming the quantitative increase in primary education special attention should be given to the qualitative progress of primary education and the policy of consolidation of education should be followed. In spite of great opposition of the people, the Government implemented the suggestions of this Committee, which brought about a set-back in the expansion of compulsory education.

At the time of provincial autonomy in 1937, Congress Ministries were formed in 6 out of 11 provinces. The Congress made vigorous efforts to expand compulsory primary education in their provinces. They established primary schools in those villages, where there were no primary schools. Local institutions were given additional grants so that they could meet the expenditure in making the primary education compulsory. Gut's schools were also opened at the places where people demanded it. These efforts of the Congress Ministries led to a great expansion of compulsory education. By the time independence was achieved, provision had been made for compulsory education of boys in 229 cities and 10,017 villages for girls in 10 cities and 1404 villages.

Post-independence Scene

The independent India felt the great need of expansion of education at all stages and specially at the stage of primary education. Therefore, the national Government took active and sincere steps to make the primary education free, universal and compulsory. The principle of compulsory education was declared through Article 45 of the constitution of India. It was also made clear that this education would be of basic type. On this basis, Board of National Education was established. Our Government has been making vigorous efforts to expand compulsory primary education in all corners of the country. Under the different Five-year plans, huge amount has been spent for the development of Primary Education.

Difficulties and Rectifying Measures

For the expansion of Primary education, the Central Government has been giving the financial help to the Provincial Governments. The States which intend to expand primary education are given 34 per cent of the total annual expenditure in this connection in the form of financial help. Thus, we see that the primary education has made a great progress, but because of certain reasons it cannot be said to be encouraging and satisfactory. The main reason for this is that there are many problems and difficulties in the field of primary education, which are creating obstacles. We will now discuss the different problems and their solution.

Defective Policy of Education

It was made clear in 1950, in the Constitution of the independent India that within a period of 10 years from the commencement of the Constitution, States shall endeavour to provide free and compulsory education to all children until they complete the age of 11 years. It is a matter of great regret that the Government has not achieved complete success in this regard. In 1950-51, 42.6 per cent of the children of the age-group of 6 to 11 years were receiving education. This percentage increased to 83.6 by 1979-80. Similarly in 1950-51, 12.7 per cent pupil in the age group 1-4 were receiving education while this percentage was 4.02 in 1979-80. Till date, the percentage of the children receiving education between the age group of 6 to 11 years is 83 while that of age group of 11 to 14 is 63.

These statistics clearly indicate that the Government has not been able to achieve the prescribed goal. The main cause for this is that the policy of the Government is based on idealism. Basic education has been accepted as the form of national education. Being inspired with this aim, work has been started to convert primary schools into basic schools. But in a country like India which has a vast population and where there is too much shortage of money, the implementation of the expensive scheme of basic schools is difficult. The Government has also accepted the gravity of this problem and has admitted that it is not possible to implement the scheme of basic education in the whole of India within a short period. But, still the Government has been spending most of the money on basic education. In such a situation, we may say that Government policy is based on idealism and is not taking active steps to expand primary education by adopting a practical and realistic attitude.

Proper Policy of Education

The first and foremost necessity is this that the Government should first evolve a definite education policy. The Government has already admitted that the national education will be basic type of education. But along with this, it has also been admitted by the Government that it is not possible to implement the scheme of basic education in the whole country within a short period.

In such a situation, the best policy can be that expansion of compulsory education and basic education should be separated from each other. Whatever education that is being imparted in primary schools should be made compulsory. Slowly and gradually according to convenience, primary education should be converted into basic education. If the Government does not build its compulsory educational policy on this principle, it is futile to hope that compulsory education would be universal in the near future.

Problems Related to Politics

So far the Government has not been able to devote its full attention towards removing the political difficulties. The main reason for it is that since the attainment of independence the Government had to face many problems and many of them still exist, e.g. the problem of native States, the problem of the refugees, the problem of Kashmir, the problem of different linguistic States, the problem of 100% the problem of China etc.

Role of Government

The political problems that we have mentioned above are mostly such which still exist and may continue to exist for a long time. It is also possible that the Government may have to face some more problems in the near future. However, this does not mean that the Government should not pay proper attention towards public education. If the Government is responsible to solve the political problems of the country, the Government is also duty-bound to solve the problem of public education. In spite of the fact that the Government has to face so many problems, the indifference of Government towards education cannot be justified by any means. Some scholars have even remarked that the political situation also demands that the Government should implement the scheme of compulsory, free and universal education within the shortest possible time.

According to K.G. Saiydain, "While the political situation demands the immediate introduction of the scheme, the politicians are not keen enough to take it up." The Government can be exonerated of this charge only when they devote their proper attention and perform their duties towards the expansion of primary education. Nothing less than this will satisfy the people.

Defective Education Policy

In most of the States of India, the responsibility of the primary education is on the municipalities and the district boards. At the time when the responsibility and the work of primary education was entrusted to these institutions, it was hoped that these institutions will speed up the work of the expansion of primary education. In the course of time, however, it has become clear that these institutions have not risen equal to the occasion. Ordinarily, there is lack of working capacity, interest and money in these institutions. All the Acts relating to compulsory education have become out of date. There is no such central institution or power which may compel these institutions to implement these Acts.

Reforms for Education

In fact, it is the responsibility of the nation to educate its citizens. It is, therefore, necessary that the Government of India should take upon itself the sacred work of primary education. If on account of some reasons, the Government cannot shoulder the responsibility, then it should establish such a powerful central institution, which may compel the district boards and the municipalities to start the work of compulsory primary education in their respective areas within a definite period.

Teachers' Dearth

Yet another problem of primary education is the non availability of the desired number of really trained teachers. This poses a very difficult and serious problem before the Government. As compared to the city schools, there is great shortage of such teachers in village schools.

Training of Teachers

As pointed out earlier, the desired number of really trained teachers are not available for making education compulsory but this problem can be solved. In the beginning, the teachers of essential qualification can be selected as teachers, no matter whether they are trained or not. Thereafter, a definite number of teachers from among the above mentioned teachers can be encouraged to increase their qualifications or they can be sent to training schools to undergo the training on Government expenses. It cannot be a wise step to wait for making the education compulsory till the time when the desired number of trained teachers may be available. It is rather more essential that the salaries of the teachers should be increased. They should be provided more facilities and they should be attracted towards teaching work by conferring upon them more honour and respect

Low Teaching Standards

There is a great shortage of really trained teachers in primary schools. Besides this, the primary schools are not using the proper and necessary implementation of teaching due to shortage of money. It is because of these reasons that the education is uninteresting and its standard is low. Hence, it fails to attract children and their guardians.

Grants-in-Aid and Teachers' Training : The first essential requirement that is necessary to raise the standard of teaching is that only trained teachers should be appointed in primary schools. To implement this, it is necessary that the number of training schools should be increased. It should also be kept in mind that the training schools should be established not only in the urban areas but also in the rural areas so that men and women of the neighbouring places may be attracted to receive training in them at less expense. Probably, it would be the best if the Government or local boards meet the whole expenditure of the training of the teachers. It may, however, be added that it would be only sheer imagination that only the appointment of trained teachers would raise the standard of teaching. It is also necessary that the primary schools should be given liberal grant-in-aid to enable them to purchase teaching implements. Enthusiastic and trained teachers generally find themselves unable to do much due to lack of the necessary means of education.

Lack of Finances

Dearth of money is yet another serious problem that confronts the primary schools. During the British period the Government met 30 per cent of the total expenditure incurred on primary education. In the independent India, this amount was increased to 34 per cent. This scanty help given by the Government cannot be said to be adequate for making education compulsory.

Suggestions : The expansion of primary education is not taking place properly due to shortage of money. It has been estimated that if compulsory basic education for the children of 6 to 14 years of age in the whole country is made, it will require an annual expenditure of about Rs 300 crores. To spend so much money on education is beyond the capacity of this poor country. Rupees 93 crores were spent on primary education in the First Five Year Plan but this amount was reduced to 89 crores in the Second Five Year Plan because of need of money for other development work. In the Fourth plan Rs 241.3 crores were spent while the proposed outlay for the Fifth plan was Rs 743.0 crores. The allocation for primary education in the Sixth Five-year plan was 835.73 and in the Eighth Five-year plan it was 920.14.

In the situation of this shortage of money, our aim should not be to achieve qualitative increase in primary education but we should rather make efforts to educate as many children as possible so as to make them get rid of illiteracy. In this connection, Gokhale has rightly remarked, "Primary purpose of mass education is to banish illiteracy. Quality of education is a matter of importance that comes only after illiteracy has been abolished."

Keeping in view this thing it would be desirable to end partially if not completely the expenditure that is being incurred on converting primary schools into basic schools. The emphasis should first be laid on the compulsory education and not in the form of basic education. Some Indian educationists are of the view that the expenditure of primary education can be met by reducing the term of primary education upto 4 years. Australia, Germany, Japan, Egypt, China and Russia expanded primary education among the common people by fixing the term of primary education for 4 years. Sri Desai, an eminent Indian educationist, has suggested that in order to reduce the expenditure of compulsory education, fees should be taken from the children of rich persons and private primary schools should be allowed to take fees from the students. If the Government accepts these suggestions, the financial problem of compulsory education can be solved at least to some extent.

School Buildings

Another problem in the way of compulsory education is the establishment of schools. It becomes very difficult to solve this problem in villages, if not in cities. India is mainly a rural country but still there are thousands of villages where there are no schools. In order to make the education compulsory, the establishment of Primary Schools is necessary in nearly 4 lakh villages including the villages having a population of less than 500. It is not easy to collect money to establish so many schools. Moreover, it would not be beneficial to establish schools in the villages having population less than 500. This poses a serious and complicated problem before the administrators and educationists of the country.

Allied to the problem of the establishment of schools, there is also the problem of buildings of the schools. At present in our country, there are only 20 per cent such buildings of schools which can be called proper and adequate. The rest of the schools are being run in houses, temples, buildings of rich persons, residence of teachers etc. These schools lack sufficient space for seating all the children much less to talk of their games and sports. Many schools are situated in a very busy locality and undesirable environment. Moreover, these buildings are such that adversely affect the health of the students because of inadequate supply and provision of the sun and the air. These problems can be solved only by building new buildings which require a huge amount of money but as pointed out earlier, it is very difficult to collect the amount needed for building schools.

Suggestions : Following suggestions have been put forward to solve the problem of establishing and building of schools:

(i) The problem of establishing schools in rural areas is very difficult. There is great shortage of money for establishing new schools. Besides this, many villages are small and at distant places. If money can be arranged for building schools, then they should be first built in those villages where they are most urgently required. As regards the small villages, some villages in the middle of them should be selected so that it may be convenient for the children of other villages to attend school there.

(ii) Problem of the lack of teachers and schools can be solved through shift system. Although this system cannot be accepted as an ideal one, yet because of the lack of teachers and school buildings for the present it will be better to adopt this system. According to the shift system, different students can be called to receive education into two shifts. The first shift can be run from 7.30 to 11.30 a.m. and the second shift can the run from 1.00 p.m. to 5.00 p.m. Different countries of the world have adopted shift system in their early stage of expansion of education. The more prominent of such countries are Germany, France,

Portugal, United States of America, Japan etc. Even today, this system is prevalent in Australia, New Zealand, Turkey, Egypt, China, Ceylon, Denmark, etc. This system should be made prevalent in India also. If the time of the shifts is kept, keeping in view the season and the needs of the farmers and the workers, then the problem of establishment of schools and buildings can be easily solved in India. Of course, the teachers will have to work more in this system. But if they are given more salaries they will have no difficulty in taking up this additional work.

(iii) In order to speed up the progress of compulsory education, the Indian educationists have suggested that the number of students in each school should be increased. At present, the teacher has to teach on an average 35 students in each class. In many western countries, each teacher had to teach more than 36 students in the early stages of education. For example, till 1922, the number of students in each class was 60 in England and so was the case in Italy upto 1932. The United Nations Organisation recommended 60 students in the primary classes of China. Therefore, in those primary schools of India where one teacher teaches the students of one class only the number of students can certainly be increased. Of course, in those schools where one teacher teaches more than one class it would not be proper to introduce this system.

Uncompatible Curriculum

The curriculum of the primary school is narrow and unsuitable to the local needs. It, emphasis is given on bookish knowledge and the principle of 'learning by work' to develop the constructive powers of the student is disregarded and ignored. In order to remove these defects of the curriculum, the Government has decided to convert primary education into basic education. This will certainly remove the defects of the curriculum but the expensive scheme of basic education cannot be enforced at one time in the whole country and hence the seriousness of the problem cannot be undermined.

Suggestions : As mentioned earlier, the curriculum of the primary schools is one sided and uninteresting. Because of not being related to the local environments, it has no utility. It is true that by implementing the scheme of basic education, the Government is endeavouring to make the curriculum interesting but this work will take a long time. Therefore, for the time being, the education of crafts should be given in the primary schools in accordance with the local needs and requirements. This will not only increase the interest of the children in education, but they will also be benefitted by the knowledge they thus acquire. It is not necessary that the education of crafts should be imparted by some scholars or trained teachers. The services of local and experienced persons can be utilised to perform this work.

Stagnation and Wastage

Another great obstacle in the expansion of primary education is wastage and stagnation. Out of hundred students of class I^{st} in 1957-58, only 61 students reacted in class II; in 1958-59, 49 students reached in class III; in 1959-60, 42 students reached in class IV in 1960-61. The percentage of wastage and stagnation in these four classes was 58. The recent studies made in some districts have revealed that the wastage and stagnation in class I^{st} are 46.5 and 43.9 respectively. The rest of the children left studies either after their failure in the examination or in order to assist their guardians in earning their livelihood. Unfortunately, the lack of buildings, etc. are the reasons because of which the schools fail to attract children to complete their education. It is of utmost importance that the wastage and stagnation in primary education should be checked otherwise there will be no possibility for the success of any scheme of expansion of education.

Suggestions : The problem of wastage and stagnation can be solved through the following ways and means:

(a) Educational system should be reformed.

(b) Teaching method should be made interesting.

(c) Good school-buildings should be built.

(d) The environment inside and outside the school should be reformed.

(e) The curriculum should be reformed.

(f) Educational system should also be reformed.

(g) Efforts should be made to develop the health of the students.

(h) The guardians or the parents should also be educated.

(i) Social problems relating to education should also be solved.

We have simply mentioned some suggestions in brief here because later on we will discuss the problem of wastage and stagnation in detail in a separate chapter.

Obstacles of Nature

There are also natural obstacles in the way of expansion of compulsory education. Because of less population in Himalayan region, Kashmir, Garhwal and Almora etc., the villages in these areas are situated at distant places. So is the case with Rajasthan. Besides this, there are many areas in Madhya Pradesh and South India, which are covered with forest and the population of these places is scattered in small and distant villages. There is lack of means of transport in the above mentioned regions and because of the severe cold, heat or heavy rains, their difficulties further increase.

Suggestions : It is very difficult to conquer natural obstacles mentioned above in a big country like India. However, after the attainment of independence, many of these problems have been solved. There has been praiseworthy increase and progress in the means of transport under the Five Year Plans. Roads have been built in many distant villages and the work in large scale is still being done in this connection, but there are many places where the natural obstacles create problems for the children for receiving education. It would be rather more desirable to entrust the responsibility of the education on some local persons in order to avoid the problem of children going to distant places to receive education.

Evils of Society

There is no corner of India which is not infested with social evils such as superstitions, illiteracy, faith in ancient convention and customs, child marriages, untouchability, Pardah system, etc. These social evils create innumerable obstacles in the expansion of compulsory primary education. Without having any regard or care of the Child Marriage Prohibition Act, many persons still marry their boys and girls at a very minor age and deprive them of the fruits of education and knowledge. Although, citizens have been granted the right of equality by law, yet in some schools or the other many Harijan students are still not admitted in many schools. Even today some Hindus and Muslims firmly believe that either girls should be given no education or they should be given only little education. Because of the prevalent pardah system, there are still many persons, who oppose the system of coeducation even in primary schools.

Suggestions : It may be suggested that despite the prevalence of these evils, the work of the expansion of education should not be slackened. It should be rather increased because social evils are flourishing because of illiteracy and ignorance. Education develops the mind of the man and his logic power. In the course of time, education will itself root out all these social problems which appear to be formidable at present. Beside this, the Government and the social workers should try to bring about consciousness among the people in regard to disadvantages because of the prevalence of social evils through the means of pictures, speeches and other such works. Lastly, the educated young men and women should volunteer themselves to remove the social evils around their neighbourhood. This will go a long way to remove social evil from our society.

Language Problem

Last but not the least is the problem of language. There are about 826 languages and 1952 dialects in the country. It is a serious problem before the administrators and educationists as to which language should be the medium of instruction for the children speaking different languages, and dialects. The Constitution of India mentions 14 languages, which cannot be made the medium of education but there are many other languages, which cannot be given that status.

Suggestions : Kothari Commission has suggested the mother tongue should be the medium of instruction at the primary stage. All the regional languages should be developed. It is also suggested that the teaching of Hindi should be compulsory right from the primary stage so that it can be medium of instruction in all the states in the near future.

Educational Programmes for Backward Castes : Most of the children of scheduled castes, scheduled tribes and de-notified tribes do not get even the primary education. Though untouchability is prohibited but in remote villages, we still find the caste barriers and children of schedule castes, scheduled tribes and de-notified tribes are subject to hatred and so they are not given due attention.

Special Type of Schools

The establishment of special schools is necessary in the areas where there are the people of scheduled castes and tribes and de-notified tribes. Sufficient attention is being given to this in the independent India. The Government has been taking every possible steps to establish special schools for the students of such tribes and is providing facilities of free education, scholarship, books, writing material, etc. Under the different Five Year Plans huge amount has been invested for the purpose. Although the efforts of the Government are really praiseworthy, but we are disappointed to find that the number of people of scheduled castes and tribes are lagging behind in the field of education. The accountability of education of these castes and tribes who have been staggering under the weight of misery and poverty for centuries should not be left on the Government alone but people should also come forward to assist the Government in this sacred work.

19

Nursery Education

Earlier, In India Pre-primary education was the concern of the family only. It was the duty of parents to impart instructions to their children in the rudiments of their mother tongue and general good behaviour. Now, the families are incapable to shoulder the responsibility and so these things are taught to children at school. Thus, the responsibilities of schools in the field of Primary Education have greatly increased.

Most of the scholars are of opinion that Froebel is the founder of Pre-primary system of education, to 1837, he founded a Kindergarten school at Blackenberg. This was the beginning of Pre-primary education.

Initially the system of Pre-primary education was not so organized as it is today. In the great epic Mahabharata we find the example of Abhimanyu, who was taught the Art of demolishing the Circular Fort while he was in mother's womb. However, with the advent of modern period, in India too, the formal Pre-primary education was begun. For the Pre-primary education we have Froebel's Kindergarten Montessori system and Nursery system.

Nursery Schools

Froebel's system of education 'is called the play-way method. In Kindergarten school, the children of four years of age are admitted. They are taught many things pertaining to good behaviour, through various plays. Children are also taught 3 R's, through a psychological method. The first six years of the child's life are very vital. During these years, the child is able to develop many such sentiments which become almost permanent with him. Froebel studied child psychology and made it as the basis of education for children.

Montessori School

Mana Montessori was the founder of this system of primary education. In montessori school children from two to six years age are educated. They are imparted education through didactic materials and toys.

Mrs. Margret Macmillan was the founder of Nursery system education. She founded a Nursery school for physical and mental development of children. In Nursery school, children of two to four years of age are admitted. They are provided healthy environment for their development. In these schools, the trained lady teachers are appointed and children get their motherly treatment.

The Pre-primary schools provide good opportunities to young children for their sensory training and education in good conduct and behaviour. In these schools, psychological methods are adopted for the physical and mental development. The impressions and habits acquired during this period of school life last lifelong. Pre-primary schools provide medical care, healthy food and healthy environment for physical and character development. Through different types of plays, children acquire many good social traits. Children in these schools are taught language, art, music, dance and rudimentary mathematics on psychological lines.

Indian Pre-primary Schools : The system of pre-primary education in India was introduced in the third decade of the twentieth century. By 1952, there were about 330 nursery schools in the country. Upto the end of first Five Year Plan, their numbers rose to 800. Since then their number is increasing day-by-day. At present, there are thousands of pre-primary schools. We find the mushroom growth of such schools. Some of them are of good standard but most of them are befooling the public. Pre-primary schools are individual and voluntary. The government provides very little help to some of the schools. The result is that most of the schools suffer from want of necessary material equipments, good buildings and other facilities. In most of the schools, there are no trained, teachers.

It is most alarming that the utility and importance of pre-primary schools was felt as back as Sargent report of 1944 but the government has taken very little pains for pre-primary education uptill now.

New Experiments and Investigations, As a result of some experiments and investigation, pre-primary education has been divided into the following four stages:

(1) From conception to birth.

(2) From birth to 2 years of age

(3) From 2 to 4 years of age

(4) From 4 to 6 years of age.

From conception to birth, the baby is influenced by the physical and mental dispositions of the expectant mother. So in order to educate baby, mother's welfare is greatly needed, mother welfare centres are established at some places but there are steps to be taken in this field. Through these centres the expectant mothers should be provided good environment inclusive to healthy development of the child.

From birth to 2 years of age, the child learns something under the guidance of the mother. If the mother is healthy and of good nature and culture, the child shall also be influenced by the same. From 2 to 6 years of age, the child should receive education in some good pre-primary school. As we have already said, these types of schools provide the necessary environment for healthy development of children on psychological lines. Children are taught language, music, art, dance, arithmetic, general science along with manners of good behaviour through plays.

Teaching System- In our country, we have adopted the pre-primary system of education on western toes. But the need is that the new techniques suited to our conditions and traditions should be devised. Uptill now we have adopted the Kindergarten, Montessori and Nursery systems in our pre-primary schools. The need of the hour is that the children should be taught manners and social etiquettes according to our own traditions. So far young children are told stories with themes imbued with European culture. The need is to write new stories with Indian themes. We should not blindly copy the European method but adopt them if they are suited to our culture and tradition.

It is a matter of joy that some pre-primary schools on the montessori lines have started in our country. The Child Education Society of Bhavnagar has been the pioneer in this field. Some other societies have come forward to adopt a new system of nursery education by drawing the best from the Basic and Montessori systems. Sarvodaya Society have also come forward with many good ideas about nursery education. If we embrace a new system of pre-primary education conducive to our society and education, we shall be able to train our babies in the right direction.

20

Teacher Education

Historical Backdrop

Teacher Education in Ancient Period : In ancient period a special feature of the teacher education was that teachers used to take a personal interest towards each pupil. Sometimes so many students come to a teacher that he could not fulfil his responsibilities towards them. Hence, he used to seek the assistance of meritorious students of higher classes. They were called 'pattacharya'. They assisted their teacher (Guru) in teaching, used to be his pupils. If the teacher some times went away, the teacher used to entrust the whole work of teaching and schools to such students.

This system was, in fact, the monitorial system in which some meritorious students of the same Class and some students of the higher classes assisted the teacher in the performance of teaching and other allied works. The students, who were entrusted with this work, used to become efficient teachers and school organisers in the course of time. After having been thus trained, they used to devote themselves to teaching work in future.

Teacher Education in Medieval Period : Consequently, excepting a few rulers, they did not devote much attention to education. In such a condition, it was very difficult for them to have any idea of teacher education.

Teacher Education in Modern Period : In fact, teacher education in the systematic form was introduced in the modern times only.

Early efforts of Teacher Education in the Modern Period : In the modern period, the Educational Boards of Bombay, Madras and Calcutta for the first time felt the need of teacher education and they established a few training centres but only the teachers of primary schools were imparted training to these schools. The Native Education Society of Bombay trained 25 teachers and sent them to different parts of the province so that the standard of teaching in the primary schools might be raised. In 1812, Calcutta Society was established in Calcutta. This Society made the provision for the training of the teachers on the basis of monitorial system. In order to encourage the work of the society, the East India Company started giving Rs. 500 monthly aid since 1825. In accordance with the suggestions of Munro, the-then Governor of Madras, a Training School for the training of the teachers was founded at Madras in 1826.

Woods' Despatch and Teacher Education : Wood's Despatch of 1854 mentioned the following, "We desire to see the establishment, with as little delay as possible, of training schools and classes for masters in each Presidency in India." The wish that was expressed by the Directors of the Company in Wood's Despatch in regard to teacher education could not be fulfilled.

Teacher Education from 1859 to 1882 : Lord Stanley has mentioned in his Despatch that special attention should be devoted to the training of the teachers. After the transfer of the power it was not possible for the British administrators posted in India to ignore or disregard the orders of the Secretary for State of India. Consequently, they worked with enthusiasm for the establishment of training schools for the teachers of primary schools and as a result of their efforts many Training Schools were established in each province by the year 1882. The number of students studying in these schools was 553. The number of schools in Madhya Pradesh was 44 for men and 1 for women and the number of students studying in these schools was 118.

In 1862, Normal School system was started in Bengal. According to this system the teachers of the native schools or their relations were lent to Normal Schools. In 1874, Campbell, the Governor of the Province, prepared a new scheme for the training of the teachers, and consequently, 46 normal schools were established at the cost of Rs. 1,64,000.

In Madras, there were 32 training schools and nearly 927 students were receiving training in those schools. Likewise, provision of the training of the teachers of primary schools was made in other provinces also. In 1882, there were 106 normal schools in the whole of India and about 3,886 men and women were being trained in those schools, the annual expenditure of these schools was nearly Rs. 4 lacs.

Regular System of Teacher Education : The regular system of teacher education was detailed in accordance with the recommendations of the Indian Education Commission, 1882. Consequently, by the end of 19th century, there were six Training Colleges at Madras, Lahore, Allahabad, Kurung, Rajmundri and Jabalpur and 50 Training schools in the whole country.

Government Resolution of Education Policy, 1904 : Lord Curzon devoted sufficient attention towards education and training of the teachers. The Government Resolution of Educational Policy of 1904, after considering all the aspects of the teacher education, made the following recommendations:

(1) Provision should be made for higher training of able and experienced teachers for the Indian Educational Service.

(2) The importance of the equipment of the Training colleges is almost equal as that of General Colleges.

(3) The training period for the graduates should be only one year and therefore they should be granted degree by the University. The knowledge of teaching method and practical training should also be included in the curriculum.

The training period for the non-graduates should be two years.

(4) Theoretical training and practical training should be mutually connected with each other and there should be a practising school connected with each Training College.

(5) Training colleges should be connected with ordinary schools so that the teachers may apply the methods teamed in the Training Colleges.

The Government Resolution of Educational Policy : Government Resolution in Educational Policy of 1913 further emphasised teacher education and declared: "Under modern system of education, no teacher should be allowed to teach without certificate that he is qualified to do so."

Calcutta University Commission and Teacher Education : The Calcutta University Commission (1916-17) devoted special attention towards teacher education and made the following recommendations: (1) The number of trained teachers should be increased; (2) Research work in education should be encouraged; (3) A demonstration school should be attached with each Training College so that practical work may be done in it; (4) The subject of education should be included in the curriculum of B.A. and Intermediate classes; (5) Education Department should be established in Calcutta and Dacca Universities.

Hartog Committee of 1929 and Teacher Education : The Hartog Committee emphasised the training of the teachers of primary schools and recommended the following in this connection: (1) Education Standard of the teachers should be raised; (2) Training period should be extended; (3) Able teachers should be appointed in training institutions and their number should be increased; (4) Provision of refresher courses should be made from time to time for the teachers of primary schools; (5) In order to attract able persons in the-teaching profession, the conditions of teachers should be improved and made attractive.

Training Institution : In 1947, there were following three types of institutions:

Normal Schools : Teachers of Primary schools were given training in these schools.

Secondary Training Schools : These schools imparted training to the teachers of middle schools only, those students who passed matriculation were admitted in these schools.

Training Colleges : The teachers of High Schools were given training in these schools. Only graduates and postgraduates were entitled to get admission in these colleges.

Facilities of Training at Present

Praiseworthy works have been performed in the field of expanding the facilities of teachers training in the post-independent period. Suggestions given by the University Education Commission, 1949, Secondary Education Commission, 1952 and Kothari Commission, 1964-66 are being implemented by the Government. We will now briefly discuss the suggestions made by these three Commissions:

University Education Commission (1948-49) : Radhakrishnan Commission for the change in teacher education by telling, "A real education is not so much a matter of lessons to be learnt and memorized as of a life to be lived and purposeful activities to be shared." It made the following important recommendations in regard to teacher education:

(1) The curriculum of training institution should be reformed. Instead of bookish knowledge, importance should be given to the practice of teaching in schools.

(2) While evaluating the work of the students, special attention should be given to their success in teaching works.

(3) Only suitable schools should be selected for practice of teaching.

(4) Most of the teachers of the training schools should have sufficient experience of teaching in schools.

Secondary Education Commission (1952-53) : It made the following recommendations:

(1) Training schools should be of two types, (a) First type of schools should be for those students who have completed secondary education; (b) The second type of schools should be for the graduates. For the time being, their training period should be one year but later on it should be extended to two years.

(2) Teacher student should be trained in more than the teaching method.

(3) Provision should be made for Refresher Courses, Short Intensive Courses on Special subjects and poetical training in workshop in the training schools.

(4) No fees should be charged from the teacher-students of the training schools.

Education Commission (Kothari Commission, 1964-66) : Kothari Commission made the following recommendations in regard to teacher education:

(1) Extensive Service Department should be established in each Training Institution.

(2) Comprehensive colleges imparting training to the teachers at different stages of education should be established in each state.

(3) A State Board of Teacher Education, which should be responsible for teacher education at all stages and in all the fields, should be established in each State.

(4) The curriculum and courses of the training schools should be changed and reorganised in accordance with the changing times and circumstances.

(5) No fee should be charged from the students of training institutions and provision should be made for grant of stipends and loans to them.

(6) Facilities of correspondence courses and part-time training courses should be made available on extensive basis.

National Policy of Education

In the Education policy of 1986, due importance was given to teacher-education. It was said that all-out efforts should be made to improve the education and training of future teachers. The appointment of teachers should be on the basis of their abilities and aptitudes. Provision was made for establishing District Institutes of Education & Training, who will cater the need of non-formal education for the workers of adult education. Secondary Teacher Education Institution shall be reorganised.

Training Institution in the Present Period : At present, there are following eight types of teacher's training institution in our country:

1. Pre-primary Training Centres,
2. Primary Teachers Training Schools,
3. Secondary Teachers Training Colleges,
4. Specialised Teachers Training Colleges,
5. Education department of Universities,
6. Special Institutes for Trained Teachers and Research Work,
7. Training Institutes for Women,
8. In-Service Training Institutes.

Here, we are giving a brief account of some of them:

Pre-primary Training Centres : Pre-primary Education is in its early stages in our country. Consequently, the provision of training of the teachers of pre-primary schools is also in its early stage. In the year 1992-93 there were 205 pre-primary training centres in the country. These centres impart training to the matric and upper primary pass students for a period of one year. The curriculums of the training centres are different

Primary Training Schools : There are two types of primary schools in India (i) basic, and (ii) non basic. Consequently, there are also two types of training schools. In the year 1988-89 there were 992 in the whole country. The training period of both these two types issues the following two types of certificates (a) Junior

Teachers' certificate is conferred on those students, who take in these schools after passing upper primary, (b) Senior Teachers' Certificate is awarded to the students taking training in these centres after passing matriculation.

Secondary Teachers Training Colleges : They are of two types-some impart training to undergraduates while some to graduates. In 1988-89, the number of such colleges in the country were 992. The training period of such schools is one year in some States where as it is 2 years in some other States. The successful students are conferred a certificate of diploma by the University or Education Department. The name of the certificates or diplomas are different in different States. The teacher in these institutions perform teaching work in junior high schools and secondary schools.

These institutions are run by Education Department of the States and Universities. In some states such as Uttar Pradesh, these institutions are run by Education Department as well as by the Universities. The training period of these colleges is generally two years and the successful candidates are awarded B.Ed., L.T. or D.P. Ed.

Difficulties and Remedial Measures

Dr. S.N. Mukherjee is of the opinion, "The present position in relation to teacher-education is by no means satisfactory, in spite of the rapid progress in recent years. Numerous problems have arisen with this development" Here, we are giving a brief account of these problems and their solution:

Training not Related to School Work : It is one of the chief problems of teacher education that training imparted by the training colleges to the teachers is not related to school work. The conditions and circumstances prevailing in the training institutions are such that the teachers find themselves unable to implement in practice the educational principles which they learn here.

No Diversion Between Theory and Practice : The question arises as to why there is so much difference in practice and the theory and how this difference should be removed. It is not much difficult to find out the reason. There are very few Training Colleges who have some 'Demonstration School' connected with them. Consequently, the teacher-student are not able to determine the educational principles and method for their students. They do not get sufficient opportunity to test in practice the principles and methods of teaching which they have learned and consequently their teaching lacks practical experience.

Consequently, their ideas are not clear and they are unable to impart successful teaching in their schools. What is still worse is that generally their professors are not capable of having a clear conception of things because of the fact that this quality can be developed only when they have the opportunity of testing their principles in practice. Pointing out the solution of this problem, Sri K.G. Saiyadain has aptly remarked: "Practice and theory must both be visualised as growing entities, theory illuminating practice constantly modifying theory.

It is Therefore, very essential that an administration school fully equipped with all the necessary means should be attached with each Training College which should be run on experimental basis. If the teacher-student gets the opportunity of testing into practice the theories and principles of 'teaching learned' in training colleges, they will be able to perform their work more successfully and efficiently.

Undue Emphasis on Theory : Yet another defect of the prevalent Teacher's training is that undue emphasis is given on theory. On the contrary, they are given very little time for practical work. During their training period they teach nearly 50 lessons. As is well-known, generally each teacher has to teach 6 or 7 hours every day. Thus, the teaching of 50 lessons is the work of only one week is completed. In other words we may say that during their training period they are allowed one week for teaching class, whereas they remain busy in study of theoretical subjects from July to April. This clearly shows their lack of practical experience.

Curtailment of Theoretical Courses : The above mentioned problem can be solved only when the theoretical subjects are curtailed. The teacher-student should be taught only those subjects which may prove useful in their teaching life and may help them throughout life. This cannot be said to be a wise practice that they bid farewell to their books and the knowledge acquired after the completion of their examination. The curtailment of theoretical courses will automatically make available to them sufficient time for teaching works. It will be more desirable for teachers to spend 3 to 4 hours every day during the whole of their teaching period so that they may become efficient in teaching profession.

Neglect of Human Aspect : Yet another serious problem of teacher education is that their education neglects human aspect and more emphasis is given on technical aspect. During the training period so much emphasis is given on the methods and capacity of teaching that they do not get proper opportunity to apply their critical mind in solving the problem of education relating to its aim, purpose and values.

Values of Training Centres : It has been unequivocally admitted that there is neglect of human aspects during the period of training of teachers but educational institution do not consider themselves responsible for this. They contend that so little time is given to them for training that they find themselves unable to devote to the human aspect. The argument may appear to be plausible on its face but, in fact it is completely baseless. If we accept this excuse and retain the existing position in the training institutions, it will mean that we believe in the wrong values and do not make any endeavour to reform it. In the works of Sri K.G. Saiyadain, "It is essential for the training colleges to revise their values and avoid the misfortune of the man in the cave who could see nothing of the fascinating vista around because his vision was bounded by the four walls of the prison. There is an adequate appreciation of the social and agricultural background, which must be set right."

Unconditional Environment : The Environment in which the teacher-students study during their training period lacks freedom.

Free Environment : In order to solve the above problem, it is necessary that the Training Institutions should be freed from the binding of strict roles and strict control on the life and activities of teacher student The Training Institution should be organised into such free and active communities, in which the teacher students may work under those circumstances and inspirations which our country wants to establish in our institutions. If this is not done, the teacher student coming out of training college will not be benefited. If they receive their training in unfree and unconductive environment, they will continue the same defective process in which they have received their training. Besides this, they will continue to retain the wrong conception which they have developed during training period.

It is heartening to note that the work of organising the Basic Training Colleges into community centres has started and more freedom is being given to the teacher-students of post graduate training colleges. However, much remains yet to be done to give a real and effective form to this movement.

Selection of Candidates for training : Selection of suitable-candidates for training is also the main problem of teacher education, some years ago when there was not a strong desire among the persons to become teachers; trained teachers were not more than their demand, the position was not as serious and difficult as it is today. There are two aspects of this problem.

(a) The number of persons desirous of seeking admission in training college has unprecedently increased, and

(b) There are not sufficient posts for all the trained teachers. It is, therefore, necessary that only suitable persons should be selected for training in view of the welfare of the teacher as well as the teaching profession.

Some Suggestions : In order to solve the above mentioned problems, K.G. Saiyadain recommended the following:

(i) With the help of training colleges, education Department of each State should ascertain through at least one survey in 5 years as to how many men and women teachers will be required in the State and the scheme of admitting the students in training colleges should be prepared on the basis of this public demand.

(ii) Short-term courses should be organised for old and experienced teachers who on account of some reasons have not been able to take admission in training colleges.

(iii) As regards the persons who wish to take admission in training colleges after completing their education in colleges or universities, only suitable and promising persons who may become able and efficient teachers, should be selected.

(iv) Better and more efficient means should be adopted to select new students for admission.

(v) The person desirous of entering into teaching profession should keep in mind that they should not enter into Training Colleges after acquiring scattered and unconnected knowledge of different things, which may not in any way help them in their future profession.

(vi) For the examination of degree, teaching of science should be made an optional subject as is already prevalent in some universities.

Difference between Basic and non-basic Courses : At present two types of training institutions are working in our country, basic and non-basic. The curricula of both these courses are different. Basic system emphasises activity, method, community life and practice, its theoretical aspect is weak. On the contrary, the non-basic system emphasises theoretical knowledge and teaching method. The aspect of practice is only subsidiary in this system, thus, there exists defects and weakness in both the systems.

Integration of Basic and Non-basic Courses : The basic and non-basic system should be integrated in such a way so that their defects may be removed and a new and efficient system may be evolved. Keeping this in mind, the All-India Conference of Training Colleges has suggested the following for integration of the said two systems:

(i) The theoretical part of the general training course should be minimised and the desired revision should be made in it.

(ii) More importance should be given to practical work and it should be reorganised in such a way so as to impart training of community life, craft and correlated teaching.

Low Standard of Teachers' Education : The teaching standard of our training colleges is very low and so able teachers are not produced. Kothari Commission was of the view, "Existing programmes of teacher education are largely traditional, rigid and divorced from the realities of schools and existing or proposed programmes of Educational reconstruction.

Reorganisation of Teacher's Education : All out efforts should be made to re-organise the teacher's education so that the standard may be raised. In this connection Kothari Commission was for integrated curriculum of general and technical education in colleges and universities. The curriculum should be framed keeping in view the conditions of the country. While framing the curriculum individual and technical needs of the mind. In training colleges new and progressive means of examinations should be introduced. Keeping in view the suggestions given by the Kothari Commission, in the draft of the fifth plan, it has been said, "The curricula of the training schools and colleges will be reoriented so as to ensure deepening of the prospective teacher's academic and professional preparation."

Conclusion : The problems of teacher education which we have discussed above explicitly indicate that the work of teacher education is not progressing properly in our country and its utility is also doubtful. However, these problems are not such as cannot be solved. The necessity is however this, that the educationists of the country should compel the Government to remove the defects prevalent in the field of teacher education within the shortest possible time. If these defects are not converted into reality. The role of teacher is most significant in educational revival and he can perform his role properly only when he is given proper and efficient training.

b) More importance should be given to practical work which should be reorganised in such a way as to impart and [illegible] [illegible] [illegible] [illegible] [illegible].

[illegible] of Teacher Education: The [illegible] of teacher training colleges is very low and so are [illegible] [illegible] [illegible] Commission [illegible] of [illegible]. Existing programmes of teacher education are largely traditional, rigid and divorced from the realities of schools and extent of proposed programmes of educational reconstruction.

Reorientation of Teacher Education: A [illegible] [illegible] [illegible] programme of teacher education so that the standard may be raised. [illegible] Commission was [illegible] [illegible] of general and technical education, in colleges and universities. The curriculum should be [illegible] keeping in [illegible] the conditions of the country. While [illegible] [illegible] individual and [illegible] needs of the [illegible] training colleges [illegible] programmes should be [illegible] [illegible] [illegible] as suggested by the Education Commission [illegible] of the [illegible] has been [illegible]. The [illegible] in training schools and colleges will be reorganised so as to enable [illegible] of the [illegible] [illegible] [illegible] [illegible] organisation.

Conclusion: The problems of teacher education [illegible] [illegible] [illegible] India [illegible] the work of teacher education [illegible] the progress of our country and its ability [illegible] [illegible] these problems are [illegible] [illegible] solution. [illegible] is however [illegible] that [illegible] [illegible] should compel the government to remove the defects [illegible] the field of teacher education within the shortest possible time. If these defects are [illegible] [illegible] [illegible] the role of teacher is most [illegible] national [illegible] [illegible] [illegible] his role properly [illegible] when [illegible] given [illegible] [illegible] training.

21

Social Education

The Backdrop

Before making a brief discussion of the history of Social Education, it may be made explicit in the beginning that the education which we call social education since 1949 was previously called adult education.

Adult Education Before 1921 : Efforts made for the expansion of adult education before the year 1921 were just negligible. Of course, some night colleges were established in different parts of the country but their aim was to impart primary education to the children who worked in the factories and did not get time for studies during the daytime. In 1901-02, there were night schools imparting adult education in Bombay, Madras and Bengal only. But these schools could not flourish because of the indifference and apathetic attitude of the Government and the number of such schools continued to decline by the year 1917. The Government of India Act, 1919 granted extensive rights of vote to the Indians. Hence, adult education naturally increased among the common people because it was felt that Indians could not exercise properly their franchise due to lack of education, consequently, night schools and night classes were organised in United Provinces, Punjab, Bombay, Madhya Pradesh, Bengal and Madras.

From 1921 to 1937 : The Government of India Act, 1919 was enforced in 1921, and the 'transfer' subjects were entrusted to the Indian Ministers. Education was also a transferred subject. Indian Ministers took deep interest in resolving the problem of adult education.

Consequently, entering efforts were made in different provinces to make the adult literacy popular among the people. Not much time had passed since sincere efforts had begun in respect of the expansion of adult literacy, these efforts received a major setback because of the worldwide Economic Depression of 1927. Because of the lack of money, both the Government and the people lost inspiration and encouragement to work for expansion of adult education. Consequently, the number of adult schools continued to decline. In the year 1937, the number of men and women schools of this type was reduced to 20 and 11 respectively.

From 1937 to 1947 : The fate of adult education again took a turn for betterment when Congress Ministries were formed in 1937. In their programme of expansion of education, the Congress Ministers gave an important place to adult education. Being encouraged with this, the Government of India also showed its interest towards the expansion of adult education for the first time by appointing an 'Adult Education Committee' in 1939.

State Education System

A brief discussion of the efforts made by the Congress Ministers in different provinces for the expansion of adult literacy is given below:

Assam : The work of expansion of adult literacy was entrusted to Education Department in the province of Assam. With the help and cooperation of its subordinate offices, the Education Department of Assam made proper provision of adult education.

Bengal : In this province the Government granted financial help to the schools organised by the Gram Sabhas and thereby encouraged the adult education.

Bihar : The movement of adult education made great progress in the province of Bihar. The movement named 'make your home literate' was launched and libraries and reading rooms were opened in thousands of villages.

Bombay : In 1917, 'Provincial Adult Education Council' was established in the province and under its supervision the work of adult education was started in the city of Bombay. This scheme achieved so much success that with the aim of the expansion of adult literacy in the city of Bombay, Bombay City Adult Education Committee was also established. In 1938, Bombay Government appointed an Ad-hoc Education Advisory Board which rendered praiseworthy service in removing adult illiteracy in the province of Bombay. Sri S.R. Bhagat was the Chairman of this Board.

Orissa : The work of adult education received a great impetus during the rule of Congress Ministries in this province. But the work of adult education received a setback immediately after the resignation of the ministry.

Punjab : The work of adult literacy could not make much progress in this province. However, the Government distributed thousands of books among the adults free of charge.

Uttar Pardesh : The Congress Ministry of this Province gave a great impetus to the work of expansion of adult education. Centres of adult education were established at different places and provision was made for the reading rooms, libraries and other types of facilities in order to encourage and inspire the adults to become literate.

Post-independence Situation

Adult education has been given a place of priority in the independent India. By changing the name of adult education to social education, not only its nature but its scope has also been extended. It was decided that along with making the adult illiterates literate, they should also be given the education of citizenship.

Thus, under the social education the scope and view of adult education was made wide and extensive.

The Twelve Point Scheme : In order to develop the qualities of citizenship among the adult illiterates and to make them conscious of their rights and duties and to expand their knowledge, the education minister of the government of India presented a twelve point scheme in a press conference organised on May 31,1948.

Conference of Provincial Education Ministers : A Conference of Provincial Education Ministers was organised in February, 1949 at Delhi to discuss the Twelve Point Programme mentioned above. After a thorough and detailed discussion in the conference, it was decided that within a period of three years at least 50 per cent of the adult persons belonging to the age group of 12 to 50 years should be made literate but this programme could not be implemented because of the financial difficulties of the Central and the State Governments.

Five Point Educational Programme

The Government of India made a Five Points Programme:

(1) Expansion of literacy;

(2) Propagation of the knowledge relating to rules of health and sanitation;

(3) Financial upliftment of the adult persons;

(4) Consciousness or awakening of the people towards the feeling of citizenship, rights and duties,

(5) Provision of healthy entertainment in accordance with the need of the society and the individual.

First Five Year Plan : It was decided to spend Rs. 7.5 crores for social education in the First Five Year Plan. Many provinces made the provision of social service works and some provinces even made a commendable progress in this respect. The work of social education received an impetus in public work organised with this aim in view. For example, many such work organised by Gram Panchayats, Cooperative Societies and Professional Unions or Associations, etc.

Second Five-Year Plan : Under the Second Five Year Plan besides improving the methods of social education, classes of social education were expanded at different stages. The State Government started many centres of literacy and social education training institutions of workers and organisers of social institutions and established libraries, colleges and audio-visual institutions. A sum of Rs 10 crores was provided for social education under the Second Five Year Plan. Besides this, a sum of Rs 10 crores was spent on social education through National Extensive and Community Development Schemes.

Third Five-Year Plan : A sum of Rs 15 crores was spent on social education under the Third Five-Year Plan. Under this plan also, efforts were made to expand and encourage social education. In villages, schools, Panchayats and voluntary organisations, work in the field of social education was done.

Fourth Five-Year Plan : Under the Fourth Five-Year Plan a movement on extensive basis was launched for the development of adult education. It was decided to connect the adult literacy with the life and activities of the people so that villages may be developed. A special emphasis was given on expanding literacy by creating awakening for its utility. In order to make the drive of literacy effective, the provision of libraries was being organised to rural areas and a large number of schools were being established for expanding literacy in different languages. As special emphasis was given on the following things during the Fourth Five-Year Plan, training of workers of literacy and library; establishment of adult schools; night schools and colleges for training of the workers, establishment of National Adult Education Board and thereafter State Boards. A sum of about Rs 64 crores was spent on the scheme of social education under the Fourth Five-year Plan.

Fifth Five Year Plan : The Non-formal education Programme was introduced for the first time in the Fifth Plan. Full time institutional education was introduced to meet the requirements of illiterates and semi-illiterates. This programme was integrated problem-oriented, environment and how the young could adjust to it, family life, education, health and hygiene, literacy skills and initial functional training leading to employment and self-employment. In the Fifth Plan the proposed outlay for social education was Rs. 3,500 crores.

Sixth Five Year Plan : Due to the fall of Congress Government at the centre in the year 1978, the draft of the Sixth Five Year Plan (1978-83) was prepared by the Janta Government. The Government allocated Rs. 200 crores for the progress of social education. On October 2, 1978, the National Social Education Programme was introduced in the formal manner. The aim of this programme was to provide social education to 10 crores illiterate people by the year 1983-84. There was again a change of Government at the centre in the year 1980. The Congress Government prepared a new draft for the Sixth Five Year Plan (1980-85) and Rs 128 crores were allocated for the expansion of social education.

Seventh Five Year Plan : Under the Seventh Five-year Plan Rupees 360 crores were allocated for social education and decided to complete the unfinished programmes of Sixth Five year Plan. The target was to make every adult literate, which however, could not be achieved. Under this plan the programme of continuing education was implemented and it was connected with Industrial Rural Development Programme.

Eighth Five Year Plan : Rupees 184.76 crores were allocated for the development of Social Education under Eighth Five-year plan and it was decided that adult illiteracy shall be definitely removed from the country. It was also decided to make hectic efforts for continuing education.

In the education policy of 1986, it was declared that social education should be according to the national objective. More educational centres shall be opened in rural areas, programme of continuing education shall be properly enforced and full use of radio, television and film shall be made for collective teaching.

Social Education: the Expansionary Phase

A National Centre for Fundamental Education was established at New Delhi for imparting social education to higher officials and for doing appropriate research in the chief problems of social education. The Library Institution of Delhi University performs the same function in the field of libraries. A Social Education Institution for workers was established at Indore. A provision has also been made for providing constant educational facilities for the establishment of public colleges and Vidyapeeths for imparting education to the adults in rural areas. A Central Film (Documentary) Museum was established which has more than 4974 films on different subjects of education and culture and which are provided to the members of educational institutions free of any charge. Nearly, 1,045 educational institutions and social organisations are the members of this Museum. A quarterly magazine entitled 'Audio-visual education' is also published.

The Central and the State-Government also organised Conference of Audio-visual workers. A Central Audio-visual Committee has also been established. Besides establishing training institutions, public centres of literature and research centres have also been established. This institution also makes available knowledge and information regarding Audio-visual education. Under the National Council of Educational Research and Training, a department of Adult Education has also been established. This department performs the functions of imparting training to the higher officials involving in the work of social education, helps to develop suitable teaching methods, conduct research work on selected problems and furnishes different types of information.

Meaning and Concept

The meaning of the phrase, 'Adult Education' has been defined in different ways. As is very clear from the phrase, adult education means making the adults literate. As a matter of fact, the meaning of adult education is much wider than this. While clarifying this, Sri S.N. Mukherji has remarked, "Adult education may be defined very broadly so as to include all instructions, formal or informal imparting to adults. In India, adult education has two aspects- (1) Adult literacy, i.e. education of those adults, who never had any schooling, and (2) Continuation of education of the literate."

(*Education in India Today and Tomorrow*)

According to K.G. Saiyadain, "Adult education ... includes political and civic as well as moral education."

Modern Concept : In the 15th Session of the Central Advisory Board of Education, which was held in Allahabad in January, 1949, Maulana Abul Kalam Azad expressed the new view- point of the Government of India towards adult education. According to him, the aim of adult education should not be confined only to run adult illiterates into literates but it should extend to make each citizen a wise member of the democratic set-up. The viewpoint of adult education underwent a change and from that time it was called social education. A great change has come in the meaning and definition of social education. The scope and range of adult education has greatly extended and it has now assumed the form of social education.

The Meaning : While clarifying the meaning and definition of social education Maulana Abul Kalam Azad expressed the following words while delivering the inaugural address to UNESCO Seminar on rural adult education, held in December, 1949 in Mysore, "By social education, we mean education for the complete man. It will give him literacy, so that knowledge of the world may become accessible to him. It will teach him, how to harmonise himself with his environment and make the best use of the physical condition in which he resides. It is intended to teach him the unproved crafts and modes of production so that he may achieve economic betterment. It also aims at teaching him the rudiments of hygiene both for the individual and the community so that our domestic life may be healthy and prosperous. Last but not the least, this education should give him training in citizenship so that he obtains some insight into the affairs of world and can help his Government to take decision which will make for its progress."

According to Humayun Kabir, "Social education may be defined as a Course of study directed towards the promotion of consciousness of citizenship among the people and the promotion of social solidarity among them. It is not content with the introduction of literacy among the grown-up illiterates but aims at production of educated mind among the masses. As a natural corollary, it seeks to inculcate in them a lively sense or rights and duties of citizenship both as individuals and members of the community."

It is clear from the above mentioned definition that social education is a regulated subject which increases the capacity of the individual for participating in collective works. It creates consciousness among them for a proper evaluation of citizenship. It attracts them towards duty and behaviour. It is only through social education that the adult can increase his income within his limited means and can make his contribution in the building of society.

Aims and Objectives

Aim of Social Education : Since the attainment of independence, it has been sincerely felt that for the establishment and stability of democracy in India, it is necessary to educate the Indian people. Consequently, the newly established first Education Ministry of the independent India gave an important place to the education of adults in its programme. Consequently in 1949, a Committee headed by Sri Mohan Lal Saxena was appointed to advise the Government in connection with the expansion of adult education. Having found the aims of adult education narrow, this Committee advised the Government that this education should be called 'Social Education'. This suggestion of the Committee was accepted by the Government. This Committee determined the following aims of social education:

(1) To awaken the adults towards their rights and duties and develop the feeling of social service in them.

(2) To create love in them towards democracy and to educate them the administrative system of Government,

(3) To acquaint them with the existing problems before the country and the world.

(4) To develop the feeling of glory towards Indian culture through the education of history, geography and culture.

(5) To provide them the opportunities of pleasure and cultural acquaintance through music, dances, poetry and dramas.

(6) To make them aware of moral values throughout the medium of collective discussion and reading and writing.

(7) To impart them proper knowledge of reading, writing and ordinary mathematics and encourage them for expansion of knowledge.

(8) To teach them to utilise their leisure properly to achieve their economic progress through the learning of different handicrafts.

(9) To continue their education through libraries, debates, discussions, Education Committees and public colleges.

(10) To develop in them feeling of cooperation.

Purpose of Social Education : The purpose of social education has been divided by the Government into two categories:

(a) Individual, and (b) Social.

Individual Purposes : (1) Mental development; (2) Development of professional capacity; (3) Physical development; (4) Development of Social Skill; (5) Cultural development; (6) Self Development

Social Purposes : (1) Promotion of Social cohesion; (2) Conservation and improvement of national resources; (3) Building of cooperative groups of institutions; (4) Inoculation of social ideology.

Need of Social Education : The above-mentioned aims and purposes have not been determined as a result of any chance or incident but after having seriously considered the needs of the individual and the society of the country. In consequence of these needs, the need of social education has been felt According to Dr. R.S. Pani, "Social education is a many-sided endeavour, since its aim is primarily to develop in an individual a live sense not only of the privileges but of the responsibilities of citizenship him a democratic secular state like India." We will now briefly discuss the need of social education.

Need of Illiterate Adults : Indian Constitution has granted the right of equality and equal rights of freedom to all the citizens but many of the citizens are not able to exercise their rights on account of their illiteracy. Keeping in view of these requirements of the illiterate adults, provision of social education has been made and the chief purpose of social education is to make illiterates the literate adults.

Need of Complete Education : The education which is imparted in the schools and institutions of higher education cannot be called complete because it does not develop the necessary abilities in the persons that they may lead their lives successfully in all the fields. The main defect of the education imparted in the schools is that it does not give any type of training in respect of health, family and proper utilisation of leisure. After entering into life the individual feels, the need of this type of training. Social education fulfils this need of persons.

Need of Recreation : In the modern period, like the citizens of other countries, the needs of Indians have also increased. In order to fulfil these needs, they remain busy to earn money from morning till night. After the hard labour throughout the day, it is quite natural that these persons should have a wish to have means of some type of entertainment. So far as the cities are concerned, lack of means of entertainment is not a problem. There is great lack of means of entertainment in the villages. Social education has also taken upon itself a task of providing different types of entertainment to the rural people.

Political Need : The present time is the period of reorganisation, rehabilitation, development and progress for our country. We have established a secular welfare democratic state in our country. We have to make it strong and stable which can be possible only when its foundation is fine and strong. This foundation is, in fact, the whole people of the country, on whom depends the responsibility to elect able State Governments and it is only on them the welfare of the nation depends. To achieve this aim, it is necessary that the common people of India should be given proper education and proper literature should be made available to them for study. As we emphasise the education of boys and girls and youths, in the same way, we will have to make proper provision of education of adults of India. Unless we are able to bring about the consciousness among the adults, we will not be successful to achieve our cherished goal. Therefore, the social education, which has taken upon itself the task of educating the adult Indians is of utmost importance.

Social Need : It is clear from the definition of the society that cooperation is an essential element of society. The whole structure of the society rests on the foundation of cooperation. It is only this cooperation which not only protects the society but also builds and develops it. The existence of all the institutions, committees and organisations of the society depend upon cooperation. We can be successful in making the society progressive only with the help of cooperation.

Economic Need : The majority of Indian people is poor. The condition of the rural people is comparatively poor and more miserable than the urban people. They do not have even sufficient means to fulfil men-needs of clothing and food. Unless we are able to remove the slur of poverty from the forehead of our country, we are not entitled to call ourselves progressive. Being inspired with these ideas, the Government of India has devoted their attention to the financial uplift of crores of poor Indians and keeping in view this need it has been decided to raise their economical status by giving them different types of training through the programme of social education.

Need of the Country : If the people of the country are not educated, then it is not possible to make a full use of constructive power of the country. There is great need of education for acquiring strength and then making use of it. An uneducated person does not know as to what powers he inherits in him and how can he make use of them. It is completely true in regard to India that huge public power of this big country is not being properly used. The provision of social education has been made keeping in view this need in mind.

Difficulties and the Remedial Measures

We will now discuss the different problems confronting social education and some suggestions to solve them.

Illiteracy : India is the second most populated country of the world, next only to China. According to the census of 1991 population of the country is 84.39 crores and out of them only 52.11% are literate. Thus huge population of Indian people are growing in the dark because of their illiteracy. In view of the existence of so widespread illiteracy, to hope any type of social, economic and political development is just like to build a castle on the sand.

Liquidation of Illiteracy : Although the liquidation of illiteracy of the adults is not a simple task yet success can be achieved by adopting some methods. We can resolve this problem only when we stop having golden dreams of placing them on the high peak of culture and humanism and make up our mind to make them literate within the shortest possible time.

Moreover, in the beginning we should concentrate on teaching of writing and simple mathematics. In the 5th Educational Conference held at Washington on October 29 and 30, 1936, Dr. Edwin Embree rightly remarked:

"Reading is the first commandment even among the basic three R's."

In order to teach reading and writing to the adults, it is not necessary the method which is adopted should be proper and complete from the scientific point of view but we should adopt the method, which may give equal and best results.

This type of method was discovered by a Missionary of America named Dr. Frank Laubach to educate the people of Moros tribes of the Phillipine archipelago. First he selected 5 to 6 such words which were generally used. Thereafter, he selected some more words and with their help build sentences. Thus, with the help of the charts he taught 17 letters within a day to each adult. Each family adult who learned the chart was sent to teach the members of his family and his neighbours. Thus, within a period of 5 years, 70,000 adults out of 1,50,000 adults of the province of Lana were taught not only to read but also to write.

Dr. Laubach visited India in 1935, 1937 and 1938 and

demonstrated his method for teaching in Marathi, Telugu, Bengali, Hindi, Tamil and Gujarati languages. The Missionary of Moga in Punjab achieved tremendous success by adopting this method. It is a matter of great regret that this method propounded by Dr. Laubach is out of the country now. If the method propounded by Dr. Laubach is adopted by the people, India can be made literate within a very short period.

Obviously, the liquidation of illiteracy is the responsibility of our Government. It is, therefore, necessary that either through the successful method experimented by Dr. Laubach or any other method which is seemed to be proper should be adopted to completely liquidate illiteracy from our subcontinent.

Kothari Commission has suggested for compulsory National Service Programme for adult education for all the schools and colleges. The Commission has also suggested for the appointment of village sisters, introduction of condensed courses and follow up programme.

Curriculum : The second problem of social education is of its curriculum. Because of the improper and unsuitable curriculum, the work of social education is not making much progress. The curriculum which is used for the education of the children cannot be used for the adults because their interests, needs and view-points towards life are completely different. Again, same curriculum cannot be determined for all the adults because some of them are totally illiterate and for the curriculum which can teach them the knowledge of the letters is necessary; some are half illiterates and for them teaching of some special subjects is necessary; and lastly there are some non-literates who know some reading and writing and in order to inculcate the feeling of citizenship in them, the curriculum including subjects such as civilization, culture, history, geography, civics, etc. is necessary.

Construction of Curriculum : The proper and suitable curriculum can be prepared only after carefully and minutely studying and considering the needs of complete illiterates, and non-literates because the aim of social education is not only to expand literacy but also to achieve the complete development of the adults. Hence, the curriculum should include all those subjects which may ensure their political, economic, social and cultural development. Not only one but several curriculum will have to be prepared keeping in view the needs, interests, mental tendencies and standards of the adults of different ages. Although the curricula will be different yet their subjects will ordinarily be the same, subject to their short or detailed studies keeping in view the needs of adults of different age group.

It has been pointed out by several educationists that it would be proper to prepare the curricula considering the curricula of some such countries where the conditions of adults are generally similar to that of Indians. From this point of view, the curricula of Denmark and China can be accepted as ideal.

In the curriculum of adult education, the first importance should be given to the teaching of writing and reading. When the adults acquire sufficient knowledge of writing, and reading then provision should be made for imparting education of mother tongue, mathematics, history, civics, economics, geography, culture, animal husbandry, general science, hygiene, literature, physical education, etc. The education of some other subjects may also be imparted in accordance with the local needs. Each adult should be trained in some or the other crafts, so that be may he able to make it a means of additional means of his income.

Method of Teaching : The problem of determining a suitable method of teaching adults is also not less complicated. If the teaching method has any element which appears to them uninteresting or which is against their reeling of 'self, freedoms, principles or habits then such a teaching method will certainly prove to be unsuccessful. Dr. V.K.R.V. Rao is of the opinion, "An adult may be illiterate, but his mind is grown-up and his interests are already cultivated. We are not writing on a blank slate, when we are dealing with an adult." That is why, so far it is not possible to determine a single method of teaching for the adults.

Suitable Method of Teaching : In order to determine a suitable method of teaching for the adults, it is necessary to study minutely their psychology. The teaching should be such as may be interesting and may attract them to receive education. The educationists of our country are very much active in this direction and they have evolved some suitable methods. We will now briefly discuss some of such teaching methods:

Letter Acquaintance Method : In this method the adults are first made acquainted with the knowledge of the letters. This system is prevalent in our primary schools.

Sentence Method : In this method the adults are first made acquainted with the knowledge of two words and thereafter by joining them the letters, given in the form of different sentences.

Laubach Method : A Missionary named Dr. Laubach has evolved a new method which is known as chart method. This method has been experimented in different parts of the world, to this method education of the whole sentence is given with the help of the chart.

Story Method : Sri Sangam Lal Agarwal has the credit of evolving this method. In this method, the education of the letters is given through certain stories based on the construction of letters.

Simple Word Method : This method has been evolved by Sri Pathak. In this method, prominence has been given to the songs. The songs are first sung and then the letters and the words are recognised by seeing them in the charts.

It is generally accepted that all these methods are suitable for the education of the adults. While adopting all these methods, it is necessary that the letters of Indian language should be made easy so that the adults may have convenience to write, understand and recognise them. It is also pointed out that Roman letters should be used for all the Indian languages. This will give the adults the knowledge of European languages along with their own languages and the obstacle which are there in the unity of the country on account of diversity of the languages will also come to an end. Kamal Ataturk solved the problem of illiteracy of the people of Turkey by making use of the Roman letters and thereby developed the feeling of unity in them.

Dearth of Teachers : Yet another problem confronting the expansion of social education is the dearth of teachers. The teachers who are appointed in the adult schools, are ordinarily the teachers of primary schools. They do not possess necessary ability to teach the adults. They are ignorant of the psychology of adults. They are not trained in the suitable teaching method of the adults.

Supply of Teachers : Although it cannot be denied that the problem of having a desired number of suitable teachers is in fact, difficult but at the same time it may be contended that this problem can be resolved through constant and firm efforts. The first and foremost work in this connection is that the teachers to be appointed for imparting of adult education should be acquainted with the psychology of the adults. Besides this, the teachers to be appointed in the adult schools of villages, should have sufficient knowledge of agriculture, animal husbandry, cottage industry, hygiene, spinning and weaving etc., so that the rural adults may benefited by their teaching.

It will take a long time before we can have the supply of the desired number of teachers for adult schools. However, it would not be proper to postpone the work of social education until the desired number of suitable teachers are available. The volunteers should be invited to do teaching work in adult schools.

Under the guidance of Mahatma Gandhi, the volunteers successfully and properly performed the work of imparting education to children of the village in the District Champaran. The same ideal can be adopted for educational institutions, employees of the offices, members of N.C.C. and A.C.C. and other selfless social workers take inspiration from the example of Mahatma Gandhi and adopt the principle of 'teach one each one' then in the interim period we will have sufficient number of teachers for the adult schools and the problem of liquidation of illiteracy will be successfully solved in the near future. Dr. Kothari has suggested for compulsory National Service Programme at all the levels of studies for the expansion of adult education.

Suitable Literature : The responsibility of social education cannot end only by making the adults literate. It is not sufficient only to teach reading and writing and simple mathematics to the adults. If they stop receiving regular lessons after having received this type of education, then they will again become illiterate after some time. It is, therefore, necessary that after giving them preliminary education some literature should be made available to these Neo-literates. The Neo-literates should be made available to such type of literature as may develop their capacity to examine things, power of criticism and the social feelings, so that they may be able to distinguish between the best and worst in the field of art, truth and untruth in the field of knowledge and good and bad in the field of conduct. It is a problem to prepare such type of literature of the Neo-literates.

Production of Suitable Literature : According to K.G. Saiyadain, "The work of social education is greatly handicapped by the paucity of suitable reading materials, graded to appeal to the adults." There is urgent need for producing large number of booklets, folders, charts, journals, newspapers, wall papers and other illustrated material which will capture adult's interests.

This work can be performed and completed with the help of learned writers. They should be encouraged with every possible way to prepare suitable books and booklets for the adults. Illustrated newspapers and magazines should be published. Monthly magazines should be published containing news relating to games, health, culture and news of the world because there is utmost need of such magazines for the neo-literates. All the State Governments of our country are taking active steps in this direction. The report of the Literary Work in the production of Literature for Neo-literates 1958 of U.P. has made some important suggestions in this connection. According to the said report, while preparing literature for the Neo-literates following 5 things must be kept in mind:

(a) Aims of social education; (b) distinction of age; (c) distinction of sex; (d) distinction of religion; and (e) demand and need.

'Literacy House', Lucknow, 'Adult Education Council', Mysore and 'National Education Council' are doing commendable Job in this direction.

Agencies of Education : According to "Teacher's Hand Book of Social Education", "By agencies of social education is meant the bodies or institutions which deliver the goods, which contract the 'consumer' of social education and satisfy their needs." A special caution is required for selecting these means of social education because if they fail to attract the ' attention of the adults then they will prove to be completely useless. A wise selection of the means is not simple task. That is why, persons having specialised knowledge of adult psychology, are engaged to solve this problem.

Proper Agencies of Education : Different types of suitable means can be suggested for increasing the knowledge of the adults. In this connection. Report of the Literary Workshop in the Production of Literature for Neo-literates 1958 of U.P. has suggested the following: (a) descriptive prose, (b) poetry, folk- song and riddles, (c) drama, dialogues, (d) Stories, (e) Newspapers, (f) interesting discourses, and (g) reading, etc.

The utility of the above mentioned means of education cannot be doubted but we have to admit that the chief aim of these means is only to achieve intellectual development of the adults. But, if the work of social education will be confined only to this, then it will not be possible to achieve the complete development of the personalities of the adults and which is the main aim of social education. Therefore, other means will also have to be used for giving education to the adults. The following means can prove sufficiently effective:

(a) Audio-visual aids, radio, cinema, gramophone, dramas, etc.

(b) Collective songs and dances

(c) Literary and debating conferences and seminars

(d) Historical and cultural programmes, etc.

The Central Ministry of Education has laid special emphasis on the use of the audio-visual aids.

Lack of Funds : According to Census of 1991, the total population of India was 84.39 crores and out of them only 52.11 per cent were literate. We can Just have an idea as to how much money is required for making so many adults literate. Suppose one teacher can make 30 adults literate within 6 months. Thus, he can teach reading and writing to 60 adults in a year. Consequently, for making all the persons adults literate we will need lakhs of teachers and a large number of adult schools. It is clear from this that the availability of funds is a great problem for making adults literate.

Solution : Generally this argument is put forward that sufficient money cannot be made available for making literate all adults in our poor country. Shri K.G. Saiyadain has rejected this argument. According to him, there is only one type of poverty which cannot be removed and that is the poverty of enthusiasm. If we make sincere efforts, other types of poverty can be removed. It is the responsibility of the Finance Department of the Government and the farmers of the National Schemes to make provision of the necessary money required for the purpose of adult education.

Responsibility : Another problem of social education is as to who should be responsible for social education- Central Government, State Government, Education Department, District Boards or Public Educational Institutions. The Central Government has shifted this responsibility on the State Governments and thus they have tried to free themselves from the responsibility of 'social education'. But the solution of the great problem of social education does not seam possible through this shifting of the responsibility.

Joint Responsibility : All the defects and complicated problems of social education cannot be solved by the Central Government, State Government or any other institution alone. It would be the joint responsibility of the Central Government, State Government and the different institutions of the people of the country. It is only then this problem can be solved satisfactorily in a near future. According to K.G. Saiyadain, "It is obviously a responsibility which neither the Education Department nor the Government Machinery as a whole can take on by itself, and needs the closer and most cordial cooperation of all agencies, official and non-official and of all individuals of good will and social sense who are interested in the welfare of India. There is so much work to be done and it is of such varied kind that there is scope for every one who cares to join the cavalcade of service students, teachers, men of leisure, political leaders, writers, labourers, craftsmen, professional men everybody."

Absence of Coutinual Education : Last but not the least is the problem of absence of continuation of Education. According to Kothari commission, "The very purpose of the literacy campaign will be defeated, if it does not continue in some form to keep the process of learning alive."

Provision of Continuation of Education : According to Kothari Commission, "In conditions of rapid change and advancing knowledge man must continue to learn in order to live in full." So hectic efforts should be made for the continuation of education of adults. Kothari Commission has suggested that in schools provision should be made to impart the education of such subjects which the adults want to study further, part-time teaching should be organised and institutions like Central Adult Women Welfare Council, should be setup in large number.

22

Continuing Education

Education is a life long process. Formal education has contributed a lot in the expansion of primary, secondary and university education but due to its rigidity, it is not able to meet all the educational needs of the modern scientific and technological era. So a need for such an educational system was felt which may be flexible and within the approach of everybody. The result was the distance education. Distance education is the coordinated form of formal and non-formal education and it has good points of both of them. Some scholars have termed it as Open Education and others as Correspondence Education. However, the term Distance Education is more appropriate.

Meaning and Definition

Distance education is in fact a form of Open Education. It is a device by which people residing in remote regions receive education according to their interests and aptitudes. In this form of education, teacher has little importance. The education is imparted through information, correspondence, radio and television. It is true that in this form of education teacher and taught are not before each-other and teacher does not directly observe the activities of students but students are benefited by the planning and direction. It is a from of education in which teacher does not take the responsibility of oral teaching but becomes instrumental in imparting knowledge to those who want to get it at the place of their own choice.

Thus, in distance education teacher and taught remain apart. They have no or very little contact. It is the education which is planned by an educational institution or organization. Generally, we do not need any class room or school for teaching but in the teaching of practical skills we have to use them. Radio, Television, Video-cassettes and film strips are used for teaching. Basically, distance education is learning centres education which derives facilities to students to receive education at place of their choice.

The Significance

In modern times all the developed and many under developed countries have adopted the system of distance education and this system has drawn the attention of most of all education lovers. In India equipments for providing education are inadequate and because of the rising population, the number of illiterate person is increasing day by day. It has not been possible for us to meet the educational needs of all those who desire to receive education. The utility of distance education has so much recognized these days that 60 countries have jointly established on International Council of Distance Education. The traditional education can benefit only for job. If a student is admitted in some school or college he shall have remain there till he finishes the prescribed course successfully. During this period, a number of teachers teach him at a particular place and according to a fixed timetable. Under this traditional system, the poor are deprived of the facilities of higher education because in existing system, higher education is quite expensive. A large number of persons reside in rural areas and it is very difficult for them to receive higher education.

This is an age of democracy. In a democratic set up it is very necessary to give benefit to all. If many people can not go to schools, colleges and universities, we shall have to take education to their very door steps. If all can not get education and traditional centres of education, we shall have to device ways and means for taking education to them. And under these circumstances, chances of distance education are greatly needed.

The present system of education was started at the time when there were very few persons to receive education and for them the oral system of teaching was considered as quite suitable. In present times, the techniques of imparting education have been so much refined that it has become quite easy to provide education to all. The progress has enabled people of any social and economic status to receive education without difficulty. If people receive education through these techniques they not only become more enlightened, but the entire nation shall be benefited. The method of distance education is of democratic outlook and it is a new method for providing education to all.

The utility of distance education is from the following point of view:

(1) As we have already said that the demand of education is increasing day by day and it is not possible to meet this demand through formal education and so distance education is greatly needed.

(2) Education is a long-life process. We can get formal education for only few years, but distance education can be received throughout the life.

(3) In present times the education is not confined to a class of people. The principle of education for all has been excepted and so expansion of distance education is essential. In our country a large number of girls, handicapped persons and children of poor families are devoid of formal education. So it was felt to device a system of education by which people can get education at their home and so need of distance education was greatly felt.

(4) In order to take the advantage of modern technology, distance education is essential. Due to the development

of technology radio, television, video-cassettes and computer are not only the source of recreation but they can also be of great use for increasing our knowledge.

(5) Quite a large number of persons after completing their formal education go for a job or any other employment and leave their studies. Distance education helps a lot in increasing their skill and ability.

(6) Distance education is greatly needed for the equalization of educational opportunities so that lower class of the society can get the opportunity of education through it.

(7) It is a matter of great shame that still about 48% of our population is illiterate. We have adopted many programmes for the removal of illiteracy and the programme of distance education is one of them. Distance education has been greatly instrumental in our adult literacy mission.

(8) Distance education is essential for the help of formal education. In modern times, it is very difficult to get admission in the institutes of higher education and so we have to take the help of distance education.

System of Correspondence

The beginning of distance education is from the correspondence system. By introducing many modifications in the correspondence system, the path towards distance education has been made smoother. It has been possible due to development of educational technology. One of the chief disadvantages of correspondence system was the total absence of the teacher in it. However, in distance education the students get at times, the benefit of the presence of teachers and it has made distance education more acceptable. Some regional or local centres are opened were students get the advantage of consulting some teachers. The chief purpose of distance education is to make higher education available to those who have been deprived of it because of their adverse circumstances. Under the distance education system students residing any where in the country can receive higher education.

In our country first the correspondence courses were started but now the distance education is day by day taking the job of correspondence course. Indira Gandhi Open University has doing a commendable job for educating those who could not get higher education due to the one reason or the other. Other Open Universities and regional centres of Indira Gandhi Open University are contributing a lot in this direction.

Nature and Scope

As we have already said that in distance education, there is no provision of face to face classroom teaching sometimes through contact programmes some arrangements are made for classroom lectures for two or three weeks. In place of classroom teaching correspondence lessons are sent to students. In addition to these lessons, some supplementary material is also provided. A team of experts prepares these materials according to the needs. The lessons are generally good and the students are able to grasp them. The nature of the lesson is as such that the students can not acquire so much knowledge by consulting one or two books on the subjects.

In addition to correspondence lessons, radio, television, video cassette, tapes are used. Attempts are also made to make distance education more useful through broadcasting information, library facility, mobile teaching squad etc.

Critical Appraisal

Some people have criticized the working of open universities through distance education on the ground that it will lead to deterioration of academic standards. These persons are of the view that a student who receives the university degree through courses based on distance education can not be equal in competency in knowledge to the students who have earned University degree by studying according to the traditional method in classroom situation under the guidance of teachers and help of good books. In reply to this criticism, the supporters of Open University system say that the lessons of the Open University are prepared by a panel of expert teachers and they are of the nature that one can not get the same knowledge through a lecture of a teacher or reading by one or two books.

Some critics of the distance education and open universities are of the opinion that the lessons and reading materials of distance education are nothing but just a disconnected assemblage of fragments of certain books and so students are seldom able to grasp to them. However, lessons and reading material supplied by Indra Gandni Open University have shut the mouths of these criticise. The material supplied by the university is of very high standard. Still there is no denying that fact that open universities can not fully replace the traditional universities. There are some subjects which can be taught only, traditional universities for research work too open universities can not match the traditional universities.

The distance educations is criticised that in distance education use of radio, television, video and cassettes, tapes is most essential and in a country like India where there is so much power shortage and regular failure of electricity, teaching through these method is nothing but a fools paradise. For this criticism one can say that we can solve the problem if the programmes are broadcasted several times. In due course of time we may be able to solve our problems of power shortage in electricity failure and then this criticism shall have no weight.

Pursuing Further

Education is the around development of a person. It is a life long process. Education is for refinement and enlightenment. It is a continuous process. No one becomes educated by nearly receiving some literacy. An educated person is one who can utilise his education for solving his different problems and who can benefit others by the same. It is the education which develops one's intellectual and cultural horizon.

In India, people are generally not so keen to obtain knowledge as people are in developed nations. Many people in our country take admissions in Schools, Colleges and Universities but dropout in the middle of the session without completing the prescribed course of studies. Some do so due to their adverse circumstances and some due to their bad companies. Thus, there is a large number of persons who are not able to complete their formal education. However, their desire to acquire further knowledge is not killed after some times they may like to continue their education. For them, continuing education is a boon. Under these circumstances, it is the duty of the government and social leaders to provide facilities of continuing education to dropouts, farmers, labourers and half educated individuals.

Persons in Occupation

Persons engage in agriculture, industries, sciences and different services are all contributing in the national development in one form or the other. All the people employed in service or business have the great importance in the field of development of the nation. All these persons on the basis of their varying experiences learn many things automatically. But in addition to their particular skills and experiences they need to acquire some such knowledge which may enable them to become enlightened. This knowledge may be in political field, economic field or such other fields. It is only through the continuing education that this knowledge may be imparted to them.

Any person, engaged in any job may have many such interests which are not directly related to his job. These interest gradually fade away when he does not get opportunity to develop them further. On the other hand, if he gets opportunity to develop them, he may sharpen his interest to such an extent that he may be able to produce some striking things in the area of his interest. If a person is provided with the facility to use his leisure in workshop of his interest, he may contribute a lot to the society. It is only through continuing education one may utilize his leisure in a creative manner. On the other hand, if he has nothing to do during his leisure time he will waste it in reading some cheap literature, deteriorating to his character and personality. Thus, continuing education is helpful in checking his deterioration and to put him on right path of further progress.

Persons engaged in one or the other industries drift away from the latest developments taking place in the world in other areas than their own due to their environment in their jobs. For them too continuing education is essential. Persons engaged in health services, family welfare enterprises and other types of social services can also be benefited by continuing education. They can be imparted knowledge about the latest development with the help of books or public lectures. Provisions should be made for continuing education for Gram Sewaks, Block Development Officers, Doctors, Lawyers and Engineers and others busy in their specialized areas. For these persons libraries and study centres should be opened where they may get the opportunity to increase their knowledge. Cinema, Radio, T.V. and other audio-visual aids also play the vital role in the field of continuing education.

Continuing education should be planned for literate and illiterate farmers and labourers of rural areas and urban areas. Through the continuing education we can make our citizens engaged in services and business more enlightened, cultured and progressive.

For Illiterate and Semi Literate Persons : As we have already said that continuing education is not only helpful for those who are engaged in some jobs or business but it also helps the illiterates and semi-literates to achieve knowledge and contribute their might in the development of the nation. After the achievement of independence, our government have started many schemes for spreading literacy among to illiterate persons. Throughout the country, thousands of centres for adult and social education have been opened and crores of rupees have been spent for the purpose in different Five Year Plans. A large number of libraries have been opened for the semi- literate person. Radio and T.V. are also contributing their might for the purpose. A large number of programmes are relayed for the education of these persons. Many primary schools run the classes of adult and social education in the evening.

In accordance with the directives of National Policy on Education, 1986 (NPE) and the implementation strategies envisaged in the Programme Action, the Government has formulated a comprehensive programme known as National Literacy Mission in the field of adult education. The objectives of National Literacy Mission are to impart functional literacy to 800 lakh illiterate persons in 15-36 age group,.300 lakh by 1990 and an additional 500 lakh by 1995. At present, there are 513 projects in operation in various states and union territories.

Voluntary agencies have been playing an important role in the Adult Education Programme. There are at present 382 voluntary agencies working in the field. In addition 40 Shramik Vidyapeeths and 16 state resource centres are functioning in different states to cater to worker's education and to provide technical resource support to the programme.

Launched in 1986, the Mass Programme of Functional Literacy covered over 4.20 lakh learners. During 1987 a still ambitious programme has been adopted involving both students and teachers of schools and colleges with inputs for research studies on the success of the programme. The programme has been designed keeping in view the needs and language of learners.

Inspite of the great efforts, we have not been able to achieve our targets. Investigations have revealed that illiterates and semiliterate adults have special interests in such subjects as, (1) ancient history, (2) basic religious matters, (3) the diseases which generally attack animals and destroy agriculture and gardening, (4) the fundamentals of economics, (5) short but healthy novels and interesting stories, (6) folk stories, (7) folk songs, (8) psychology of adults, (9) fundamentals of philosophy, (10) first aid, (11) prevention of ordinary diseases, (12) matters regarding health and sanitation. (13) psychology of child behaviour, (14) information about bringing up young children. (15) music, (16) liking, habits of people of other lands, (17) modern international and national events, (18) the modern history of the country and (19) modern scientific achievements. This list of subjects reveal that an adult wants to understand many things about life. It is through continuing adult education we may be able to satisfy his lust for knowledge.

For Literate Persons : In our country' hectic endeavours have been made for adult education but very little work has been done for those adults who had to leave primary school studies prematurely. In a report of UNESCO about 60% children of Asian countries happen to abandon their primary education before successfully competing it. In our country no adequate facilities are available to retain literacy. Of course, there are some books for their continuing education but they too are not made available to all the persons. These books are not very useful.

The result is that there is quite a large number of persons, especially women, who are keen for their education but they have no opportunities. It is the duty of the government and social workers to come forward for their continuing education. The government and the educational agencies should not only publish the good books for their continuing education but also made them available to needy persons.

23

Professional Education

Requirement and Significance

In modern era, emphasis is given for the inclusion of technical and vocational subjects in the curricula of education. The main cause of this is that the need for vocational and technical education is being greatly felt. Sri Humayun Kabir is of the opinion that the basis of prosperity of any nation is the scientific and vocational education. If this education is successfully imparted in the country, it will certainly achieve progress. The examples of the United States of America, Germany and Japan confirm this view.

In the modern period, here are four elements: (1) capital, (2) raw material, (3) materials and (4) technical education are considered the basis of prosperity of a nation. We have to accept without any hesitation that there is lack of capital in India because the foreign rulers have exploited our nation and the natural means of this country have been used by them to their self-interest for a long time. Consequently, India has to face many famines and there prevailed widespread poverty in the country. However, our country does not lack raw material and mineral substances. A large quantity of deposits of iron, manganese, oil, copper, bauxite, mica, etc. are lying in the lands of India. Besides this, there are best means of producing electricity in the country. But the use of these things can be made only when there are large number of persons who have thorough knowledge of technical, vocational subject and different sciences in the country.

In the Science Policy Resolution of Government of India on 4th March, 1958, great emphasis was laid on technical education. It lays, "The wealth and prosperity of nation depend on the qualitative utilisation of its human and material resources through industrialization. The use of human material for industrialization demands its education in science and training in technical skills. India's enormous resources of manpower can only become an asset in the modern world, when trained and educated."

Developmental Phase

Technical and Vocational Education in Ancient India : In ancient period, technical and vocational education had expanded greatly in India but this education was not imparted in the schools. The works and professions of different cites were definite, some of these persons had the knowledge of different types of crafts and were engaged in the production of things. Education of different crafts was given by these persons to their sons and disciples. In Muslim period, the form of technical and vocational education was nearly the same as in ancient India.

Detraction of Indian Industries : The technical and vocational education that was being imparted in India in a conventional way was responsible for the progress of different trades and industries. The trades and industries received a major setback under the British rule. The British merchants opened their first factory in Masaullipattam. They acquired political strength after their victory in the battle of Plassey in 1765. From that period to 1947, they ruled unchallenged over the subcontinent of India. A French traveller named Bender who travelled India near about 1700, described the prosperity of Indians during that period. But slowly and gradually, because of the constant exploitation by the British, trades and industries were destroyed and poverty engulfed the majority of Indians. In such a condition, the system of technical and vocational education that was imparted by a father to his son or disciple met with an end for ever. This condition continued for a long time. Thereafter, the condition began to change slowly and gradually.

From 1882 to 1902 : The national leaders of India were of firm conviction that technical and vocational education was utmost necessary to remove poverty from the country. This demand was made by the congress in its Session which was held in the year 1887. Later on, the demand was repeated again and again in other Sessions. But the British Government continued to reject this demand because of their vested interest. In 1902 there were only 80 technical and vocational schools out of which only few could be called really technical schools.

From 1902-1921 : During this period also, the Government of India did not pay any attention towards technical and professional education. Of course, much was done by accepting the recommendation of Sadler Commission of 1917. Technical and vocational subjects were also included in the curricula of high schools in different provinces.

From 1921-1937 : After the establishment of the dual rule in 1921, demand of the people for technical and vocational education received great momentum. It was demanded that the provision of this type of education should be made in India. In order to take a decision in this matter, a special Committee under the Chairmanship of Lord Lytton was entrusted this work.

This Committee studied the problems and difficulties of the Indian students, studying 111 foreign countries and made many suggestions to remove them. The most important suggestion of the committee was that the technical, vocational and industrial institutions should be established in India and provision should be made for imparting higher education to Indians in their own country. Hence, it was necessary that different branches of this type of education should be developed within the shortest possible period.

The institutions that were established in consequence of this recommendation were the following:

(1) Harcourt Butler Technological Institution, Kanpur.

(2) College of Engineering and Technology, Jadavpur.

(3) Government School of Technology, Madras.

There were nearly 535 technical, vocational and industrial schools in the whole of India in 1937.

From 1937 to 1947 : As pointed out earlier, vocational and technical education was totally ignored before 1937, but the expansion of this type of education took place with great speed after 1937. The following were three main reasons for this:

(1) Upto the Second World War, the demand of such persons increased who had acquired technical education.

(2) New industries had been established in India for the production of war material and industrial persons having received technical education were required for these industries.

(3) The demand of persons having received technical education increased for implementing the post development schemes prepared the Central and the Provincial Government.

The expansion of technical education was natural in consequence of the above mentioned reasons. But the expansion of this type of education that took place during this period cannot be called satisfactory because in 1941-42 only 264 students and 22 students were studying in graduate courses of technical education and chemical technology respectively.

From 1947 to 1969 : The post independent period witnessed the tremendous progress in the field of technical and vocational education along with the rapid growth of industrialisation in the country. There was the provision of imparting vocational and technical education to only 6,600 students in the year 1947. This number increased to 4,35,796 in the year 1963. Besides this, facilities were also provided to 25,000 students for engineering and technical degree and to 49,000 for diploma in the year 1966.

Vocational and Technical Education during the First Five Year Plan : Special attention was given to the expansion of technical and vocational education during the First Five Year Plan. It was decided to develop Indian Institute of Science, Bangalore, to establish 14 colleges of engineering to make provision of teaching of some special vocational subjects and to establish guidance centres for the students receiving professional and technical education. In addition to this, schemes were also prepared for the establishment of Industrial, Technical and professional schools, conversion of crafts schools into Junior Technical high schools, establishment of Junior multipurpose schools, development of general secondary schools into technical high schools, giving of proper place to agricultural education in the curriculum, conversion of commercial, vocational and technical schools into colleges and grant of scholarship to the students for receiving higher education in foreign countries. Provision was also made for providing more facilities to impart training to the artists and craftsmen and to establish trained centres in villages.

Second Five Year Plan : In view of the increasing demand of the technical and vocational workers, special importance was given to the expansion of vocational and technical education during the Second Five Year Plan. With this aim in view, 48 crores rupees were allotted for technical and vocational education in the Second Five Year Plan. This sum was more than two times the sum (23 crores) which was granted for this purpose during the First Five Year Plan.

During the Second Five Year Plan, the Indian Institute of Technology, Kharaghpur was completely developed for graduate and postgraduate studies. Provision was made for the study of graduate courses of 1,200 students and postgraduate and research work for 600 students. The Institute of Science, Bangalore was developed for Air and Naval Engineering, Power Engineering, Internal Combustion Metallurgy and Electrical Research and other types of vocational and technical education.

In the centres established for vocational and technical education under the First Five-Year Plan, provision was made for the post graduate course in engineering, technological and research work. The work started under the First Five-year Plan for developing degree during the Second Five-Year Plan. The rest of the money was spent in establishing higher institutions of vocational and technical education in western, northern, southern regions of the country. Two of such types of institutions were established at Bombay and Kanpur.

During the Second Five Year Plan, facilities for the education of engineering and technology in Delhi Polytechnic were expanded. Besides this, 9 other institutions of degree stage and 20 institutions of diploma stage were established in other parts of the country. The scheme of training of foremen was implemented with the cooperation of industrial institutions. The number of scholarships were increased from 630 to 800. Some seats were reserved for meritorious students in technical and vocational Institutions. Hostels were built for 13,000 technical students and for 3,300, students of Junior technical schools, Indian School of Science and Applied Geology, Dhanbad was further developed and expanded.

In consequence of these efforts, by the end of the year 1960-61, 57,000 graduates and 6,800 diploma holders in the engineering and technical education were made available to the country. This number was doubled and tripled to the number of graduates and diploma holders respectively made available during the First Five year Plan.

Third Five-Year Plan : It was envisaged that 45,000 graduates and 80,000 diploma holders would be required during the Third Five Year Plan. This requirement was nearly fulfilled. In order to meet the little shortage of the diploma holders, additional facilities were provided in the beginning of the Third Five-Year Plan. During the period of Third Five-Year Plan, the number of students admitting annually in the degree courses was increased by 6,000 by admitting of 5,000 in engineering colleges and by imparting education to the rest of 1,000 through part time or correspondence courses. Thus, number of students admitted every year increased from 13,200 in 1961 to 19,200 in 1966. Likewise, the number of students admitted in diploma courses was also increased by 15,000 by admitting 10,000 students in Polytechnic and education of the test of 5,000 students through part-time or correspondence courses. Consequently, the number of the students, which was 24,000 at the end of the Second Five Year Plan increased to 9,000 at the end of the Third Five Year Plan. A sum of rupees 142 crores was allotted for implementing the programme of the development of the technical and vocational education.

Fourth Five-Year Plan : During the Fourth Five-Year Plan, an additional capacity of 4,000 seats for degree and 3,400 for diploma courses was created. The other programmes implemented during the Fourth Five-Year Plan increase in number of students in technical schools, expansion of technical schools of diploma stage, establishment of close cooperation between the developing industrial centres with the technical institutes, imparting facilities to technical students to achieve practical knowledge in big industries and facility for part-time and correspondence for the persons engaged in technical jobs.

Fifth Five Year Plan : In the Fifth Plan top priority was given to vocational and technical education, the proposed plan outlay for technical education was Rs 164 crores. It was same in the draft of Fifth Five-Year Plan, "The main stress in the Fifth plan will continue to be on the consolidation and improvement of the quality of the technical education system."

The aim was to provide technical education to 25,000 students at degree level and 50,000 at diploma level. In the draft of the plan, it was said, "The main stress will continue to be on the consolidation and improvement of the quality of the technical education system."

Sixth Five Year Plan : The Janta Government under the Sixth Five-Year Plan (1978-83) allocated Rs 150 crores for the expansion of technical and vocational education. The Congress Government in its revised draft allocated Rs 278 crores for its expansion under the sixth plan.

Under the Sixth Five-Year Plan emphasis was laid on maximum utilization of existing facilities, improvement of technical education at all levels and evaluation of the number of technical hands required in the forthcoming ten years.

Seventh Five Year Plan : Under the Seventh Five Year Plan Rs 681.79 crores were allocated for technical and vocational education. The existing institutions were expanded and hectic programme for vocational education upto higher secondary stage was implemented. Efforts were also made to improve the quality of technical and vocational education.

For the vocationalization, a centrally sponsored scheme was introduced. The scheme was implemented in all the states except Tripura, Daman & Diu, Dadra and Nagar Haveli and Lakshadweep.

Eighth Five Year Plan : Under the Eighth Five year plan Rupees 278.63 crores were allocated for technical and vocational education. Upto the year 1991, 44,000 technical schools and 12543 technical courses were recognised in which about 6.27 lac students were moulded towards technical education of +2 stage.

Education Policy of 1986 : In the educational policy of 1986, a well thought scheme of vocational education was propounded, it was proposed under the 10+2+3 scheme that generally the vocational curriculum shall be started at upper secondary (+2) stage but there will be flexibility to start it from class 8. It was proposed that upto 1990, 10% students and upto 1995, 25% students shall receive vocational education. Upto the end of 1991-92, 12,543 schools were allowed to start vocational courses so that at +2 stage 6.27 lac students may get vocational education which was 9.3% of total number of students enrolled at this stage.

Difficulties and Remedial Measures : We will now discuss the different obstacles and problems and their solutions:

Wrong Attitude : In India from very ancient period a very respectful place has been given to intellectual labour and physical labour has been given a very low place. It was only on the basis of work of labour that the caste system had been built in our country. Youths of higher castes and families are generally indifferent to receive technical education. Consequently, this type of education has not made the desired progress.

Solution : The solution of this problem is not easy. If the Government and the social workers start the movement then the youths of this country can be attracted towards the technical and vocational education, but the movement alone will not bring about the desired results. This will certainly bring about the change in the attitude of the people but only this will not be sufficient. The Government will have to provide facilities for the studies of those students who wish to receive technical education. It is, therefore, necessary that the Government should grant scholarships and make proper provision for their employment after receiving tins type of education. It may be mentioned in the end that with the vigorous efforts of the Government and social workers, a significant change has come in the attitude of the people and now a large number of Indian youths are desirous to receive technical and vocational education. Thus, much has been achieved during post-independent period, but much remains yet to be achieved. We should always remember the words of Carlyle, "Labour is life. The true epic of our times is tools and the man."

Dearth of Institutions : Although many technical and vocational institutions have been established after independence, yet their number cannot be said to be sufficient The awakened Indian people have now realised that the young person receiving technical education have a very bright future. But because of the shortage of such institutions and lack of facilities, 60 per cent of the students are not able to get admission and hence they are greatly disappointed.

Solution : This problem can be solved only when more technical and vocational institutions are established in the country and technical education should be imparted at all the stages. At present there are less than 800 good engineering and technical institutions in the country. These institutions are very few for the country like India having so huge population. It is, therefore, the duty of the Government to establish new technical and vocational institutions to cope up with the increasing demand.

Narrow Curriculum : The curriculum of our technical and vocational schools are very narrow because only technical subjects have been included in them. No place has been given to liberal education in them. Consequently, after receiving technical education, the youths are not able to acquire knowledge of human relation and social objectives of production.

Solution : In order to remove the defects of the curriculum, it is necessary that proper place should be given to general and liberal education in it. This is heartening to note that this problem has attracted the attention of the Government and the curriculum of the technical and vocational institutions are being broadened by including the subjects of general and liberal education.

Unsuitable Medium of Instruction : Yet, another serious problem that confronts technical and vocational education the unsuitability of the medium of instruction. In almost all the technical institutions of the modern India, English is the medium of instructions.

Solution : It may be frankly remarked that in order to solve this problem, administrators and politicians of India will have to give-up the dual policy. They will have to make Hindi or regional languages of different States as the medium of instruction of technical and vocational institutions. Of course, it cannot be denied that many difficulties will come in the way because neither do we have books on technical subjects in Indian languages nor have we evolved a suitable vocabulary for it. But if we firmly resolve to solve it and work sincerely for it, those difficulties will be removed in due course of time. We should emulate the example of other countries such as China, Japan, Russia, Germany where the medium of instruction is not English but their own languages. If it has been possible for these countries to adopt their own languages as medium of instructions, why can it not be possible for India to do the same?

Less Importance of Practical Education : In our technical and vocational schools, importance is given to the theoretical education rather than to practical education. Consequently, the graduates of engineering and technology are generally not skilled in practical works. Hence, they have to face many difficulties and have to depend upon their subordinates and less educated officers to learn practical works. This entails loss of their prestige.

Solution : It is necessary that importance should be given to practical education in our technical and vocational institutions.

We should follow the example of technical and vocational institutions of Europe and America in this connection. In these countries, the students are given adequate knowledge of practical works by sending them in workshops, factories etc. and when they enter into their career they do not have to depend upon others.

Lack of Continuation of Education : After having completed their technical and vocational education the young persons are employed in some industries, etc. For some time their minds are full of knowledge which they have recently acquired but slowly and gradually they begin to forget many things. This brings about lack of efficiency in their work. The efficiency of technical personnel depends upon the quality of industrial technical knowledge that he possesses. But he lacks the knowledge, or forgets much of the things that he learned, then his efficiency will naturally decline. This is due to the fact that there is no provision for continuation of education after completion of their education.

Solution : This problem can be solved through the following two methods:

(a) Provision should be made for part-time instruction to the person engaged in technical and vocational works. Prominence should be given only to theory in this education because the persons concerned become efficient in their practical works by doing work in the factories and the workshops in which they are employed.

(b) Another method of solving this problem is through the method of providing refresher courses to such persons. It is remark to suggest here that each skilled or semiskilled person should be compelled to take benefit of this type of profession at least in a year or once after two years.

Dearth of Teachers : Main problem of technical and vocational education is the dearth of teacher. Kothari Commission was of the view, "The existing shortage of teachers in engineering colleges is disturbingly large." The main reason for this is that the meritorious and able persons, having received technical and vocational education have moved elsewhere.

Solution : This problem can be solved only by the Government. It is the responsibility of the Government to give due importance to this problem and do the needful to make available the services of good and skilled persons in these institutions. This can be done only when the scales of pay of such teachers are increased and the conditions of their services are improved and made more attractive, for encouraging to note that this problem has attracted the serious consideration of the Government and the Government is making every possible endeavour to solve this problem.

Special attention proposed to be given to solve this problem under the 8th Five-year Plan. It has been decided to increase the faculties of postgraduate courses and research work and the teachers, who have been doing teaching work will be given financial help by the Government to improve their educational qualification. The scales of salaries of such teachers have also been increased but much remains yet to be achieved in this connection.

Kothari Commission's Recommendations : The Kothari Commission has recognized the importance of industrialisation and has discussed the steps to be taken for industrialisation and prosperity of the nation. The success of industrialisation depends upon the ability and skill of the workers. Hence, while emphasising the development of vocational, technical and engineering education the Commission has made many important recommendations. According to it, 20 percent of the students after receiving their education at the secondary stage and 50 per cent of the students after receiving education after class X must adopt professional courses by the year 1986. It is clear from the determination of this objective that the Commission laid down a great emphasis on vocational and technical education. We will now briefly discuss the suggestions of the Commission in regard to different aspects of vocational and technical education.

Training of Semi-Skilled and Skilled Workers : In regard to training of semiskilled and skilled workers, the suggestions of the Kothari Commission are as follows:

(i) Facilities already existing in the industrial training institutions should be further extended and the minimum age of students admitted in these institutions must be of 14 years.

(ii) Junior Technical schools should be renamed as technical High School and they should organise such courses which should be terminal in their nature.

(iii) Emphasis should be given on production in the training given in Industrial Training Institutions and Technical Schools. For training courses of the skilled workers the qualification for admission should be below high school and for proper utilisation of the existing facilities, they should be connected with polytechnic schools.

(iv) For the students who leave schools, faculties should be provided for part-time professional and technical training through Correspondence Courses and Short Intensive Courses, etc.

Technical Training : The Kothari Commission was of the view that the need of technicians is as much as that of engineers for industrialisation. With the aim in view, the Commission has made the following recommendations in regard to the expansion of training for the technicians:

(i) At present the proportion of the technicians and engineers is 1 : 1.4. This should increase to 1 : 2.5 and 1:3 and 1:4 in the year 1975 and 1986 respectively. The curriculum of the technicians should be reorganised and extended.

(ii) More importance should be given to practical works in the schools conducting diploma courses. Emphasis should also be given in industrial experience in diploma courses.

(iii) Polytechnics should be established for industrial schools. In the polytechnic schools established in the rural areas, education connected with agricultural industries should be imparted.

(iv) The teachers of the Polytechnic schools should be appointed from among the workers of the different industries and the educational qualification for the appointment of such teachers should be fixed comparatively lower than other teachers. The salary of the teachers should be based not only on the basis of their ability but due consideration should also be given to their industrial experience.

(v) Training should be imparted to the students in suitable environment. The students and teachers should be encouraged to make small things during vacation to decorate the laboratories of the schools.

(vi) Emphasis should be given on the education of science and mathematics during the first two years in the Polytechnic schools and their curricula should be developed. The subjects of natural psychology and management, costing and estimating etc. should be included in the curriculum of the technicians.

(vii) The curriculum of the Polytechnics should be reorganised under the Fourth and Fifth Five-Year Plans keeping in view the regional and national requirements.

(viii) At certificate and diploma stages in polytechnics, provision should be made for the courses according to the interests of the girls and they should be encouraged to take the subjects after passing the lower secondary stages.

(ix) Every possible effort should be made to check and minimise the wastage taking place in the polytechnics and they should be made more useful.

(x) Provision should also be made for post-diploma courses in some polytechnic schools. Only those technicians should be admitted in these courses who have acquired industrial experience for some years after having passed diploma courses.

Other Types of Vocational Education : In this connection Kothari Commission gave the following suggestion:

(i) Different Types of courses should be introduced at the higher secondary stage. At this stage along with the polytechnics, scientific, commercial and other courses should be organised. Education of home science, nursing, social work, etc. should be imparted to the girls.

Education of Engineers : In regard to the education of Engineers, the Commission has made the following recommendations:

(i) The conditions of such schools connected with the education of engineering whose standard has declined should be improved and they should be converted into the institutions of training of technicians. If their condition has deteriorated beyond repair then they should be closed down.

(ii) For the education of some branches of engineering such as electronics and instrumentation, etc., only able and talented B.Sc. pass students should be selected and their curricula should be properly modified.

(iii) Practical training should be imparted in the third year to the students of degree courses.

(iv) In workshops, emphasis should be given on production works.

(v) The curricula at the degree and diploma stage should be determined keeping in view the changing needs.

(vi) Subjects of courses should be modified according to the advice of the expert committees. The subjects of chemical technology, aeronautics and astronautics should be developed.

(vii) Provision should be made for the organisation of Extensive Summer Institutes for the teachers.

(viii) In engineering colleges, the teachers of science and technological departments should be given the same salaries as are given to the teachers of other departments.

(ix) In order to make the teaching profession attractive, proper scales of pay should be introduced and able Engineers should be encouraged to do research work along with their teaching work.

(x) The system of frequent transfers of teachers in Government Engineering Colleges should be stopped.

(xi) In technical institutions, teaching and training programmes should be organised on extensive basis for graduates and post- graduate students.

(xii) Conventionally should have no place in the postgraduate course. The students admitted at the postgraduate stage most possess at least one year's industrial experience.

(xiii) Special courses of higher stage should be organised of national level.

(xiv) The system of admitting students in engineering schools by taking money should be completely abolished.

Man-power Requirement : Provision and organisation of vocational, technical and engineering education should be made keeping in view the requirement of man-power. The wastage taking place in this education should be checked and the interesting distinction and discrimination on socio-economic background should be removed.

Medium of Instruction : At the Polytechnic stage, regional languages should be made the medium of instructions. At the higher stage, the medium of instruction can be determined keeping in view the conveniences of the students. Provision should be made for preparation of good textbooks in regional languages.

Practical Training : For practical training scheme, the selection of the students and the trainees should be properly made. The number of training centres should be increased. If on account of some reasons, some public apprentice schools are being closed, then the Central Government should take them into their own hands.

Cooperation with Industries : In the view of the Kothari Commission, cooperation of the industries is necessary for vocational, technical and engineering education. At present, more than 3000 trainees are receiving training in different industrial institution. Their number should be increased to 5000, the Central Government should render necessary help to the industrial institutions so that they may appoint able training officers, who may impart best type of training to the student trainees.

Correspondence Courses : The Kothari Commission was of the view that the work of imparting vocational, technical and engineering education through correspondence courses should be immediately started. However, the Commission hastened to add that complete and proper arrangements should be made before the start of the work and these courses should be started only after properly testing preparations and arrangements.

Administration of Vocational : Technical and Engineering Education- In this connection, the commission has made the following suggestions:

(i) An institution such as University Grants Commission should be established for this type of education, in which representation should be given to vocational, organisational, industrial institutions and concerning ministries.

(ii) This institution should work in cooperation with Planning Commission and the Institute of Applied Man-Power Research.

(iii) The Industrial Institutions should be accorded the status of universities but their individual names and special features should not be changed.

(iv) The Directorate of Technical Education should be established in each State under the Board of School Education.

(v) Eminent educationists should be appointed on the post of the President of the Board of Governors in Regional Engineering Colleges.

(vi) The Principals of the colleges should have full authority to provide educational facilities in their institutions.

24

Education for Every One

One of the chief aims of the constitution is to provide equal opportunities of education to all. How the equal opportunities be provided is the burning problem of the Modern India. Now, it is greatly felt that the backward classes of the society may improve their condition through education. Now, there is a social awakening towards education. Many scholars are working on the problem of changing the structure of education to provide equal opportunities of education for all the persons. Those who believe in the ideal of social justice, equality, and democracy must try to contribute their might for providing equal opportunities of education irrespective of caste, creed or sex.

The tendency to limit the educational opportunities is prevalent in the country since a long time. Often it is said that only those, who have the capability of receiving education should receive the education. How can those get the education who have no capabilities ? The leaders of the society never exerted full zeal and zest to make all the people educated. However, the attitude changed in the later half of the 19th century and in the 20th century some efforts were made in the field of equal opportunities of education. After independence, in our constitution we adopted the concept of universalization of primary education. Since then, many steps have been taken in the field of providing equal opportunities to all sections of the society but still there is lot to be done in this direction.

Reasons for the Dissymmetry in Educational Opportunities **:** There are many factors in the field of providing equal opportunities of education to all the persons of the society. Here, we are giving a brief account of them:

1. There are some places in our country where there are no primary, secondary schools, what to say about the institutions of higher education.
2. In the modern times, emphasis is on the development of education. But we have the unbalanced planning. There are some places where there are plenty of opportunities but there are other places where there is no such provision.
3. Another reason of the inequality in the field of education is that the major portion of our population is living below the poverty line and the children of poor families are unable to get suitable opportunities.
4. The elementary or primary education is free but at the later stages of study there is need of the huge amount and the children of poor families can not afford to have expensive education.
5. At different stages of study, there are different types of schools. The students, studying in below standard schools at lower stage of study, find it very difficult to get admission at the higher stage of study. Generally, the students studying in the rural areas have to run from pillar to post to get admission in the university.
6. The dissymmetry also arise due to the family atmosphere. The students residing in the dirty places of city or village find it very difficult to receive higher education. Their parents are illiterate and stop the studies of their wards if there are any type of hurdles.

7. The great difference between the education of boys and girls is also one of the chief causes of this dissymmetry.
8. Educational difference between the advanced classes and backward classes is also one of the potent cause of this dissymmetry.
9. There are no good arrangements for the handicapped students and so there is a great dissymmetry.

Hurdles in Equalization of Educational Opportunities

1. First, the main hurdle is that how the turn 'Equalization' be defined.
2. It is a problem before the educationists and administrators that the equal opportunities be provided to all the sections of the society.
3. In addition to social injustice, how can the intellectual and economic wastage can be stopped, is one of the burning problems.
4. Considering the needs of the student, how can their mental status be raised, is another problem.
5. Even if we provide the equal opportunities for all, it is not possible to achieve the equal results because the environment of family and schools is one of the potent factors of intellectual development of the students.
6. As it is totally impossible to ignore the environmental factor from the educational ability, so it is not good to provide the similar type of education to all the students. However, it can not be presumed that all the students living in dirty places are incapable.
7. There is no set criteria for judging the high capabilities of students,
8. The amount of the scholarships given to the students at every level is the same, whether they are living in big cities or small villages. This similarity does not appear to be just.
9. In technological institutes, the admission tests are held

only in English language and so the English medium student get the advantage and thus the very spirit of equal opportunities is lost.

10. The handicapped students do not get the opportunity of suitable educational standard due to the lack of resources and facilities.
11. Equal opportunities for women education is also a difficult task due to our pre-notions about the women education. Some parents do not allow their daughters to have higher education because they think that it is a sheer wastage.
    Some steps for the equalization of educational opportunities:

Certain concrete steps can be suggested for the equalization of educational opportunities. They are:

1. First of all, steps should be taken to remove the shortcomings of society, community and family from the educational point of view.
2. The whole system of education should be modified in such a way that educational environment may be created in the entire nation.
3. Changes should be made in the diversive tendencies of language, place, standard of living, culture and social systems etc. so that equal opportunities may be given to all.
4. It is very necessary to make adequate changes in the system of educational evaluation so that there may be no possibility of favouritism.
5. The aims of education should be modified according to the needs of the time.
6. Equality in education should not only mean to achieve equal results but due importance be given to the efforts to raise the standard of education.
7. Unhealthy environment is the greatest hurdle in the field of the development of the child, so efforts should be made for the total environment to be more clean.

8. The evaluation of equality should be judged from the ratio of equality. So ability should be judged from the point of view of standard of living *etc.*
9. We shall have to change our attitudes towards women-education of backward classes, schedule castes and schedule tribes and handicapped persons. We shall have to remove all the hurdles and evils of the society of such persons and then only we shall be able to give the practical shape to equalization of educational opportunities.

Kothari Commission has made it clear that in India two types of inequalities are found in the field of education (a) in the education of boys and girls and (b) in the education of developed and backward classes, in older to remove these inequalities, the Commission recommended that upto the end of Fifth Five Year Plan lower Secondary Education should be made free and thereafter in the period of 10 years higher secondary and university education should be given free to the poor and meritorious students. The Commission also emphasised the need of reducing the cost of education. In the libraries of educational institutions, sufficient number of textbooks should be kept and meritorious students should be granted financial help to enable them to purchase the textbooks.

At the secondary education stages 15 percent students should be granted scholarships. By the year 1976, five percent of the students of postgraduate course should be granted scholarship. This percentage should be increased to 25 by the year 1986. The Commission also recommended the adoption of a system for granting educational scholarships. A system of university scholarships should also be started. 500 scholarships should be granted to the students, who should be selected to receive education in foreign countries.

Kothari Commission also suggested that within 20 years more than 10% handicapped persons should be educated. The Commission gave more emphasis on the women education and recommended for the organization at the national level to provide jobs to women. The Commission also recommended for the expansion education amongst the scheduled tribes.

Under the educational policy of 1986, there is great provision of equalization of educational opportunities. Under the policy, there is provision of universalisation of primary education, vacationalization of secondary educational, job-oriented scientific education, and specialization of higher education. There is also provision of open university system. It is expected that with the proper implementation of this policy, our goal of equalization of educational opportunities shall be achieved.

Education for the Disabled

India is a developing country but still a vast majority of the people are below standard. The number of handicapped in the country is also very great. One will find these handicapped people begging on the streets here and there. The provisions for the teaching of these people should also be made with great zeal and courage.

The handicapped people can be divided in three categories:

1. Mentally handicapped,
2. Physically handicapped, and
3. Socially handicapped.

The number of mentally retarded people in the country is very great. Physically handicapped people are also of different types: some are lepers, some are blind and some dumb and other physically handicapped. There are also people who are socially handicapped. These people are so poor that for them it is not possible to think of any type of education.

Steps Taken

During the pre-independence period, almost negligible efforts were made for the education of handicapped. There were only few organisations that used to take some steps in this direction. The government was not interested in their-education. However, after the independence, the national government came forward with the active programme of the welfare of these people. A number of schools and colleges were opened for the education of these people. Amongst the prominent are (l) National Centre for the blind, Dehradun, (2) National library, New Delhi, (3) Training Centre for the Dumb, Hyderabad, (4) School for the Blind, Dehradun, (5) Training Centre for the Teachers for the Handicapped at Bombay and others. The education budget for the education of handicapped is increasing day by day. Indian government spent 23.06 lakhs rupees on the education of handicapped in the year 1955-56. The amount rose to Rs. 60.07 lakhs in the year 1970-71. In 1974-75 Rs 1 crore were spent for the education of handicapped. At present, the annual budget is more than three crore rupees.

Major Difficulties

The government has made all out efforts for the education of handicapped but still there is a lot to be done in this direction. There are certain hurdles in this field. Many of our schemes are not completed due to the lack of funds. The allocation of funds made by the Centre and State Governments are very meagre. The number of handicapped is in lakhs but the financial allocation is not up to the mark. The number of educational Institutions for the handicapped is also not sufficient. There is great need for the increase in the number. The teachers of the school of handicapped are not fully trained. There is a great dearth of good teachers in this field. The curriculum should be village oriented, so that handicapped persons can perform certain functions in the villages. The administration of the schools of handicapped is also not up to the mark.

It is true that some things have been done for the education of handicapped but the number of handicapped is so great that still all efforts appear to be negligible. All our attempts should be made in this direction.

The vast majority of the people of India consists of those persons who are backward in all fields. The caste system of the country has done a great loss in the upliftment of people of India. There are backward classes, scheduled castes, scheduled tribes and tribal people who are educationally very backward. In article 341 and 342 of the Indian Constitution, there is a list of scheduled castes and scheduled tribes. From the educational point of view, they are far behind to those who belong to the upper class. Some efforts were made for the education of scheduled castes, scheduled tribes and tribal people in the pre-independence era. In the Macaulay's declaration of 1835, it was said that the doors of the Government colleges shall be opened only for those who belong to the higher class. However, in 1858, doors of these colleges were also opened for the people of scheduled castes and scheduled tribes. Hunter Commission in the year 1882 said that the education of the scheduled castes, scheduled tribes was totally neglected.

The Commission recommended for the opening of special types of schools for these people. Hunter Commission also recommended that hectic efforts should be made for the education of tribal people. Upto the year 1921, 1922 only 6 per cent of the population of backward people were getting elementary knowledge. The percentage at the higher level was 0.1 and 0.2. In the year 1921, Mahatma Gandhi said that every effort should be made to educate the people of scheduled castes and scheduled tribes.

In 1902 the number of children of tribal people getting education in different Provinces was 4,534 in Madras, 7,667 in Bomaby, 30,302 in Bengal, 3,204 in Central Province and Barar and 16,094 in Assam. In 1936-37 the number rose to 15,603 in Madras, 29,102 in Bombay, 25,597 in Central Province Barar and 40,934 in Assam. The above data fully reveal that almost negligible efforts were made for the education of children of these people.

Era after Independence

After the dawn of Independence, the Government greatly felt the need for the propagation of education for all the people of the country. In Article 45 of the Indian Constitution it was said that within ten years the education for all the children of the country upto the age of 14 shall be made compulsory. Article 15, 17, 19, 25 and 46 are related for the raising of social status and propagation of the education for those who were greatly neglected. Article 17 is in connection with the untouchability. Article 46 is in regard to the economic development of backward people. In article 25 it is said that the doors of religious institutions of Hindus shall be opened for all the people. In article 29, it is said that the doors of Government and Government aided institutions shall be opened for all the people of the country

Under the Five Year Plans, provisions were made for the education of backward people and scheduled castes. In the first Five Year Plan Rs. 17 crores were spent for the education of scheduled castes. However, Rs. 53 crores were spent for the purpose under the Third Five Year Plan. Upto the year 1971 the percentage of scheduled castes receiving education was only 5. Hectic efforts were made for the education of scheduled tribes. Certain efforts were also made for the propagation of education in the tribal people of the country. The result of these efforts was that by the end of 1981,14.03 percent of the total population of scheduled castes and tribes became literate. Until now about 16 percent of their total population is literate.

Difficulties and Remedial Measures

As we have already said, a huge amount has been spent for the propagation of education amongst the scheduled castes, scheduled tribes and tribal people but still there is a lot to be done. There are some hurdles in this field. Among these people, there is no environment of education. Still there are thousands and thousands who do not think that is necessary for them to send their children to the schools. Those children who go to the school at primary level leave their education at the secondary level. Untouchability is a crime in our country but still it persists in one form or the other. There are still villages where the children of scheduled castes cannot receive education with the children of upper castes due to threat of upper casts. The economic condition of the people of scheduled castes, scheduled tribes and tribal people is also very poor and so they do not understand the need of education. Under these circumstances, a huge amount spent for the education is wasted: It is true that the Central Government as well as the State Governments of different provinces are making hectic efforts in this direction but the money allocated for the purpose is utilized somewhere else. The Government has also made provision for the scholarship for the students of scheduled castes and scheduled tribes. They are given free education up to the University level, but there are very few who utilise this opportunity.

As we have already said that with a view to remove these hurdles an environment should be created amongst the people of these castes and tribes and they should realise that education is a must for their development. The Government endeavours are not enough. More and more social agencies should come forward for this great task.

Drop-outs in Education

A large percentage of children between the age group of 6 to 11 years in our country are not sent to school due to their domestic circumstances. There is also a large percentage of such children who are sent to school but they dropout before completing their primary education. Because of the unprecedented growth in population in our country, the number of such students is increasing day-by-day. These illiterate children are curse for our democratic set-up. For such students a scheme of non-formal education has been started. In order to understand this scheme, it will be essential to know the difference between formal, informal and non-formal education.

Education Pattern

Formal Education : In formal education, there is a prescribed curriculum. There are prescribed textbooks and prefixed timetable and set rules for admission and examination. The duration of the session is also prefixed. Due to these rules and regulations the convenience is seldom taken account. The teacher does not have any liberty to make any change in the already prescribed rules and routines. The children have to sit in a group under a fixed timetable and they are taught something according to the prescribed curriculum. Thus, the formal education is not so much for children and it is for the facility of teachers and administration. In this type of education, children are taught experiences of others in order to give them a basis for their happy future life. Generally, the education given from the primary stage to the University level is called formal education.

Informal Education : Unlike formal education there are no set roles and regulations in informal education. Every children picks it up in natural and social environments. In his natural environment consisting of trees, plants, birds, animals, hub, mountains, forest, gardens, summer, winter and rainy seasons, a child happens to learn many things on his own. Similarly in a social environment which includes family, neighbourhood, Markets, plays, television, radio, cinema, railway station etc. the child happens to learn many things himself. There are no prefixed aims in learning. In fact, a person is motivated by his needs in learning many things consciously and unconsciously and expands his experiences. Chance and incidentalness play the vital role in this type of education. However, this type of education and learning is not less important than formal type of education and learning. It is the reason that all the great educators of modern times have emphasized the necessity of enriching the natural and social environment of the child to the utmost extant so that he may learn many things by himself.

Non-formal Education : Non-formal education is also free from the traditions of rules and regulations but there are goals to be realized through it. In this type of education, certain curriculum and procedures of evaluation have to be followed, but for following them, there is no fixed place and time duration. The procedures for this type of education are also quite flexible. In this type of education, the convenience of students is given more importance and convenience of teachers and administration is given secondary consideration. Thus, non-formal type of education is entirely organised according to the needs and convenience of students. Consequently, a child may receive this type of education while busy in his home, duty or while doing some thing for earning his bread. Some times non-formal education functions as competition to primary education in the sense that it teaches those things to non-school going children which they might not have learnt if they had attended the schools. However, it is to be noted that non-formal education is in education which may replace primary education. It is only complementary to it for those children who are deprived of the facility of going to primary schools, because of their adverse home circumstance. It is also for those children who have dropped out of primary schools before receiving in full It is also to be kept in mind that non-formal education is altogether different from adult education.

The Distinction

The purpose of adult education is to make adults learn within a stipulated period of time and then to educate them into the basic elements of life in general. In adult education, the life occupation is accepted as the basis of the education. In this education an adult acquires knowledge in formal manner, and non-formal education after acquiring some seasonable literacy programmes are organised for developing experience where knowledge and literacy is made practical and purposeful as the programmes are based on the real life. In non-formal education, literacy alone is not the chief goal. In fact, the entire education is so organised as to make closely related the personal mode of life and also the occupation relating to some industry or craft within the easy reach of children. Due to this close relationship, even after acquiring adulthood the individual shall remain not only literate but also remember his acquired knowledge and experience.

Curriculum and Syllabus

It is not very difficult to draw and outline of the curriculum for non-formal education. The basis of organization of the curriculum is the local needs, industries and crafts suitable for the boys and girls concerned. The rural environment is different from the urban one and so the curriculum of rural children shall be different from the other children. The needs of boys are different from the girls. We shall have to take into account the varying needs of the boys and girls for framing their curriculum. The interest, capacities and age of children too should be kept in view.

Agriculture and rural industries are accepted as the basis of curriculum organization of rural children. Urban industries, mills, factories and other kinds of livelihood are the basis of curriculum organization for urban children.

For the organization of curriculum, the help of experienced workers, farmers, teachers and others is also taken. The cooperation of the voluntary organizations of the neighbourhood should also be sought for procuring the necessary help at times. The materials, such as lanterns and baskets and Jugs etc. may be lent to the village people at the time of their special social functions. This will create a feeling of brotherhood in them and the people shall consider the centre as their home.

Main Motivational Factors

As we have already stated that the boys and girls coming to the centre should be grouped in sections according to their age and capacity. They should be educated on the basis of following motivations:

1. Intellectual, 2. Political, 3. Religious, 4. Social, and 5. Economic.

1. Under the intellectual motivation, children should be prompted to learn on the basis of their interests. They should at least pickup the preliminary knowledge of those subjects which are taught to children of primary schools.
2. Under the political motivation, the boys and girls should be taught the rights and duties of citizenship. They should be given the elementary knowledge of working of Village Block, Panchayat, District Board, Municipal Board, State and Central Government. Newspapers, radio talks and Television programmes should be made available for the purpose.
3. Under the religious motivation, children should be encouraged to have the feeling of religious tolerance. Equality of all religions should be the basic ideal before them.

4. Under the social motivations, attempt should be made to wipe out the distinction of caste, colour and creed from the minds of Children. Children of Scheduled castes and Scheduled tribes should not be discriminated and all out efforts should be made for their upliftment. The spirit of equality and brotherhood should be infused amongst the children.
5. Under the economic motivation, the children should be made to learn that education is for their economic development. It will brighten their future and increase their working efficiency and help in raising the standard of their life.

For making the above motivations as the basis for educating children, it is essential to enlist the cooperation of able teachers, conveners and supervisor, along with acquiring reading materials. The non-formal education in India is at a very preliminary experimental stage, in some states different kinds of work has been done in this direction while it has yet to be started in most of the states.

25

Modern Trends

Donald K. Adams had written well about the modernisation process. We produce below some extracts from his paper.

There are a number of interpretations of the character of modernisation, for it is filtered by the distinctive lenses of the observers. In this complex and still, somewhat mysterious process, however, there is perhaps a fairly general consensus that the following changes take place.

Technology will change towards the increased application of scientific knowledge; agriculture will move from subsistence farming to cash crops to commercial production, in Industry the trend is away from muscle power to the use of machines which derives power from other forms of energy, in religion there becomes a secularization of belief pattern; in ecological arrangements movement of urban concentration in familiar patterns, a reduction in size and number of functions in education, growth in quantity available and variety of curricula offered.

Some scholars, however, do distinguish between the notions of modernization and development Modernisation, one argument goes, refers more to the values, attitudes and styles and living of people, while development is more fundamentally an application of technology in processes of production and distribution.

From this interpretation, it follows that modernization may towards development. That is, the effort expended in producing and acquiring modern clothing, entertainment, and services detracts from the accumulation of capital through savings and thereby limits investment in agriculture, industry or infrastructure. While this distinction has merit, we will primarily rely on the term "modernisation" to describe, processes we are discussing.

Perhaps most controversy exists when an attempt is made to describe the political requisites for modernization. James Coleman, for example, gives the following definitions of political development.

The acquisition by a political system of consciously sought and qualitatively new and enhanced political capacity as manifested in the successful institutionalization of:

(1) New patterns of integration regulating and containing the tensions and conflicts produced by increased differentiation, and (2) New patterns of participation and resource distribution adequately responsible for the demands generated by the imperatives of equality.

The emphasis on 'New pattern of integration' and 'new patterns of participation' is perhaps quite standard in the definition of most political scientists. Coleman, in describing the modern participatory state' identifies to possible models, the totalitarian and the democratic.

His preference for the latter is obvious and he finds the democratic model viable for a modern society; that is, he believes that a democratic polity is better vehicle for bringing about and sustaining development and social change.

Some political scientists such as Word and Rustow are more cautious, whereas they emphasize that developed politics is characterized by interest and involvement, they do not argue that political development necessarily implies democratic decision making.

Indeed, in commenting on the communist belief that all societies move along a single path toward one preordained goal, these authors conclude that of this artless and simplistic notion society does not gain invalidity as we change the sign on the finish line from 'communism' to 'Democracy'.

What political scientists call Participant Political System, that is, nations with elected public officials, multiple political parties and the like, are often associated with higher incomes. However, successful economic performance has been associated with authoritarian Government as well as the democratic ones.

There appears then, to be little direct evidence to suggest that the more participant forms of democracy ensure rapid economic growth. More likely there are common social individual elements underlying transformation of political and economic institution.

While democracy may neither be a prerequisite to, nor a necessary outcome of modernization, several scholars note that the nature of modernization does appear to be supportive of democratic institutions. As the result of empirical inquiry, Adelman and Morris conclude: "It is reasonable to assume that before fully participant nationwide democratic institutions can evolve, certain levels of mass communication, urbanization and literacy, for example, must be achieved and nationalist, positivist attitudes must be sufficiently diffused throughout the society."

This position is in keeping with the finding of a number of empirical studies including those of Daniel Lemer and other social scientists who study the communication process which suggest that modernization consists of a sequence of phases beginning with urbanization, followed in order by increased literacy and the spread of mass media. The latter phase, Lerner has argued, is a requisite for democratic participant political system.

Education fits into this process in a variety of ways. In itself, it has become one measure of modernization and presumably undergrade development of the economy, polity and so forth. By way of example:-

Schools also inculcate pupils with the disciplined attitudes and motivations requisite to the demands of industrialization. Human capital is more valuable than physical and we can give you the differential value in percentage points.

Educated people produce more on the job, adjust more quickly to the demands for new skills and are more committed to their work. An investment in education becomes an investment in the health of the economy.

Demographic and Economic Changes

Not only does education generate economic growth but also accomplishes miracles in other faces of society. Schooling curbs population growth because the better educated are more rational and see the folly of large families. Educated women want few children and have few children than uneducated women.

In terms of migration, even a little schooling makes rural youth seek the city and the scent of higher education makes the city youth look to universities abroad. University training abroad reduces the student from the less developed nation into the abundant carefree life of the rich nation, where he stays and inspite of occasional conscience pangs, lives happily ever after.

Education and social structure modernization means a more equitable spread of the wealth and an open social structure where the main constraint to an individual's upward mobility is lack of talent. The educational system promotes opportunity for the poor, it is the great leveller of society.

Within the schools, universalistic and achievement oriented teachers make regard only on the basis of talent and once the talented are appointed with a diploma they are guaranteed success and respect in the greater society.

Thus, the obvious policy for poor nations is to expand rapidly enrolments and provide a longer period of compulsory education to maximize the school's influence.

Planning for Education

This story cannot end without a reference to educational

planning. Overwhelmed by the power importance of education and impressed with the growth in our understanding of its complexities, we have succumbed to our own wisdom and advocate formal, elaborate uncompromising planning.

From the classroom to the national level, we tabulate projects and endeavour to mould the system that it may produce to its capability. The stacks of national plans lying in ministries of education all over the world represent the ultimate, if mute, tribute to our confidence.

This is, of course, but a capsule description of the most romantic tales of the century.

Planning for Future

We are living in a fast changing world. Due to advanced science and technology man has acquired such powers as could be helpful in wiping out poverty, ignorance and sickness from the world. Scientists have visualised life future changes that are likely to occur as a result of scientific and technological advancement.

Shadow of Coming Events

According to Dr. Phillip Handler (1971). We have attained such scientific and technological knowledge as would enable us to stabilise world population and improve conditions of living. In the terms of educational technology, Dr. Handler states-

"In the near future, each individual will have a private, pocket size, two-way television instrument and immediate personal access to a computer serving as his news sources. It will be his personal communicator with the world at large, with his bank, his broker, government agents, shopping services, and so on."

The future impact of science and technology on human society has been visualised by Dr. Handler. According to him, "Less than five percent of the working population will be engaged in primary agriculture with no more than another 20 percent engaged in other primary productive activities such as food processing, mineral extraction, construction or manufacturing."

"The bulk of the labour forces, then, will engage in activities currently classified services, rather than production of goods. The principal pursuits of mankind will be cultural, recreational or devoted to the expansion of knowledge and understanding."

"Most of the diseases which have been man's most ancient enemies will be matters of historic interest only. Each individual may look forward to about four score year of vigorous, healthy pain-free life before succumbing to the ravages of old age."

There is an explosion of knowledge in the modern world and this is also creating problems for education. Whatever we knew in 1901, was doubled in 1950. Our accumulated knowledge in 1950 was doubled in 1960 and in 1970, this was again doubled. Thus, human knowledge due to advanced science and technology has been multiplying itself leading to the explosion of knowledge.

Another important fact to bear in mind is that due to advanced science and technology the modern world has shrunk and its size has become small. We have such means of communication as enable us to know and reach any corner of the world. According to Wilbert E. Moore:

"In these times, scarcely a day passes without the newspaper and the mass media reporting a new or continuing crisis of great international import in some little known part of the world. The technology or communication and travel has, it is said, shrunk the size of the world. The politics of international tension has made that small world a dangerous place for human habitation."

The Menace

The modern science and technology can be useful if they are utilised properly. But at present man does not possess the wisdom to use this scientific and technological power properly. A number of crises have appeared due to human selfishness, short-sightedness and hunger for power. It has already been noted that with the help of science, span of life has increased and there is also a postulation that if mankind has to survive in the future, efforts must be made to check population growth and to develop such a world understanding as will lead to the development of a world wide government which will be responsible for maintenance of world peace.

Prof. James A. Parking Chairman and Director of the Centre for Education Inquiry, New York has stated that almost all the universities of the world are faced with five crises. These are:

(1) Crisis of number.

(2) Crisis of finance.

(3) Crisis of relevance.

(4) Crisis of priorities.

(5) Crisis of scepticism.

Crisis of Number : The population of India is now about 88 crores. More than half of this population is below the age of 18 years. Thus, in India there is a need for many more educational institutions. According to Kothari Commission (1964-66), "The total number of teachers exceeds 2 million. The total student population, which is now (that is in 1966) about 70 million; will more than double in the next 29 years, and by 1985, it will become about 170 million or about equal to the total population of Europe. The size and complexity of these problems argue the need for rapid action in involving an appropriate educational policy...."

The crisis of numbers in the educational world is a universal phenomenon. According to Dr. James A. Parking. "While experience differ from country to country, on the average the number of students entering higher education had doubled in the decade from 1960 to 1970. If there were no other problems, miss astonishing growth would, by itself, result in almost intolerable strains in most institutions of higher education in most countries."

If education has to be an effective instrument of planned social changes, it must adopt itself to the changing needs of society. The modern age is essentially a technological age. In order to live in this age every man must acquire technological knowledge and skills. The Kothari Commission has rightly emphasized the need for science-based education.

Crisis of Finance : Due to increase in number of pupils more educational institutions are needed and in order to run them more finances are required. Educational institutions all over the world, even in a rich country like U.S.A. require more finances because costs of education have risen tremendously. Previously, universities were receiving financial support mostly from private funds. Now a days they have to look for financial assistance from the government. University autonomy all over the world is being threatened due to governmental interference through its control over academic expenditures.

This is not a good sign because education can be an effective instrument of social change only when it is allowed full play and not controlled or interfered by any vested interest

Crisis of Relevance : In a static society, change is very slow and social patterns continue in the same form for a number of generations. Means of production and distribution are simple and social institutions perform their functions mostly undisturbed.

Due to rapid changes brought about by scientific and technological advancement much of knowledge and learning which was considered useful in a traditional and static society has become irrelevant and meaningless in a modern and dynamic society.

In India, the question of relevance has been raised in the form of student unrest. Students all over the world are dissatisfied with the kind of education which is given to them because it does not prepare them for life. Students today want much education as will enable them not only to understand their past but also, equip them for future. Contents of many courses in our universities are meaningless in the present context. We want to build a socialistic society and from this point of view it is necessary that there should be equal educational opportunity for all. Such education will be an effective instrument of planned social changes as will fulfill the needs and aspirations of youth.

Crisis of Priorities : The time has come to think of priorities with a view to bringing about desirable social change. In our educational system again there is a need for such changes as will emphasize first thing first. In other words, whatever was considered good in the past may not be regarded so now because of changes in political, social and economic conditions of life. Today, the need is to provide such education as will enable young men and women to be self employed. The educational system needs to be based on work-experience. In other words, learning by doing and earning while learning is necessary, if education has to be an effective instrument of planned social changes.

Crisis of Scepticism : There are times when doubts are raised in the accepted beliefs, ideals and principles. In a healthy society individuals are permitted to express their view without fear. Unfortunately those in power in our universities and other educational institutions do not like to hear the voice of dissent. They were only to be denoted by a passive group of teachers and pupils, but this is no more possible. In a fast changing world where ideas flow from one corner to the other easily and quickly, it is not only difficult but rather impossible to exercise control over expression and exchange of ideas.

One of the functions of the university is to encourage new thinking so that new avenues of thought are discovered. Due to lack of courage and initiative, educational leadership in most of the countries of the world is for the status quo. Most of the people, who are responsible for making education an effective instrument of social change lack foresight initiative and boldness to leave the beaten path and lead the new generation to the brave new world.

Crisis of Culture

Due to rapid scientific and technological changes, we are faced with a cultural crisis. In other words, we have come to the point which requires concise formulation of our moral and social values. It has been observed that when a traditional society proceeds towards industrialisation there are three alternatives open before it.

(l) The first is that it may continue to hold its traditionalism and refuse to assimilate the values, ideas and attitudes typical of an industrial society.

(2) The second alternative open to such a society is that it may remain uncertain in regard to its policy matters and permit a kind of drift in all matters. Such a policy is very harmful for it does not help its progress and leave the individuals at the mercy of the prevailing democrats. In many societies of the world we find there are two trends. That is, some societies look behind and receive inspiration from their ancient but without caring for the present or the future. This is typical of some of the societies in the east. In some of the western societies where tradition is weak and there is no deep sense of history, a feeling of uncertainty for the people who refuse to take up a position.

(3) The third alternative, perhaps the most desirable alternative is to resolve the cultural crisis and adopt a world view which will include "all mankind and emphasize essential unity of all religions. In other words we need a spiritual regeneration in this world today."

Along with this we have to strengthen democratic institution and safeguard political and social freedoms. These are the three alternatives which are before the world today. As it has been pointed out earlier, the first two alternatives have no value. The third alternative of world community should be our good and the task of education is to pave the way for such a society as will be based upon the concept of the good of all and a glorious future.

Masses in Power

Education of the future must take into account the rapid industrialisation in the world to bring about the supremacy of the masses specially in industrial society. As a matter of the fact industrial society has become a mass society characterised by mass production and mass communication. It seems that the masses have a lot of comforts for things are produced on a mass scale and there are such media of communication as to enable the masses to know about a thing quickly and conveniently. What is missing in this set up to the human factor.

Modern man finds himself lonely in the crowed while a large

number of people are engaged in large scale productions, the totality of life in society is lost. Individuals have become more or less mechanical and the masses are working towards an end which appears to be meaningless for them. In such a mass society the main problem is to rehabilitate the individual in terms of his potentialities, his need for novelty of experience.

The problems of the masses today are being solved at the economic and political level by various social techniques and mechanisms. Nonetheless, the individual is losing his freedom to think and to act as he desires. The means of mass production are mostly in the hands of a few people who manipulate the economic system and try to have the largest amount of profit leaving only a little for workers in the fields and factories.

So long as we fail to plan for prosperity on a mass scale as the modern man remains ignorant. In spite of all the means of mass communication, the problem for education will remain.

Thus, on the one hand we get that supremacy of the masses as emerging and on the other hand we observe that masses are losing their human touch on account of mechanisation in the fields of production and distribution as well as in their lives for, as stated above, he feels himself lonely in the crowd.

Power Groups

Due to industrialisation 'we find that groups of people engaged in various industries are getting organised. There are workers' unions, labour organisations, professional guilds etc. This has become necessary, for without an organisation the interest of a group cannot be safeguarded and its difficulties removed. These organised groups exercise pressure on political parties and legislatures to serve their interests.

Organised groups are active and influential not only in the social and economic fields but also in political spheres. In western societies where industrialisation has reached to a high level, we find a two party political system. The party in power has a strong opposition. But in such societies as are gradually getting industrialised, the two party system has not emerged in a satisfactory manner.

In India, the party in power is very strong and the opposition is rather weak. Such a state of affair is not desirable in a democratic society. It is imperative that organised groups not only safeguard their own interest but also see that there is a healthy opposition to the government in state Legislatures. The education of the future should facilitate it

New Class in Power

The impact of industrialisation, science and technology on society has also brought a new class in existence. In pre-industrial era the elite belonged to a feudal aristocracy and states depended upon the landed property of the high caste of an individual. Now-a-days, the basis of social status is the capacity to earn.

We find that people who do not have high status traditionally are becoming influential in their groups on account of their high rate of profits and economic prosperity. In other words, the emergence of a new class on the basis of industrialisation has upset the traditional class and caste status and created new categories for social significance.

In this connection, it may be mentioned that industrialisation has not only created a new class of people who are rich and powerful in spite of their lack of status, it has also created a high degree of mobility, we find people moving from region to region in search of lucrative jobs and prosperity. Thus, it is not uncommon to find that in a new industrial society people from far and wide come and settle down.

They build their new traditions, breaking almost completely from their social past. It is desirable to examine the implications of these new relationships in an industrial society and devise such a system of education as will bring about integration and develop healthy social relationships.

Leisure Problem

In an industrial society, where we have mass production the

problem of leisure is acute, for people work less and produce more. In those countries where population is on increase mass production has led to unemployment. But in some Western countries where population is under control the problem of unemployment has not been so acutely felt. Nonetheless, workers today have more leisure, for there are machines which require less number of people to produce more. That is why, a modern worker is comparatively paid more and given enough leisure.

The problem of leisure become serious when the worker does not know what to do in his spare time. Since he has been working in a large mechanical set-up, his approach to life also becomes somewhat mechanical and he gradually loses human touch. It is extremely necessary to see that the right type of education is provided for the proper use of leisure. The mass media of communication like cinema, radio and television are there not only for information but also for recreation. It is desirable that the mass media of communication are not be exploited and misused by vested interests and thereby impoverish the masses culturally.

As a matter of fact, the problem of leisure is related to the problem of culture for millions. Previously, culture was considered to be the sphere of new and the rest of the people were left to their footways. Now a days, mass media of communication have assumed great importance in view of the large scale publicity and propaganda carried out by business organisations, political parties and other organised groups. The masses are bewildered and they fail to recognise the subtle nature of propaganda. Therefore, a worker at leisure is constantly bombarded with all kinds of propaganda material and he is culturally deprived of or displaced.

It is extremely important that there should be a well organised scheme of education for leisure and informal agencies of education should devote some time to the spread of culture in the masses.

It is a sad commentary on the state of affairs today that while we have all the means to wipe out hunger, ignorance and disease from the world, we lack the necessary ideals and moral value to organise our efforts to apply modern means of production and communication for public welfare purposes.

Planning and Freedom

One of the strong agencies in the modern world is that of democracy. People at large are gradually realising that there cannot be any real peace or progress without democracy. It is rightly said that the world of today is gradually becoming democratic. The forces at work are numerous, some of them are helping the democratic forces and some are against democratization. As a matter of fact, in every society positive and negative forces are at work all the time. It is the task of education to help the positive social forces and weaken the negative forces.

Purpose of Democracy : It may be noted here that the concept of democracy has also been undergoing gradual change. Now a days, while it is accepted that all people are equal, they are also different in some sense. In other words, the concept of equality does not mean that individual differences should be wiped out and all individuals in spite of their mental abilities should be given the same kind of education.

Today, it is realised that the purpose of democracy would be better fulfilled if there are opportunities for self-growth to the maximum. For example, if a child has superior intelligence he should be provided with such type of education as will be challenging enough as well as interesting for him.

Thus, in a democracy while the principle of equality is accepted, it is at the same time realised that individuals with superior abilities should be provided with special opportunities for self- growth. This requires a kind of planning in education which will meet the requirement of all sections of people.

Fundamental Freedoms : While we accept the principle of planning in the context of democracy, it has to be emphasised that there are certain fundamental freedoms which must be assured for all. In a democracy, freedom of worship, speech, opinion and to hold meetings for social and political purposes are generally recognised and granted.

But these freedoms are not enough. While people may have political freedom they may not have social and economic freedoms.

It is, therefore, necessary that freedom in a democracy should mean freedom from want, ignorance, disease and unemployment. This is the welfare aspect of a democratic society.

Social Responsibilities : In the context of freedom and planning, another important factor is the consent of people and sharing of social responsibilities. It is one of the features of a democratic society that people agree to planning and collective action so that social and political freedoms can be safeguarded.

People surrender their certain rights to the State in order to provide for such mechanisms as will ensure proper distribution as well as production of goods and other requirements of life.

In a democratic society, the, State cannot perform its duties without willing cooperation of the people. That is why, democratic societies plan for such educational system as ensures democratic attitudes among the people.

One of the important democratic attitudes is that of cooperation and participation. People cooperate and participate in the democratic process of society when they feel a sense of responsibility for the actions of the Government.

The famous definition of democracy which emphasises the government for the people, by the people and of the people invariably underlines the fact that no democracy can function without a sense of identification on the part of the people with the State and democratic government.

Viewpoint of Manheim : Karl Mannheim has rightly pointed out that society is moving from lassies fair state to a planned one. But in a planned society, according to him, there can be two tendencies in regard to power and control.

One tendency could be that of democratization and the other that of authoritarianism. As we know, in a democratic set-up there is so much of freedom that sometimes certain people misuse it. In an authoritarian set-up power and control resides in the hands of a few. Thus, both the tendencies in a planned society cannot fulfil the aims and objectives of a real democratic society.

In order to meet their needs, Mannheim suggests a Third Way. The essential features of this Third Way are that the planning is not for conformity but for the variety. According to Mannheim, we can plan in such a manner as will produce harmony.

The second important feature of this Third Way, according to Mannheim, is that the planning done in such a manner as provides enough scope for individual enterprises and avoids control for the sake of it.

We have seen that sometimes when the government has got this power to control, bureaucracy introduces control without any regard for the place given for free enterprise. In democratic planning public and private sector work in harmony and contribute jointly to social welfare.

Mannheim also emphasises the element of social justice in democratic planning. Without this element, it is likely that certain sections of the society will take advantage of planning and drive extra benefits. In a militant democracy, planning of social justice is a must.

The third way of militant democracy as emphasised by Mannheim also requires the control of those people who misuse democratic freedom and try to destroy the democratic institutions of the society. It is evident that people have not only to be taught to be democratic but they must also learn to safeguard their democratic institutions of society. Their democratic rights from those who want to exploit them.

Mannheim would also like the people of democratic society to be clear in their minds in regard to the basic values governing social life. When the goals, objectives and values are quite clear to the people there is little possibility of difference in the fundamental approach to freedom and planning. Thus education in a democratic society will teach people not only how to behave as democratic nation but also translate into feelings, thoughts and action the basic value of a militant democracy.

Significance of Education

While discussing the crux of an industrial society planning, freedom and control we have also seen at places the role of education in a democratic society. Nonetheless, it is desirable that we focus our attention on the role of education in times to come.

From this point of view, the first requirement is that the scientific and technological potentialities of a people have to be developed by education. If it is desired that a society should have industrialisation in order to banish poverty and unemployment, it must try to educate its people in scientific and industrial fields.

It is not only enough that the core of curriculum becomes scientific and industrial but also there should be emphasis on the education of the talented and gifted. While the duty of the State is to spread education as widely as possible, there is also a compelling need to educate, to the highest level, the talented and the gifted.

Role of education in future society will be dynamic and not limited to one field of study or only one aspect of life. Educators have visualised interdisciplinary approach in the field of education. Peter Wilby, while discussing further education, pointed out that if education of the future has to be meaningful it must make efforts to adopt interdisciplinary courses that integrate several subjects. This will require dropping of the single subject degrees which are taken without paying any regard to the interdisciplinary relation among the different subjects of study.

Education of the future can play its role effectively, if it confines itself only to material aspect of life and ignores self knowledge, it cannot play its role according to the needs to time.

Education for Job Purpose

In an industrial society, skilled workers and technicians are in great demand. Modern machines are quit complicated and they can be well manipulated by educated workers. Thus, we need something like a technical high school to spread technical and industrial education in a society. But along with technical and industrial education we have to provide for individual differences and interests.

It is a well-known fact that all individuals are not equally interested in technical or scientific subjects. Keeping in view this fact, it is necessary that in a job-oriented education, there should be a provision for humanistic and liberal studies so that an industrial worker does not receive only one-sided education.

We know the purpose of education is the all round development of the individual. Education must enable the individual to realise his individuality first and later on it can prepare him for any vocation or profession. But to emphasise only vocational aspect of education or job-oriented education will defeat its purpose.

Formal Education

Traditionally, liberal education has been given to children. The pre-industrial society cared more for traditional and cultural view of life. Therefore, there was great emphasis on the teaching of liberal and humanistic subjects. But due to industrialisation, there has been a great demand for scientific, technical and industrial education. In view of this, a conflict has arisen between liberal student and technical education. How to resolve this conflict is a problem before educationists of the world.

Recently, there has been a move for a plan of general education. In this plan, a provision has been made for essential elements of liberal and humanistic studies. In other words, all children in an industrial society will have to study some such subjects as will provide them with liberal outlook on life.

The teaching of social subjects is to be done with a view to make children responsible citizens. It is, for example, suggested that social responsibility should be developed through teaching of social studies in a historical framework and against a universal background. Thus, it is evident that children in an industrial society should be educated in a manner as will enable them to have a fairly good idea about philosophy, literature, history and other humanistic and social studies.

In this connection, it has to be pointed out that in a democratic society every citizen has to feel responsible for the decision made by the government. It has been observed that people and government do not work in a cooperative way. The result is that people at large do not feel responsible for the decisions and actions of their government. This attitude defeats the purpose of democracy. Hence, education of the future has to be of such type as will develop a sense of responsibility among the people towards the state of affairs in the society.

Another important element in general education is that of science and its impact on life. It is generally accepted that modern science has affected thinking and brought about various changes in our outlook. Nonetheless, it is also true that some of the prejudices and superstitions still continue. We know that certain races consider themselves superior to others and scientifically it is proved that there is no racial superiority.

So the plan for general education should try to develop among the people a scientific attitude and provide them with such knowledge as will help them in getting rid of their traditional prejudices and superstitions. It has also been observed that a lot of emphasis on science has led to the development of a narrow outlook. In order to avoid this it has been suggested that there should be a course in the philosophy of science. In other words, scientists should try to understand the philosophical basis of scientific investigation and try to visualise the impact of scientific discoveries on human life.

Age of Computer

The problems created by urbanization and industrialization reveal the fact that modern man is dominated by machines. As a matter of fact, human society today is gradually becoming a victim of machines. It is led towards a king of dehumanization. By living and working with machines modern man has become somewhat mechanical in his approach towards life and society. The result is that we are faced with a danger of losing the human touch.

Thus, education of the future has to preserve human values and see that human factor is not neglected. In other words, education should continue to pay proper attention towards the harmonious development of human personality. If individuals have an integrated individuality, if personality of all persons flowers to the full, the danger to human values will be removed and dehumanization will be controlled.

Finally, the task of education of today as well as of tomorrow is to help the individual to know himself as Socrates wanted centuries age. So long as the individual is ignorant of his real self, his potentialities, his limitation and his mission of life, he cannot contribute in a creative manner towards his self growth and development of his society.

Education can help develop a sense of self-respect and esteem among their pupils by respecting them as individuals of unique abilities. As a matter of fact, a real teacher always does so. When a real teacher teaches his pupil he makes him feel his uniqueness and the things that he can do after his full development education of the future is a challenge as well as an opportunity for those who dream of a world community and world government.

Bibliography

Awasthy, G.C. : *Problems of Education in India*, Allied Publishers Private Ltd., Bombay, 1965

Bantock, G.H. : *Education in an Industrial Society*, Faber & Faber, London, 1963.

Bloom, B.S. : *Human Characteristics and School Learning*, Harper, New York, 1976.

Brown, J.W. Lewis, R.B. & Hercleread. A.V. : *Instruction: Materials and Methods*, Mc Graw Hill Book Co., New York, 1964.

Brubacher, John S. : *Problems of Education*, Tata McGraw Hill Publishing Company, New Delhi, 1978.

Chatterjee, R.K. : *Education and Problems*, National Book Trust, India, New Delhi.

Chaube, S.P. : *Philosophical and Sociological Foundations of Education*, Ravi Mudranalya, Agra, 1981.

Cook, L.A. & Cook, E.F. : *A Sociological Approach to Education*, McGraw Hill Book Co., New York, 1950.

Cream, David : *Explaining Teaching Machines and Programmes*, Featon, San Fracisco, 1961.

Dale, Edgare : *Problems of Education*, Dryden Rinehart and Winston, New York. 1969.

Dewey, John : *Democracy and Education*, McMillan Co., New York, 1961.

———— : *Education : Problems and Solutions*, Little Field-Adams & Co., New Jercy, 1961.

Eby, Frederick : *The Development of Modern Education*, Prentice-Hall of India (P) Ltd., New Delhi, 1964.

Haban, Charles, F. : *Problems of Education in the World*, New York, Dryden Press, 1945.

Hancock, Alan : *Planning for Educational Mass-Media*, Longmans London, 1977.

Kaul, B.N. : *Studies in Distance Education*, Association of Indian Universities, IGNOU, New Delhi, 1988.

Kilpatrick, William Heard : *Problems of Education*, McMillan Co., New York, 1961.

Kinder, James. S. : *Audio-Visual Materials and Techniques*, American Book Company, New York, 1959.

Kothari, O.S. : *Report of the Indian Education Commission*, New Delhi, 1966.

Kulkarni, S.S. : *Teaching Learning Process: A Systems Analysis*, UNESCO Regional Office for Education in Asia, Bangkok, 1975.

Lowman, J. : *Mastering Techniques of Teaching*, Prentice Hall India, New Delhi, 1987.

Mac Iver, R.M. & Page, C.M. : *The Problems*, Macmillan, London, 1950.

Matheson, Alastair : *The Communication Materials and Methods*. McGraw Hill Book Company, New Delhi, 1964.

Mc. Whinnie, Donald : *The Art of Education*, Faber & Faber, London, 1961.

Menon, Narayan : *The Communication Revolution*, National Book Trust, India, New Delhi, 1976.

Mohanty, J. : *Current Trends in Higher Education*, Deep & Deep Publications, New Delhi.

———— : *Educational Guidance, Measurement & Statistics*, Takshashila, 1996.

———— : *Educational Technology*, Deep & Deep Publications, New Delhi, 1991.

———— : *Studies in Educational Broadcasting*, Deep & Deep Publications, New Delhi.

Munn, Norman L. : *The Fundamentals of Human Adjustment*, Houghter Miffin Co., Boston, 1965.

Ottaway A.K.C. : *Education and Society*, Routldge and Kegan Paul, London, 1962.

Rao, V.K.R.V. : *Education and Human Resource Development*, Asia Publishing House, Bombay, 1966.

Raymont T. : *The Principles of Education*, Orient Longman, Calcutta, 1957.

Rewntreu, Desk : *Educational Technology in Curriculum Development*, Harper and Row Publishers, London.

Ross, James S. : *Ground Work of Educational Theory*, George S. Harrap Co., Ltd., London, 1954.

Rusk, Robert R. : *Philosophical Bases of Education*, University of London, London, 1956.

Sampath, K. : *Problems of Education*, Sterling, New Delhi, 1981.

Schramm, Wilbur : *Educational Problems : Today and Tomorrow*, The Funds of Advancement of Education, Newyork, 1962.

Sharma, G.D. & Ahmed, S.R. : *Methodologies of Teaching in Colleges*, UNESCO UGC & NIEPA, New Delhi.

Vedanayagam, G. : *Teaching Technology for College Teachers*, Sterling Publishers, New Delhi, 1989.

Report

Report of the Education Commission (1964-66): Education and National Development, Delhi: Government of India Press, 1966.

Report of the Committee on Emotional Integration. Ministry of Education, Govt. of India, 1962.

Report of the Secondary Education Commission (1953), Ministry of Education, Govt. of India, 1958.

Report of the University Education Commission (1948- 49), Delhi : The Manager of Publications 1950.

N.C.E.R.T.: Teacher Education, New Delhi.

Index

❑❑❑